LIVE IT UP!

50 COOL, UNIQUE, and WORTHWHILE

WAYS to SPEND YOUR TIME

KELLY JAMES-ENGER

Random House Reference

New York   Toronto   London   Sydney   Auckland

Please address inquiries about electronic licensing of any products for use on a network, in software, or on CD-ROM to the Subsidiary Rights Department, Random House Information Group, fax 212-572-6003.

This book is available at special discounts for bulk purchases for sales promotions or premiums. Special editions, including personalized covers, excerpts of existing books, and corporate imprints, can be created in large quantities for special needs. For more information, write to Random House, Inc., Special Markets/Premium Sales, 1745 Broadway, MD 6-2, New York, NY, 10019 or e-mail *specialmarkets@randomhouse.com*.

Visit the Random House Reference Web site: *www.randomwords.com*

Printed in the Singapore

10 9 8 7 6 5 4 3 2 1

Library of Congress Cataloging-in-Publication Data

James-Enger, Kelly.
    Live it up! : 50 cool, unique, and worthwhile ways to spend your time / Kelly James Enger.
      p. cm.
    ISBN-13: 978-0-375-72197-7 (alk. paper)
    1. Life skills—Handbooks, manuals, etc. 2. Occupations.
  3. Recreation. 4. Leisure. 5. Social action. I. Title.

HQ2037.J35 2006
646.7—dc22

                                                    2006051137

For my son Ryan
And his birth parents, Jodi and Kyle, for making me a mom

Acknowledgments

This book couldn't have been written without the involvement, support, and assistance of a number of people. First, I must thank Jena Pincott, my editor at Random House, who first approached me about doing this book, and my agent, Laurie Harper, who's always in my corner.

I'm also indebted to my two research/writing assistants, Maureen Callahan and Mark James. Their work has influenced and strengthened the book in so many ways, and I couldn't have made my deadline without them! Kudos and thanks to both of you for such great work.

I've also been tremendously fortunate to have the help of Diana Gerardi, who not only takes wonderful care of our baby boy, but also served as a proofreader for the manuscript. Thanks, Diana, for all you do, including giving me the twenty-something perspective.

Special thanks to the friends who saw me through a tight deadline, including Cindy, Abby, Jill, Polly, Kris, and Sharon—you've all helped keep me sane.

And finally, thank you to Erik, my partner in marriage and life—for all you do, and for taking this boat ride with me. I wouldn't want to do it with anyone else.

Contents

Teach and Live Abroad

Has the thought of living overseas always appealed to you? Ever wanted to visit foreign places and learn a new culture or language? Consider teaching abroad. You get paid to live in a foreign country and can immerse yourself in local culture for months, even years, if you like.

THOSE WHO DO, TEACH

Your first consideration is where you want to teach and live. Maybe a particular country has piqued your interest, or perhaps you've heard you can make great money teaching in certain countries, such as Japan, and still have time for travel and fun.

If you're already a teacher and want to live abroad, consider yourself lucky. Teachers have an easy time landing jobs overseas. Even if you're not certified to teach, all is not lost. You can probably still find a teaching gig "over there," wherever "there" is.

Certified Teachers

Teachers with K-12 certification have a wide range of options. They're qualified to teach at a variety of schools, but it's figuring out how to contact those schools that's the hard part. To keep abreast of overseas teaching jobs, current listings, articles about overseas schools, and instructions on how to secure an international teaching job, check out *The International Educator*, a newspaper published four times a year with a special "jobs only" edition in late June (*http://www.tieonline.com*).

The better schools almost always insist on interviews. Schools that enroll a high percentage of the host country's native students, or that pay lower salaries, may hire by correspondence, and therefore may be a possibility for inexperienced teachers. Be aware that these schools probably pay less than others and may offer less than ideal facilities.

Research the school well before leaving. Most are quite reputable, but there are a few exceptions. You can apply directly to schools, or attend recruitment fairs, where interested applicants are interviewed. Usually you'll apply to recruitment agencies in September; if you make it through the process, you'll interview at a recruitment fair in the winter, and receive a job offer in the spring.

Before going to interviews at recruitment fairs, do some research on the countries in which you're interested. If you already know about the local customs, languages, and the like, you'll impress the recruiters and may get the job.

Here are some recruitment fairs from which to choose:

- *Department of Defense schools* (http://www.dodea.edu/offices/hr/news/default.htm). These schools are located on U.S. military bases in thirteen countries around the world; you'll find their atmosphere to be much like that of American public schools.

- **Private international schools.** There are about 1,000 private K-12 English-speaking schools that educate the children of expatriate diplomats and businesspeople living abroad. You may have a few native students as well. This environment is similar to that of a private, elite school in the U.S., and your best shot at getting hired is to go through one of the two largest job fairs, which take place in February each year. Apply as early as possible, as some fill before December:

  International Schools Services (http://www.iss.edu). This is a very selective program; you must have a bachelor's degree, teaching certificate, experience living overseas, and be willing to go to any country for a two-year commitment.

  University of Northern Iowa's Overseas Placement Service for Educators (http://www.uni.edu/placement/overseas). This nonprofit organization represents more than one hundred schools and organizations.

- **Smaller recruitment fairs.**

  Ohio State University. There is no Web site; call (614) 292-2581 for information. The university hosts a fair for between twenty and thirty schools in February of each year; some require teacher's certificates, some do not.

  Search Associates (http://www.search-associates.com). This agency holds fairs in February, March and June in Massachusetts, California, and Washington, D.C.

There are also volunteer organizations that place teachers. Most provide for expenses and give a stipend to two-year, or long-term, candidates; the most well-known is the U.S. Peace Corps (*http://www.peacecorps.gov*). (See Chapter 18 for more info.)

The Fulbright Teacher Exchange Program (*http://www.fulbrightexchanges.org*) is a one-for-one exchange of participants who are fully integrated into regular host country schools. Teachers and administrators are eligible, but you must have a current full-time teaching or administrative position at the time you apply. Another program, the Fulbright Scholar Program (*http://www.cies.org*) provides grants for college and university faculty and independent scholars to teach or research abroad.

Another program you may want to consider is Teachers for Africa (*http://www.ifesh.org/teachers.html*). This mentoring program places teachers and administrators in sub-Saharan African countries, where they help train local teachers. You receive health insurance as well as a stipend of $800–$1000 U.S. dollars per month, which is a whole lot for that area of the world.

BUT I'M NOT A TEACHER YET!

Don't be discouraged if you are not certified to teach. There are plenty of opportunities for you out there anyway. English is the new "lingua franca" for worldwide commerce, higher education, and diplomacy, which means there are increasing opportunities for native speakers to teach English worldwide. Most positions require a one-year commitment and, usually, a bachelor's degree. English as a second language goes by many acronyms, such as ESL, EFL, TEFL, TESL, and TESOL, and teaching it is a great way to live abroad.

In the past, all it took was your ability to teach English, and you could get a job in many foreign countries. Now most schools require teachers to have training or certification in teaching English to non-native English speakers. There are many ESL programs out there, so choose carefully and ask for references from recent graduates.

Reputable U.S.-based ESL training programs include:

- *American Language Institute TEFL Graduate-Level Certificate* (*http://www.americanlanguage.org/amtefl.html*). The American Language Institute at San Diego State University offers a 120-hour graduate-level certification course for people wishing to teach abroad; plus lifetime job-placement assistance is provided.

- *School for International Training TESOL Certificate* (*http://www.sit.edu/tesolcert/*). This 130-hour, four-week course in Brattleboro, Vermont, focuses on teaching demonstrations, practice teaching, learning theory, and lesson planning.

- *TEFL International TESOL Certificate* (*http://www.teflintl.com*). TEFL International is based in Thailand and Oregon and offers intensive four-week training in locations around the world.

Once you receive your certification, your school will help you with job placement; to find overseas jobs teaching English, you can also search online at:

- http://www.eslteachersboard.com/
- http://www.tesall.com/jobboard/index.pl
- http://www.eslcafe.com/joblist/

BEFORE YOU LEAVE . . .

Once you've found a job, you'll need to take care of a few more incidentals, including the following:

Passport

Don't have a passport yet? Visit a passport agency such as a post office, courthouse, or library and fill out an application. The application can also be downloaded from the U.S. State Department's Web site: *http://travel.state.gov/passport.* You have to pay a fee to obtain or update a passport; make sure you give yourself at least six weeks to receive yours.

Visa

Most countries require that you have a visa to live there. A **visa** is a stamp or seal in your passport that allows you to live in the specified country for a certain purpose. (If you're not sure when you'll return, you may also have to apply for resident status.) Obtain your visa from the embassy or consulate of the country in which you plan to live before you leave; check out *http://www. state.gov/s/cpr/rls/fco* for more info.

Work Permit

When you apply for your visa, ask about work permits for the country in which you'll be living. Some countries make you wait until you arrive to get your work permit; others require you to have one before you leave the United States.

STAYING HEALTHY

Before you leave, determine how the people in your chosen country pay for medical bills, and check whether the same rules apply to foreign residents. Some countries have the same government-sponsored medical insurance available to foreign residents; others have a national health-care system supplemented by private insurance. If many Americans live in a country, sometimes its local private health insurance agencies will offer to cover U.S. citizen residents.

If this isn't the case, you may have to obtain health insurance with a U.S. company before going abroad. If you have insurance, check whether you will be covered while living overseas. If not, switch carriers. Look for one that offers both routine and emergency care, hospitalization, and **medvac** (medical evacuation), if necessary. Carry your medical insurance card and bring claim forms with you, as they can be difficult to obtain later. Visit *http:// travel.state.gov/travel/tips/health/health_1185.html* for more information on medical emergencies abroad and overseas insurance programs.

Immunizations

Depending on where you're going, you may need to visit a doctor to get immunizations before you leave. Immunization requirements vary from country to country, so check with the Centers for Disease Control and Prevention at *http://www.cdc.gov*. (The CDC also has a traveler's hotline at 1-877-FYI-TRIP.)

Due to the HIV/AIDS epidemic, certain countries require long-term residents and students to submit proof that they are free of the disease. Contact the embassy of the country in which you plan to live to find out if this is the case; if so, ask if it will accept test results from the United States, and then get the test done here.

Prescription Drugs

Got drugs? Leave all medications in their original containers with their original labels on them to help you avoid customs hassles when entering another country. For extra peace of mind, bring copies of your doctor's prescriptions. You may also want to have the prescriptions translated.

AVOIDING CRIME AND PUNISHMENT

Living overseas means living by the laws of the land in which you will reside, not those of the United States. Be on your best behavior. Remember, most countries do not provide trial by jury, accept bail, or furnish you with half-decent housing or food in jail. Officials may not speak English and you could get stuck in solitary confinement for months while waiting for your trial.

If you find yourself in any situation that may involve local authorities or legal action, get to the nearest U.S. consulate. Although consular officers can't get you out of jail or act as your lawyer, they can help you find an English-speaking attorney or get legal advice. They can also contact your family, if requested, and help you transfer food, money, and other necessary items. If you are arrested, ask to speak with the nearest U.S. consular officer. Under international agreements, this is your legal right.

THE NOT-SO-UGLY AMERICANS

While you may have sought the opportunity to teach abroad as a way to learn about a new culture and learn new things, it's still nice to know a few Americans in a foreign place. They can help you find answers to questions or problems that Web sites and guidebooks simply don't address.

It's a good idea to register with the U.S. embassy or consulate in the country to which you plan to move. You can register before you leave at *http://travelregistration.state.gov/ibrs*. If you wait to register until you arrive in your new home country, you can register on the Web site or go to the embassy or consulate in person. This is a good place to ask about where other Americans live, and whether there are any groups you can join or events to attend. As a U.S. citizen, you're likely to find fellow Americans in nearly any country in which you live.

Speaking of Americans, you needn't worry about your U.S. citizenship. You're a citizen until you return, regardless of how long you're away from the country. The only way you can lose your citizenship is by committing an act of expatriation such as naturalization in a foreign state, taking oaths or affirmations to the foreign state, serving in another country's armed forces, being employed with a foreign government, or taking a formal oath renouncing your allegiance before a U.S. consular or diplomatic officer.

That's one of the great things about teaching abroad: You can immerse yourself in a different culture for years and still come home to the United States when you want to.

2

Start Your Own Business

Have you always dreamt of being your own boss? Or have you recently caught the entrepreneurial bug and you want a business that's all yours? If you're sick of "working for the man" or you've got a great idea for your own business, there's no time like the present to launch your own venture.

But it takes more than a great idea to succeed. It takes drive, determination, smart planning, and financing. Read on to avoid the pitfalls of starting a business, and to learn the strategies that will boost your chances of success from the get-go.

CHECK YOUR PERSONALITY

The first question you should ask yourself has nothing to do with the idea for your biz, or even how you'll finance it. It has to do with you. Be honest with yourself. Do you have the kind of drive and stamina to run your own business? Keep in mind that when you work for yourself, you give up the stability of a regular paycheck, yet the responsibilities increase, maybe fivefold, or more.

If you have trouble meeting deadlines, following through with plans, or tend to lose interest in an idea after the initial thrill, business ownership probably isn't for you. On the other hand, if you're willing to put a lot of time and energy into your venture and understand that the buck will be stopping with you, you've got a better chance of succeeding.

Keep in mind that, when you're the boss, you don't get vacation days or personal days. You will spend more time on your business than you did for any job—and probably for less money, at least at the beginning. It certainly helps to have a good support network in place—like a romantic partner, friends, and family who will cut you some slack when you miss dinner or obsess over the package design of your new product.

Finally, it helps to be healthy. Starting a business takes a lot of energy, and you can't live on espresso forever. And make sure that you're at a place in your life where you can devote the time and effort necessary to make your business "go." (If you're wondering, here's a tip: If you just got married, relocated, or had a baby, this probably isn't the right time for you.)

YOUR GREAT IDEA

Many new businesses spring out of a great idea—sometimes a unique idea. Consider your talents, background, and the problems you or others around you have experienced in your life. What problems could your business solve? If you travel for work and constantly have to kennel your Doberman, you might consider a dog-walking business. If you're the master of giving the perfect gift, what about a corporate gift-giving business? And if you've designed your own greeting cards for years, maybe you can turn your hobby into a full-blown biz.

WHO ARE YOUR CUSTOMERS?

Most new business owners don't have trouble coming up with the idea. It's taking it to the next step that causes them to falter. And that step involves identifying your customers: the people who will pay you money for your great idea.

So, who are your customers? Don't say "everyone." Narrow your market. What sex are your customers? How old are they? How much money do they make? Are they local or scattered throughout the country—or even the world? What are their problems and concerns? The more you know about your customers, the better able you'll be to sell your product or service to them.

Don't be afraid to talk to potential customers, other small-business owners, or other experts about your idea. The more information and advice you can gather, the better. After all, wouldn't you rather find out about the hole in your idea before you've invested your life savings in it? Be a sponge and soak up as much information as you can—which brings us to the next step.

PLAN LIKE A PRO

Next, you should develop a business plan. I know you want to skip this step, but it's a critical one, especially if you'll need to obtain financing for your business. Create a plan to start your business that includes all of the steps you must take, and relevant details such as the source of your financing, how much you have, and how much you need.

At a minimum, your business plan should include a detailed description of:

- *Your product or service, and what sets it apart from the competition.* How much will it cost? Why will people want to spend money for it?

- *Your primary competitors.* Who are they? What makes them successful? How can you improve on what they're already doing? And perhaps most important, why will customers choose you over the competition? (If you can't answer this question, you're in trouble!)

- *Your customers.* Who are they? What drives them? Why will they be interested in your product or service? How large is your target market? What geographic area will you serve?

- *Projected sales.* How much will you sell the first month? During the first six months? During the first year? Be realistic about what kinds of sales you can expect; it's better to assume sales will be slow, at least at first.

- *Financing.* How much money do you need to launch your business? What will be the operating costs until your business starts to make a profit? Can you handle negative cash flow (i.e., when the money is going out faster than it's coming in)? For how long? How much of a financial cushion do you have?

- *Personnel.* Do you need to hire people for your business? How many do you need? What skills do they need to have? Where will you find them?

- *Marketing/advertising.* How will your customers find out about your business? How much will you spend on advertising? How will you promote your business?

Keep in mind that it's better to think small when you're starting out. It's much easier to grow bigger than to have to get smaller, and it's more realistic when you're starting out. That's why you may want to consider keeping your day job for as long as possible. There's nothing like a safety net. (On the other hand, if you're dividing your time between your job and your new business, you may wind up shortchanging both of them. Figure out what the best option is for you.)

If you're stumped, community colleges, libraries, and chambers of commerce all offer classes on how to write a business plan. Check into what your community offers; even an abbreviated plan is better than flying without one.

GETTING HELP

Keep in mind that, no matter how small your business starts off, there are certain legalities that can't be ignored. First, you may need certain licenses or permits to operate your business, especially if you operate it out of your home. If you plan to hire employees—even if they're friends or family and only are working part-time—you also have to be up to speed on laws, including Occupational Safety and Health Administration (OSHA) regulations, federal regulations on withholding taxes and Social Security, and state workers' compensation laws.

Sound more complicated than you thought? It may be worthwhile to consult an attorney who specializes in small businesses to make sure you've taken care of all the legal stuff. You may also want to talk to an accountant. Your local chamber of commerce, library, or community college probably offers resources for would-be small-business owners; contact them to see what they offer. In addition, the Small Business Administration (SBA) and the Service Corps of Retired Executives (SCORE) can be excellent resources. Check out the following Web sites for more information:

- **http://www.sba.gov/starting_business/** The U.S. Small Business Administration has loads of information for people starting businesses that covers everything from financing to taxes to employees.

- **http://www.sba.gov/onlinewbc/** If you're female, check out the Online Women's Business Center, part of the SBA's Office of Women's Business Ownership.

- **http://www.sba.gov/library/pubs/mp-12.txt** Make it easy with this "Checklist for Going into Small Business." You can print it out and refer to it as you go.

- **http://www.score.org/** Want advice from a real expert? SCORE provides resources and support for small-business owners, including free advice from SCORE volunteers, who are current or retired business owners, executives, and corporate leaders.

SHOW ME THE MONEY

Chances are, you'll need some extra bucks for your biz. If you launch your business part-time while still working full-time, you may not need as much financing, but then you won't be able to put as much time into your start-up. At a minimum, you'll need enough to live on for six months to a year, plus the start-up and operating costs of your business.

Your start-up costs may include the costs of:

- *advertising*
- *decorating or remodeling*
- *fixtures and other equipment for your office or storefront (and the cost to install them, if applicable)*
- *insurance*
- *legal and other professional services*
- *supplies and initial inventory*
- *required licenses and permits*
- *signs*

Once your business is in operation, you'll still need income to cover operating costs, which will include the costs of:

- *advertising (it's not just a start-up expense!)*
- *delivery and transportation*
- *employee wages*
- *insurance*
- *maintenance (such as janitorial service)*
- *postage and shipping*
- *miscellaneous expenses*
- *rent*
- *supplies and other office expenses*

- *taxes*

- *utilities*

- *your income!*

Estimate how much you'll need to make to cover your business expenses, and make sure you have more than enough. If you're running short on funds, talk to friends and family for financing, or ask a local bank for a loan. Check with your local chamber of commerce or SCORE office to determine grants, loans, and other programs for which your business may qualify.

CHOOSE YOUR SPOT

If you can, consider starting your business from home. You'll save on rent and utilities. If that's not possible, consider the location of your business carefully. Cost is one factor, but so is foot traffic, accessibility, the demographics of the area, and nearby competition. Consider, too, how critical the "look" of your office is: In a retail establishment it's significant, but for other businesses it may be less important.

LET THE PEOPLE KNOW!

Finally, you need to let people know about your business. This requires both public relations (PR) and advertising. (What's the difference? You pay for ads, but PR is free—and much harder to get.) For example, you can send a press release to local media letting them know about your new biz, and join the local chamber of commerce to spread the word.

Consider newspaper, radio, and cable TV ads as well as flyers, brochures, and a Web site to promote your business. The more people who know about your business, the more potential customers you have, and the greater your chances of succeeding in your new venture.

Save the Planet

Worried about the big blue marble we all call home? You're not alone. Today more people are concerned about the environment than ever before. More importantly, they're speaking up and convincing others to put their beliefs into action. Whether you've chosen to drive an electric car, eschew the auto in favor of public transportation, or simply recycle everything you can, every little thing you do adds up. If you want to make a difference to planet Earth, read on.

A BIG, DIRTY PROBLEM

If you're already concerned about the environment, that's great. (In fact, four in five Americans consider themselves "environmentalists," or people who are interested in protecting nature.) If not, let's convert you.

Consider first that the world population is about 5.5 billion, a number expected to explode to more than 9 billion by 2050. That's a lot of people, and people eat, wear, and consume a lot of stuff. Compare that to the global population in 1900, which was a measly 1.7 billion people.

This surge in population growth means an increased demand for food and energy, as well as an increase in the amount of waste and pollution that's created—and all of that impacts the environment.

Another factor contributing to environmental problems is the production of man-made pollutants. Carbon monoxide and other gasses from the tailpipes of automobiles and trucks; industrial waste created by manufacturers; pesticides that seep into the soil and run off into the water; countless tons of manure and methane produced by huge farms; and gases produced by burning coal are all major causes of pollution, to say nothing of all the fast-food wrappers and cigarette butts that litter nearly every roadway.

Finally, the technology that has made so many of our lives easier and more convenient comes with a cost. For example, we're building more houses, more stores, and more factories, and that means more pollution and fewer resources. As communities grow larger, they require more clearing of forests, prairies, and swamps, and more highways and roads . . . and that means more cars, more drivers, and more pollution.

The problem, of course, is that with all this more, more, more, there's only one planet Earth, and her resources are in fact limited. That's the bad news. The good news is that there are dozens of things you can do in your everyday life to help make a difference and protect what's left.

LITTLE THINGS ADD UP

So, what can you do? More than you might think.

At Home

- *Use your muscles!* You don't need an electric can opener when a manual one is nearly as fast. Same goes for chopping veggies by hand instead of using a food processor. Anytime you can do it without "plugging in," do it by hand.

- *Take quicker showers.* Don't dawdle under a hot spray for twenty minutes. You waste water and the energy to heat it. And shut off the tap when you're brushing your teeth; just use water to wet your toothbrush, and then rinse it off when you're done.

- *Flush the toilet less often.* Go by this adage: "If it's yellow, let it mellow; if it's brown, flush it down."

- *Kill annoying bugs by hand with a flyswatter instead of using poisonous chemicals.*

- *Skip the plastic wrap and aluminum foil.* Wrap leftovers in reusable containers and send your friends home with them, too. You can always ask to have them returned.

- *Save plastic grocery bags.* Use them as garbage bags at home, or return them to the store to be recycled. Paper grocery bags are great for holding newspaper and other paper for recycling.

- *Save your wire hangers, too.* Return them to the dry cleaners when you take in your clothes. It will be appreciated.

- *Turn off the lights—and television and radio—when you leave a room.* Get family members to comply by asking if "Mr. Invisible" is in an empty room.

- *Forget paper towels.* Instead, use a damp rag or sponge to clean up spills.

- *Cut up your six-pack rings.* Can't live without your six-packs of soda or beer? Just cut the six-pack rings before you throw them out to keep fish or birds from getting entangled in them.

- *Readjust your personal thermostat.* During the winter, set your thermostat a few degrees lower and wear sweaters, and enjoy the balmier months of summer. Drawing your curtains or blinds during the day will help your home stay cooler.

- *Recycle everything you can.* Set aside a recycle corner to store newspapers, cardboard, aluminum and tin cans, and glass. And don't forget that things like motor oil, scrap metal, and printer cartridges are all recyclable as well.

- *Do your laundry in cold water.* You'll use one-fifteenth of the energy needed to wash clothes in hot water—and now there are even detergents specially made to work in cold water. You'll save on your gas bill as well.

- *Pull weeds by hand instead of using herbicides.* In the yard, create a compost pile to get rid of leaves and grass clippings instead of adding to a landfill somewhere.

- *Water yard plants by hand instead of letting the hose run—and run—and run.* And remember: during a dry season, it's all right to let your lawn get a little brown.

- *Opt for rechargeable batteries.* Believe it or not, all those remote controls, CD players, flashlights, Game Boys™, and

MP3 players use a whopping 2 billion batteries a year that wind up in landfills, leaking toxic chemicals. Use rechargeable batteries instead and you'll reduce solid waste and save hundreds of dollars as well.

- *Turn off your TV the hard way, by getting up and turning it off.* Using your remote control to shut off your TV doesn't really turn it off, but puts it on standby, which means it's still running on full power.

- *Repair any leaky faucets and running toilets.* Those slow drips add up to a lot of wasted water over time.

- *Turn off your screen savers.* To keep that entertaining little kitten jumping across the screen, your monitor is operating at full power and your CPU is running as well. Instead, choose sleep mode, which uses little electricity.

- *Purchase larger-sized products, which tend to use less packaging overall than smaller boxes or single-portion items.* You'll save money as well.

- *Run your dishwasher only when it's full.* The more dishes you can cram into it, the better.

- *Replace your regular showerhead with a low-flow model.* You'll save gallons of water with each shower.

- *Join a conservation organization or volunteer your time to a conservation movement.* There are hundreds of environmentally-oriented nonprofit groups from which to choose; visit *http://www.justgive.org/guide/index.jsp* and click

on "environment," or visit *http://www.charitynavigator.org* and enter "environment" as a keyword. Some of the highest-ranked national environmental nonprofits include:

Beyond Pesticides. This group works to rid the world of toxic pesticides and promotes nonchemical, nonhazardous alternatives: *http://www.beyondpesticides.org/*.

The Conservation Fund. The Conservation Fund works to protect U.S. land and water resources including wildlife habitats, rivers, wetlands, and community open spaces: *http://www.conservationfund.org/*.

Natural Resources Defense Council. With more than one million members, the Natural Resources Defense Council works to protect wildlife and wild places and to ensure a safe, healthy environment for all living things: *http://www.nrdc.org/about/*.

Public Citizen Foundation. Founded by Ralph Nader, the Public Citizen Foundation works for a number of goals including clean, safe, sustainable energy sources and environmental protection: *http://www.citizen.org/*.

Sierra Club Foundation. The Sierra Club Foundation provides financial support to the Sierra Club and other environmental organizations, funding a range of environmental projects: *http://www.sierraclub.org/foundation/*.

The Trust for Public Land. The Trust for Public Land is the only national nonprofit group that works exclusively to protect land for human enjoyment: *http://www.tpl.org/*.

Out and About—and at Work

- *Make sure your tires are always properly inflated.* You'll save on gas.

- *Leave the car at home and take public transportation whenever you can.* Or (gasp!) walk or ride your bike.

- *If you drive to work, organize a carpool with coworkers.*

- *Buying a new car?* Skip the gas-guzzling SUV in favor of an electric or hybrid car to save on fuel and reduce engine emissions.

- *Recycle your motor oil, or at least dispose of it properly.*

- *Don't litter!* Save your trash in a bag in your car and throw it out when you reach your destination. (And yes, if you're a smoker, throwing a butt out your car window counts as littering.)

- *Start a recycling center at your office if you don't have one already.* Encourage your coworkers to recycle computer paper, cardboard, soda cans, and the like.

- *Reuse office supplies such as file folders and manila envelopes.* Use scrap paper to jot notes to yourself.

- *Get rid of throwaway Styrofoam™ cups.* Suggest that everyone have a designated mug instead, and there'll be less chance of someone running off with your coffee.

- *Speaking of Styrofoam™, don't buy it.* It's not recyclable.

- *At the store, buy food without elaborate packaging.* All that extra stuff just winds up in a landfill somewhere. And skip "disposable" versions of products. They're not disposable and are almost always more expensive than the non-disposable versions.

- *Buying a new appliance?* Check the energy rating of washing machines, dryers, refrigerators, and the like, and choose the one that's the most energy efficient.

- *Buy locally grown food whenever possible.* Most stores have signs designating locally grown produce. Buying organic (i.e., buying foods that have been grown and processed without chemicals or pesticides) also helps, and the quality of the food is usually high.

- *Eat "lower on the food chain."* A vegetarian or vegan diet uses fewer natural resources than a meat-based diet, and is healthier as well.

- *Get educated about conservation issues in your community.* Take a stand on ones that are important to you.

- *Skip the fast food.* Those burger joints are responsible for a huge portion of the solid waste created in the United States, much of it wrappers that are used for just a few minutes and always seem to end up in ditches along the side of the road.

- *Buy organic clothes.* If more people purchased organic cotton clothing instead of regular cotton, there would be less pesticides used on cotton overall. Check out the Organic Cotton Directory (*http://www.organiccottondirectory.net/*) for companies that offer organic cotton clothing.

- *Carry a tote.* Even better than reusing plastic or paper bags is to start carrying cloth bags when you shop. It's easy to toss groceries or books into your handy satchel. Look for one with a cool logo or design (and it's a great conversation starter as well).

Finally, if you're serious about saving the planet, set a good example. Every action you take, even a small one, may influence someone else to make a positive change as well. Whether you talk your office mates into recycling more paper, get involved to protect open spaces, or even keep your friend from throwing his cigarette butt out the car window, you make a difference. Mother Earth says "thank you."

Move to a New City

You've had it. You're ready to pull up stakes and pitch your tent somewhere else. Maybe the object of your affection lives in another place. Maybe you've got a job offer, or the chance of better career opportunities in a different city. Or maybe you just want to live someplace you've dreamed of.

What's next? Sure, you could throw a few of your worldly possessions in your car and drive until you run out of gas, or continent. But you'll be better off if you approach your move like any other important project: Pick a location, develop a moving strategy, and follow it though. If you're looking for the new hometown of your dreams, read on.

WHERE, OH WHERE, DO I GO?

Maybe you're relocating because of a job opportunity, for school, or for love (how romantic!). That makes things a bit easier. Otherwise, you need to figure out where exactly you're moving to by considering what's most important to you. The factors that affect where you eventually choose to live may include:

- *Cost of living.* In general, it's cheaper to live in a smaller town than a big city, and rural areas tend to be less expensive than more urban ones. But that doesn't mean living in a city isn't possible. For example, Manhattan is one of the most expensive places to live and work, yet many people who work there choose to live in Brooklyn or Queens and commute to work. You just need an idea of how much you'll need to make in order to live there without having to exist on Ramen noodles.

- *Employment opportunities.* Will you be able to find a job pretty easily? What kinds of career options does the city offer? (Even if you move to accept a new job, there's a good chance you'll change positions within a few years.)

- *Housing.* Will you be able to buy a home, or find a nice rental you can afford? The cost of housing in some communities is near-stratospheric, and you don't want to move only to find that the best you can afford is a dingy one-room sublet in the bad part of town.

- *Crime.* Are you willing to live in an area that has a gang problem, or frequent robberies? Some people expect some crime as part of living in the city; others want to feel safe at all costs.

- *Schools.* If you don't have kids yet, this may not be a big issue. But if you do, or if you plan to procreate in the near future, you'll be more interested in the quality of schools where you live.

- *Health care.* What happens if you get sick? Is there a hospital nearby? Are there lots of doctors to choose from? Obviously, this is a bigger issue if you have a chronic health problem, but even if you don't, it's still something to consider.

- *Culture.* If you live for the opera and the ballet, a small town where "culture" refers to the local dinner theater may not be a good fit. Some people want loads of museums to choose from; others are happy if there's a local college or university.

- *Entertainment.* Do you like to hit the clubs and eat sushi at two in the morning? A bigger city usually offers more stuff to do, but it depends on what you're into.

- *Climate.* Don't forget this one. If you detest humidity, Atlanta may be your idea of hell. On the other hand, if you live in the Northeast or Midwest, you can count on some wild winter weather.

In addition to quizzing your friends about potential locales, there are a number of Web sites that can make researching possible new homes easier. Check out the following Web sites for information about different communities:

- http://www.bestplaces.net/
- http://www.cityrating.com/
- http://www.findyourspot.com/
- http://www.realtor.com/
- http://www.salaryexpert.com/

GET READY TO MOVE

Before You Leave Your Old Home Behind

You've chosen your new hometown, and decided on your departure date. What's left? A lot. Basically, you have to wind up your old life in your old home, and prepare to start your new life in your new place. It helps to have a list of everything you need to do. You don't want to arrive at your new apartment to discover that you forgot to have the power turned on, and that it will be a week before the lights work.

- *Give notice at your old job, if you have one.* The standard notice period is two weeks, and a polite, appreciative letter of resignation will keep you from burning bridges. You never know when you'll need a good reference.

- *Give notice to your landlord that you're moving, or sublet your apartment.* If you own a home, you'll need to sell it (hopefully before you leave).

- *Decide whether you'll move yourself or use a moving company.* Hire the latter if necessary. (If you're moving for a new job, ask if your employer will cover moving costs—a great fringe benefit.)

- *Find a place to live, whether you rent, buy, or stay with friends or family (hopefully temporarily!).* Sign the lease and any other necessary paperwork. (If you know where you'll be living, get the measurements of the rooms so you know whether your furniture will fit in your new pad.)

- *Call to hook up your utilities before you leave your old place.* (Most cities now have their own Web sites, which include information about local utilities. You can also ask your new landlord.)

- *Several weeks in advance of your departure date, contact the phone company and your internet service provider (ISP) at your new place to let them know about the move.*

- *Swing by the post office and fill out a change-of-address card.* Send a card to magazine subscriptions and other mail you want to find you.

- *Call to disconnect your utilities—gas, electric, cable, and the like.* Don't forget to cancel your ISP service as well.

- *If you own a car, let your insurance agent know you're moving.* Ask about insurance rates in your new community to get an idea of what you'll be spending.

- *Close local bank accounts, if you like, although you can always do this when you settle in at your new place.*

The Packing Process

Ask anyone. The hardest part of the move has got to be packing—and realizing how much crap—or rather, stuff—you've accumulated since the last time you moved. How can you cope?

- *Start early.* If you can, pack things you don't need every day (out-of-season clothes, kitchen stuff you rarely use, books, CDs, linens) a week or two before your move. That's easier than trying to pack the contents of your entire place in a day.

- *Purge, purge, purge, and choose carefully.* Come on, do you really need nineteen sweatshirts, even if each is a different color? If you haven't used the wok in three years, do you really want to pack it, move it, and unpack it at your new home? Make piles of possessions to give to friends, sell unwanted things at *http://www.ebay.com* or *http://www.craigslist.org,* donate them to charity, or simply discard them.

- *Pack smart.* You don't have to blacken your hands with newspaper print if you use linens, towels, even socks and underwear to wrap things like glasses, framed photographs, and other breakables.

- *Start gathering boxes, masking tape, and other packing materials.* The liquor store and grocery store are great places for free boxes; just make sure they're clean, dry, and in good condition.

- *Save your back.* You may think huge boxes will hold more stuff, but if they weigh ninety pounds, no one will be able to lift them. Medium-sized boxes are more manageable.

- *Label your boxes.* Don't just write "kitchen"—use specific labels, such as "pots and pans" or "glassware." Same for clothes. Label a box "socks and underwear" and you'll be able to find clean underwear the first morning at your new home.

- *Separate your important papers.* Put documents such as your lease, passport, and personal address book in a separate file to carry with you.

- **Get Hefty™ (literally).** Giant plastic bags are great for linens, clothes, and other fairly lightweight stuff.

- **Look into plastic.** Buy see-through storage containers that you can use post-move at your new place.

- **Take a close look at your furniture.** If it's seen better days and your budget isn't strained, why move it to your new place? On the other hand, if you're broke, even that banged-up ratty-looking easy chair may be coming along for the ride.

- **Call on your friends.** If you're not having professional movers help, enlist your friends to help you pack. Lure them with free pizza and beer and they'll be happy to help.

MOVING DAY (AKA HELL)

The day is here. Expect it to be stressful, but the day will end—eventually. Try to maintain a sense of humor, especially if you're relying on your friends and family to help you transport your belongings down (or worse, up) four flights of narrow stairs.

- **Get an early start.** Movers may run late, the elevator may be crowded, and your so-called friends may not show up until the heavy stuff is already on the truck. (Funny how that happens!)

- *Have a separate moving box for your bathroom stuff—toothbrush, toothpaste, shampoo, makeup, and the like—so you can pack it last.*

- *Make sure that you're packed and ready to go.* You'll pay movers extra if they have to stand and wait, and your buddies will be annoyed if you're still throwing things into boxes when they're ready to load up.

- *Rent a dolly for the day.* You'll be amazed at how much faster loading and unloading goes.

- *If you've never packed a moving truck or van before, rely on a friend who has.* Otherwise, here are a few handy tips: Place the largest furniture, like couches, into the truck first, and slide mattresses in along the side of the truck; use other heavy furniture to keep them in place. Mirrors, large prints, and other flat breakable objects can be wrapped in moving blankets and slid between the mattress and box springs for additional protection. Make sure that the heaviest boxes are on the bottom; lighter items and unboxed things should go on top.

If you're packing the back of an open truck, make sure that everything is safely tied down. You don't want to arrive missing a mattress.

STARTING YOUR NEW LIFE IN YOUR NEW HOME

So, you're home. It just don't doesn't feel like home yet—but it will.

- *Unpack your "necessities" immediately.* That means toilet paper and whatever else you think you'll need in the next few hours.

- *Clean your new place before you completely unpack.* There's nothing scarier than finding mystery hairs on the shower wall or walking barefoot on dark brown shag carpet. Who knows what's hiding in there?

- *If you want, set up your couch and TV or stereo in the living room, so you can take an unpacking break when you're ready.*

- *Whip out your laptop and send an e-mail blast announcing your new location to friends and family.* (That's why you made sure your new ISP would have service on the day you arrive.)

- *Unpack all your stuff!* (And question why exactly you didn't get rid of more of it already.)

- *Get a new driver's license or ID card if you're moving to another state, and new insurance, if necessary.*

- *Open a new bank account, and close your old accounts if you haven't done so already.*

- *Find a new dry cleaner, gym, dentist, grocery store, mechanic, Starbucks, you name it.*

- *Walk or drive around your neighborhood to get the lay of the land.* An after-work stroll will let you meet your neighbors. Just be friendly and you'll be surprised at how many people you'll meet.

- *Take different routes to work to get to know the locations of local stores and restaurants.*

- *Join a gym, church, or newcomers' group to meet people right away.* Establish a routine at Starbucks or the gym and you'll see the same faces, and people will get to know you as well.

Moving can signal one of the most exciting changes in your life, but it is stressful. Expect it to take a few months before you settle in and feel comfortable in your new surroundings. In the meantime, unleash your inner extrovert. You may have left behind friends, but new ones are waiting for you. You just have to get out there and find them.

5 Practice Yoga

Searching for inner peace? Want to be more flexible, less stressed, and more able to focus? Or do you just want to join one of the widest-reaching fitness movements in recent years? Try yoga, which gives you physical and mental flexibility. Whether you're looking for a kick-butt workout that will give you cut musculature, or a relaxing way to get in shape without breaking a sweat, there's a type of yoga that's right for you.

BEND, BABY, BEND

Let's start with the basics. If your idea of yoga is sitting around in the lotus position, muttering "om" while burning incense, think again. Yoga may be an ancient Indian tradition, but there are new twists on the traditional that make yoga a good fit whether you're a committed couch potato or training for a triathlon. Yoga can make you fitter, less stressed, and more flexible, not only physically but emotionally as well. You can use it to tone muscles, lose weight, deepen your powers of concentration, and become more spiritual, or just impress the hell out of your friends with your ability to pop a shirshasana (that's a head-stand to the uninitiated) unassisted.

Yoga was developed thousands of years ago in India, and the word "yoga" comes from the Sanskrit meaning "to unite." Yoga practice seeks to unite the physical body with the spiritual self. There are actually eight different major branches of yoga that include **brahti yoga**, or devotional yoga; **guru yoga**, which focuses on dedicating oneself to a yoga master; **jnana yoga**, or wisdom yoga; **karma yoga**, which focuses on self-transcending action; **mantra yoga**, which involves potent sound; **raja**, or royal, yoga; and **tantra yoga**, which is considered the yoga of continuity.

While some of these terms (like "guru" and "karma") may ring a bell with you, when most people talk about yoga they're refer-ring to the eighth branch, called **hatha yoga**, the branch of yoga that involves physical discipline. Hatha yoga includes positions, or asanas, that are performed while you concentrate on and control your breathing (pranayama) and develop mental focus and con-centration, or dharana. While all types of yoga incorporate these elements, there are a variety of different yoga schools, each of which takes a different approach to this ancient art.

There are more than 1,000 different yoga poses that range from relatively easy to extremely challenging. Some are held for a few seconds, others for minutes at a time. Attaining poses is only part of yoga practice; proper breathing and in some cases chanting or meditating are also involved.

MY YOGA'S BETTER THAN YOURS!

As more people study and master this art, yoga forms are con-tinually growing. Today, popular forms of yoga include the follow-ing, most of which were developed from hatha yoga:

Ashtanga. Also known as **sports yoga** or **power yoga**, ashtanga is guaranteed to kick your butt. This relatively new form of yoga emphasizes strength and stamina over meditation—and the poses are more difficult than those of a more basic hatha or ilyengar class—plus you move quickly from one pose to another, which makes it more demanding.

Ashtanga also emphasizes breath control as you perform the poses in a specific prescribed series. Don't sign up for an ashtanga class unless you're already in good shape, and expect to feel some soreness for a day or two after your first couple of workouts. After a warm-up you'll be put through your paces, flowing from one challenging pose to the next, breathing deeply throughout.

Bikram. Ready to sweat? Bikram yoga is performed in a 100-degree-Fahrenheit room to enhance flexibility. Poses focus on stretching the muscles in a specific sequence, and it's thought to help with symptoms of chronic pain. Like ashtanga yoga, this is a tough workout: The poses are demanding and it's not for anyone but the fittest people and yoga veterans. Bring towels and plenty of water, because you will drip with sweat by the end of class.

Hatha. This "classic" yoga is great for first-time yoga students. It focuses on simple poses, performed at a comfortable pace, with an emphasis on deep, meditative breathing. This low-key, relaxing form of yoga is a great way to wind down at night and the perfect way to begin yoga practice.

Ilyengar. Ilyengar is considered a classical, easier-on-the-body form of yoga, and is good for beginners. It's a form of hatha yoga that was created by B. K. S. Ilyengar, and is now probably the most well-known style of hatha yoga. Ilyengar uses props like blocks, pillows, straps, and chairs to allow practitioners to perform moves even if they're not particularly flexible.

Ilyengar moves focus on proper form and body alignment, and the poses are held longer than in most other styles of yoga.

There is also more emphasis on meditation and inner awareness of your physical body. An ilyengar class will introduce you to the classic yoga poses, and as you get stronger and more flexible, you can ditch the props or try other forms for a new challenge.

Kripalu. This is a flowing, meditation-oriented form of yoga that involves three stages. In the first, you focus on proper alignment and breathing, performing poses for a short period of time. In the second stage, you hold the poses for longer periods of time and incorporate meditation into the practice. Finally, in the third stage, the postures are practiced as a moving meditation, performed in a continuous flow.

Kundalini. Go deeper with this form of yoga that uses chanting, breath control, visualization, and guided relaxation in conjunction with yoga poses. This form of yoga focuses on healing the mind and body and balancing the emotions; it's named for the type of energy in the spine it's supposed to release. With kundalini, you'll focus on precise postures along with specific hand and finger gestures, chanting, and meditation; because of the intense concentration involved, it isn't a great choice for beginners.

Sivananda. This form of yoga involves a series of twelve specific postures performed along with breathing exercises and mantra chanting. Some of the poses are more challenging than others, which makes this a better class for people who have some experience with yoga.

BEFORE YOU GO

While there's a slew of yoga tapes you can choose from, it's a good idea to start with an actual class. A qualified instructor can demonstrate proper form and help correct your body position as you learn the moves. After all, the challenge of yoga is performing the asanas properly. To find a good instructor, ask around. Your local health club or YMCA may offer yoga classes; in larger communities there are yoga studios that focus exclusively on yoga training. Many community colleges also offer yoga classes, or check with your friends to see if they can make recommendations. You may also want to check out the following online resources:

- **http://www.yoga.com/** This comprehensive site includes a searchable teacher/studio directory, information about yoga products and videos, and articles about yoga.

- **http://www.yogaeverywhere.com/directory.html** A directory of yoga instructors and yoga studios throughout the United States; it includes contact information and links to other Web sites.

- **http://www.yogafinder.com/** This site claims to be the largest directory of yoga classes, events, retreats, and products.

- **http://www.yogajournal.com/directory/search.cfm** This is *Yoga Journal*'s searchable directory, and includes information about different types of yoga and the how-tos of postures.

If you're worried about how much you'll shell out for a yoga class, the cost depends on the type of facility (adult education classes may be less expensive than classes at a yoga center with all the bells and whistles) and the number of classes you sign up for. In general, you can expect to pay between $5 to $15 per class, more if you pay for classes individually, and less if you pay for a group of, say, ten sessions or more.

Before you head to class, though, keep these tips in mind:

START OFF SLOWLY. It doesn't matter whether you're in killer shape. Yoga is new to you. Better to start off easy than to be barely able to walk for three days afterward. Don't leap into an ashtanga class because you've heard it burns the most calories. A lower-key hatha or ilyengar class, or one earmarked for beginners, is a smarter choice.

DON'T EAT RIGHT BEFORE CLASS. Believe me, if your digestive tract is busy digesting food, you may feel bloated or uncomfortable during the moves—or, worse yet, unexpectedly pass gas! (And there's nothing like a loud fart in a quiet yoga room.) That's why yoga should be done on an empty stomach.

DRESS APPROPRIATELY. That means comfortable, nonrevealing clothing. You don't need to worry about your goodies falling out when you're attempting a handstand for the first time. Skip the heavy, dangling jewelry, leave your shoes outside the room, and maintain a quiet, relaxed attitude when you enter.

EXPECT TO FEEL AWKWARD AT FIRST. The positions may look easy until you actually try them. If you can't do a particular pose, just do the best you can. Don't force your body into a position that's painful. After a few weeks (or, yeah, maybe months), you'll be amazed at how much more flexible you become. You'll notice that the moves seem easier and that you can hold them longer without discomfort.

FORGET YOUR FELLOW STUDENTS. If you're already pretty fit, you may be surprised that the pudgy middle-aged woman next to you is showing you up on every move. Yoga isn't about competition, and if you're worrying about how you're doing compared to someone else, you won't be able to get into the "yoga flow."

CONSIDER BUYING YOUR OWN EQUIPMENT. With some classes, you need no equipment except a mat and comfortable clothing; others may require the use of things like foam blocks or straps to help you position your body correctly. You'll quickly find that it's more appealing to sweat on your own mat than to have to choose from a damp pile. Besides, you look so cool carrying it to and from class.

TALK TO YOUR DOCTOR FIRST. If you're pregnant or have other health conditions like diabetes or high blood pressure, make sure you get your physician's OK before you try yoga. You may also want to avoid some poses—like headstands—if you have eye problems, or positions that compress your abdomen if you're expecting a baby.

DO TRY THIS AT HOME . . . OR WORK

While a yoga class is the most effective way to introduce yourself to yoga positions, you can learn to do some of the easier poses on your own. If you're feeling overwhelmed or stressed out, a simple yoga pose can help you relax, stretch tired muscles, and improve your circulation. Give these moves a try:

MEDITATION. This simple practice will help calm, relax, and energize you, and will introduce you to breathing awareness, an essential part of any form of yoga. Sit quietly in a comfortable position. Inhale and imagine that you're lifting your breath up through the core of your body and allowing it to go through the crown of your head and then cascade over your body. Repeat, focusing on your breath; if your mind wanders, simply come back to your breath. Shut your eyes or gaze at a spot on the floor; you should be conscious but focused on the inside of your body. Try it for five to ten minutes. As you improve your ability to focus, you'll find it easier to sit and simply "be" for longer stretches of time.

CORPSE POSE. This meditative pose is both simple and challenging: simple because you don't actually move your body, and challenging because you focus on every part of it and on your breathing. Lie on your back, arms at your sides, in a position that feels comfortable to you. Close your eyes and focus on your breathing, extending the length of your exhalations. Starting at your feet, contract your muscles for a few seconds; then relax them. Move up your body, contracting your calves, thighs, buttocks, abdomen, and so on, until you reach the muscles of your neck and face. (This is a type of "progressive relaxation," an effective way of recognizing and helping eliminate tension from tight muscles.) Scan your entire body, focusing on relaxing any muscles that feel tense or tight, and breathe slowly and deeply. Start with five to ten minutes and increase your time in the pose as you wish. Just be careful not to fall asleep!

CHILD'S POSE. This is a relaxing, easy pose that nearly anyone can do. Just be cautious if you have knee problems. Start out facing down on your hands and knees, knees at hip width and hands shoulder-width apart, arms straight. Exhale and sit back on your heels so that your chest and upper body rest on your thighs and your forehead touches the floor. Relax your arms on the floor next to your body, palms up, or extend them in front of you for a deeper stretch through the shoulders. Close your eyes and hold the pose for up to five minutes.

SUPTA VIRASANA. This restorative pose is said to help straighten your spine, reduce anxiety, and quiet the mind. Start by sitting in virasana—sitting on your knees with your feet bent back along the hips. (Knee problems? Don't do it if it hurts!) Use two folded blankets to support the base of your spine, and slowly recline back and rest your elbows on the floor. If that's still comfortable, go ahead and lie all the way down; then place your arms over your head and straighten them. Breathe deeply, and hold the pose for five to ten minutes. You'll feel an inch or two taller when you get up.

Want to do yoga, but think classes are just too much trouble? Don't give up. While there's no substitute for one-on-one yoga instruction, there's a plethora of excellent videotapes and books that will introduce you to the complex and ever-changing world of yoga. (Check out the Web sites listed earlier in this section for recommendations.) Even if you never progress very far beyond downward-facing dog and the sun salutation, regular sessions will make you calmer, more centered, and an all-around happier person—good news for you and the people around you.

Pitch Your Own TV Show

6

Ever watched the tube and thought, "I could come up with a better show than this?" Are you sure the heart of a sitcom writer beats deep within you? Or do you have life experience that would make a great setup for a drama? If you're ready to pitch your own TV show, read on.

THE BASICS

First, you don't just call a production company and rattle off your idea. That's not the way the showbiz world works. If you have a TV script or concept, you should register it with the Writers Guild of America (WGA) at *http://www.wga.org*. (You don't have to be a member to register, but nonmembers pay $20 per written piece versus $10 for members.) Registering your work with the WGA helps prove that you're the creator of the work. Putting "Registered/WGA" and/or your registration number on your work lets production companies and others know that the work is protected, and that you know what you're doing (or at least that you're learning).

Write It Up

It's not enough that you want to write for TV or that you have a great idea in your head. You need to actually write the treatment (more about that in a bit). That may mean narrowing your focus if you have more than one idea bouncing around, and figuring out how you want to spend your time. Remember, too, that television shows vary in form and content. Do you want to write:

- **A drama series?** A treatment for a drama series should include a rundown of the main characters, their individual quirks, and what has brought them together (e.g., they all work at a Chicago emergency room). With drama series, character development is important, although some successful series (think *Law & Order*) focus more on individual story lines than on the characters' lives. You'll also want to include a pilot script, as well as give an idea of the direction that the series would take over a twenty-two-episode season.

- **A game show?** Do you have a new twist on *Jeopardy* or *Wheel of Fortune*? What makes your game show idea unique, and what are the rules? What type of person will the host be? What will the sets look like? Whether you're creating a new game from scratch or putting a new spin on an old favorite, it must be different from what's already out there.

- **A made-for-TV movie?** Think drama. Many TV movies address current social issues; others are based on historical events. While you may have multiple characters, your main character should be facing some sort of peril. You don't want to be melodramatic, but you can't be boring, either. If your story is fact-based (remember when all three networks came out with their version of the Amy Fisher/Joey

Buttafuoco story?), make sure you play up that angle. Keep in mind, too, that it's important for your movie to have broad appeal, whether it's true-life drama, a coming-of-age story, a historical piece, or anything else.

- **A miniseries?** Can't fit your idea into a two-hour movie? Then you may want to pitch it as a miniseries, which will be aired over more than one night. Many miniseries are based on historical events (think *Roots*) and/or based on books. Just as with a made-for-TV movie, it's important that you have a good story to tell, filled with drama and characters that viewers will care about.

- **A reality show?** The trend started with *Survivor,* but shows no sign of stopping. With a reality show, consider who the "real people" will be and what tasks or challenges they'll face. What's the overall prize? Is it the hand of a millionaire? (Oops, that's been done.) Or $1 million dollars for not being voted off the island? (Oops, that's been done, too.) Remember, you've got to come up with something new— and something that viewers will enjoy watching.

- **A sitcom?** A situation comedy is a series in which the episodes typically run thirty minutes. It usually focuses on a group of characters; even if there is supposedly one main character (think *Seinfeld* or *Everybody Loves Raymond*), the supporting cast is just as important. For sitcoms, you'll need to include a list of the main characters along with a brief description of their physical appearances, jobs, personality quirks, and so forth. Also, explain what has brought the characters together. Is it that they all hang out a local bar (e.g., *Cheers*)? Are they twenty-something friends living in New York (e.g., *Friends*)? Your treatment should address the characters and give an overview of the issues they're facing; also, include a brief list of possible episodes. If you've written scripts before, you may want to include a pilot episode script of about twenty-four pages; if you haven't, look for a partner who can take on this responsibility, or just focus on the treatment itself.

Your Pitch

Now that you've decided what type of program you want to write and pitch, let's talk about what you need to pitch your show. Your completed pitch should include an outline that sets out the following:

- *the title of the show* (duh!)

- *the format of the show* (Is it a game show? A reality show? A sitcom series?)

- *your name, and the WGA registration number*

- *the logline*—A **logline** cosists of one or two sentences that describe your show and what makes it unique. "A stand-up comedian's everyday experiences living in New York with quirky friends and neighbors" would be a logline for *Seinfeld*. "An animated comedy series about a nuclear family that pokes fun at real life" would be a logline for *The Simpsons*. Your logline is a critical part of your pitch, so make it as good as you can.

- *the treatment*—Other than the logline, this is the most im-portant part of your outline. The **treatment** provides a detailed description of your show. It should only be a few pages long, but it must provide enough information so that someone reading it understands exactly what you're pitching. If it's a **scripted show** (meaning it's written, unlike reality shows or game shows), you should include some information about the main characters and the kinds of issues they'll face. If it's a **reality show** (increasingly popular these days!), make sure you take the time to explain the concept of the show and what people on the show will be expected to do. If it's a **game show**, include the rules, prizes, and a description of the stage as well as the host's personality. Remember, the idea is in your head, and your job with the treatment is to communicate that idea in writing.

MAKING THE PITCH

How the Process Works

Keep in mind that producers' needs are constantly changing, depending on what they and networks are looking for at the moment. For example, one network may be looking for more sitcoms with cute kids; another network may be interested in real-life two-hour made-for-TV movies. If your work captures a producer's attention, he or she will do some homework before pitching the project (with a script, if appropriate) to a network or studio.

Basically, a production company or a network looks for a great idea that may turn into a great show. Your job is to give them that great idea. The production company may want to work a bit more—say, to determine a particular actor's level of interest—before it actually pitches the project. If the producer is interested, he'll option your idea from you, meaning he pays for the exclusive right to sell your idea to a studio or network for a certain period of time. That may involve hiring a writer to actually create a script based on the treatment, especially if you don't have any Hollywood writing experience. Depending on the project, the producer may also look for actors (especially "names") to star in the project.

If the project is purchased by the network or studio, consider your television-writing career officially launched! If not, it's time to get started on the next project. A **pass** on a current project (a production company or network's indication that it's not interested) doesn't mean the next project won't be successful.

Get Your Pitch Out There

There are a number of companies on the Web that claim to help you sell your work, including TVWritersVault.com (*http://www. TVWritersVault.com*). The idea is that, for a fee, they'll give you access to production companies that might not otherwise be interested (many production companies don't accept unsolicited submissions). This makes the process somewhat easier if you're willing to shell out some money to these types of companies. However, there are other ways you can pitch as well—through an agent or on your own.

Do You Need an Agent?

If you're new to the biz, you'll probably find it difficult to find an agent for your work. Agents tend to work with established writers—those who already have sold TV or film projects. But if you have an offer from a production company, you can hire a lawyer who specializes in entertainment law to negotiate a deal for you.

If you have your heart set on getting an agent, though, it's similar to approaching a production company. Send a query letter that describes your TV idea and your relevant background and experience. If you know the agent has represented projects similar to yours, mention that. Ask if you may send the treatment, and enclose a self-addressed stamped envelope for his or her response.

Do It Yourself

If you make the pitch yourself, you have three basic options: call, write, or pitch in person. Chances are that you'll be doing one of the first two, or a combination of them.

Regardless of how you pitch, highlight your unique background and qualifications. If you're pitching a game show based on chess and you're a ranked chess player, say so. If you're pitching a sitcom set in a hospital and you worked for years as an RN, play that up.

Keep track of where you pitch your project, whether by phone, mail, or in person. Write down the name of the person you speak to or contact, and any relevant comments (e.g., "says they have something similar in development already").

To find production companies and networks that may be interested in your work, you can sign up for a year's subscription to the Hollywood Creative Directory for $249.95. This includes access to the following directories:

- *Hollywood Creative Directory,* which lists film and TV producers, and studio and network executives

- *Hollywood Representation Directory,* which lists agents, entertainment attorneys, managers, and publicists

- *Hollywood Distributors Directory,* which lists networks, financing companies, and domestic and international distributors

- *Hollywood Music Industry Directory,* which lists record companies, music publishers, and music supervisors.

Check out *http://www.hcdonline.com/* for more details. If that's too rich for your blood, try a weeklong subscription for $24.95.

The National Association of Television Program Executives includes a list of NATPE members on its Web site at *http://www. natpe.org/memberresources/natpedirectory/.* You have to be a member to access the contact information, but you can use the site to search for names and types of businesses (e.g., "independent producer/content producer," "cable/satellite network") and then track down the applicable contact information on your own. The NATPE also runs an annual boot camp every summer where you can develop your TV show concept and then pitch it in person (in the "Pitch Pit," no less) to TV execs. Check out *http://www.natpe.org/calendar/bootcamp/* for details.

GET SMART—AND GET CONNECTED

Part of being a television writer is keeping up with what's happening in the industry. That means reading the "trades," or the entertainment industry magazines like *Variety* and *The Hollywood Reporter.* Both publications have news about current development and production deals. As you begin to understand how the industry works, and make connections in the biz, you may find that it's easier than you thought to sell your TV idea—or maybe find that you've got an even better one than your first.

Join the Circus

7

Been threatening to join the circus since you were ten years old—or even before that? If you've "grown up" and still have visions of clowning around, swinging from a trapeze, or even selling peanuts, it's not outside the realm of possibility. Join the circus and you may have a chance to travel the world (or at least the States) and make new friends, study under experts in the field, and make a living following your dream to entertain others.

Unless you happen to be born into a circus family, there are two basic routes by which to hook up with the circus of your choice. Most circus folk either go to school and learn the necessary skills, or join a circus at an entry-level position (think cleaning up elephant poop) and follow an informal apprenticeship to learn the ropes (pun intended). And it's tougher to do than you might think. Competition for acceptance into circuses can be stiff. It's not enough just to know your stuff. You've got to have drive, determination, and a lot of energy as well.

LEARNING THE ROPES

If you don't have circus skills, you can learn them—at a circus college, of course. There are several respected schools in the United States, in addition to internationally known programs in Europe, mentioned below.

United States

Florida State University (*http://www.circus.fsu.edu/index.htm*) offers a circus-training program on campus year-round that is open to all students; no experience necessary. Students learn skills like juggling, hand balancing, and bicycle and aerial acts—swinging on the trapeze with the greatest of ease.

On the West Coast, the Circus Center (*http://www.circus-center.org*) in San Francisco offers a two-year training program that specializes in Chinese acrobatic skills. The Circus Center also offers summer camps and workshops for both youth and adults in which you can learn everything from juggling to mastering both the swinging and flying trapezes.

Want a quicker way to get skills? Whether you're looking for pre-job training or just want to learn basic circus abilities, there are dozens of schools and programs throughout the United States that offer circus skills training. Check out some of the programs below:

- *Circus Day Foundation,* part of St. Louis, Missouri's Circus Harmony, offers circus-skills classes throughout the year for both adults and kids (*http://circusharmony. org/cdf2.html*).

- *Circus Arts Workshop,* with three locations in the Washington, D.C. area, says they'll teach you basic trapeze skills in a weekend (*http://www.circusarts.com/*)!

- **Clown School of San Francisco** helps you identify, characterize, and develop your inner clown (*http://www.clownschoolsf.org/*).

- **Trapeze Arts,** in Oakland, California, and Lake Tahoe, Nevada, teaches aerial skills in both indoor and outdoor settings (*http://www.trapezearts.com/*).

For more programs, visit *http://directory.google.com/Top/Arts/Performing_Arts/Circus/Schools/* for an extensive list of both U.S. and international schools and workshops.

Europe and Canada

Circuses have a longer history in Europe, which may explain why so many schools are based there. If you want to learn circus skills under an actual tent (as opposed to in a building), consider moving to Europe. There are many traveling shows throughout Europe, which means more opportunities for work. Montreal also tends to be a hub for circuses, and is home to the highly regarded École Nationale de Cirque (*http://www.enc.qc.ca/*), Cirque du Soleil (*http://www.cirquedusoleil.com/cirquedusoleil/default.htm*), and Cirque Éloize (*http://www.cirque-eloize.com/*).

If you want to learn as you go, check out The Academy of Circus Arts, run by Zippos Circus (*http://www.zipposcircus.co.uk*), the only traveling circus school in Europe. Here students eighteen years and older have the opportunity to develop hands-on skills living, working, and traveling with the circus. You'll discover not only your inner clown or acrobat, but hopefully a taste for the nomadic circus lifestyle as well. The Academy claims that a whopping 99 percent of its students go on to successful circus careers.

If you prefer a building-based European school, check out The Circus Space, located in London (*http://www.thecircusspace.co.uk*). The advantage to attending a stationary school rather than plunging right in to a traveling circus lifestyle is that you don't have to be on the road traveling while you're learning. You can limp back to your room, ice sore muscles, and sleep in a regular bed instead of constantly changing locales. Graduates from The Circus Space often specialize in one area of entertainment, and may prefer performing at parties or trade shows instead of making a full-blown commitment to circus work.

For more European circus schools, circus classes, and advice, check out the Circus Arts Forum Web site (*http://www. circusarts.org.uk*), or check the listing of international schools listed in Circus Yellow Pages at *http://www.circusland.com* (choose the English rather than Russian version).

BUT I CAN'T JUGGLE!

If you want to do anything but the most menial jobs at the circus, you've got to have skills. If you're serious about hooking up with a traveling circus or attending a circus school, it's a good idea to start developing those talents now.

Be the Boss

One of the most visible positions at the circus is the main emcee of the show—the ringmaster. The ringmaster introduces the various acts and guides the audience through the entertainment. In fact, in the "olden days" before modern lighting equipment made spotlights possible, it was the job of the ringmaster to direct the attention of the audience to the next act. Modern-day ringmasters tend to perform alongside other entertainers, and may sing, dance, or crack jokes—you name it. If you enjoy using inflated terms such as "amazing," "spell-binding," and "death-defying," and have a big personality and stage presence to match, this may be the perfect position for you.

Clown Around

Think of a circus and what comes to mind? Elephants, acrobats . . . and clowns, of course. Clowns often seem to be the glue holding the whole show together, but they also make their jobs look effortless. Generally, clowns need a good understanding of movement and must be physically fit; they may be called on to do just about anything from walking a tightrope to riding an exotic animal to substituting for the lion tamer. (Gulp!)

Clowns are not all created equal. For example, there are **white-faced clowns**—probably the most well-known—who literally use white makeup and dramatic eye and lip colors. Typically, the "white-face" is the leader when performing with other clowns. (Never noticed that, did you?) There is also a **character clown**, who adopts some specific role such as a butcher, policeman, or hobo. (Charlie Chaplin, as the "Little Tramp," is a classic character clown.) A third type is the **Pierrot**, or "French clown," who typically appears white-faced in a black-and-white costume, and is known for his or her melancholy demeanor.

It's not enough to practice your clowning skills on friends and family. The San Francisco School of Circus Arts (mentioned above) can help you learn skills such as juggling, tumbling, and balancing. Once you've mastered the art, the school recommends sending a seven-minute videotape of your act to every show, from Ringling Brothers to small "mud shows," or traveling circuses, for which you're interested in working.

Be a Circus Freak—for Real

No circus is complete without sideshows. People with unusual talents or strange physical appearances and weird or exotic animals were once a hallmark of entertainment within circuses—and things haven't changed all that much. If you weren't born with two heads or extra limbs, the Coney Island Sideshow

School in Brooklyn can help you acquire such skills. But be forewarned—this isn't the school, or the career, for the faint of heart! You'll learn to eat fire, walk on beds of nails without puncturing your feet, and hammer nails into your nose. (Did you know that sword swallowers overcome their gag reflex by repeatedly sticking coat hangers down their throats?) If these details don't freak you out, check out *http://www.coneyislandusa. com* for information on the school's six-day course. Amazing—you can learn to be a freak in less than a week!

Happily, not every "freak" has such extreme talents. How about becoming a juggler instead? There are many different types of jugglers, the most well-known being the "gentleman" juggler, who uses everyday objects such as hats, canes, plates, and the like. It may look all but impossible, but from the physics perspective, jugglers manipulate several physical objects in patterns based on numerical sequences. What it comes down to is faster-than-normal reflexes, good eye-hand coordination, and a willingness to practice, practice, practice. Just keep in mind that jugglers are fairly far down the ladder of entertainers in the circus hierarchy. Maybe sword swallowing is for you after all.

Flying through the Air

Circuses are always looking for people with athletic backgrounds. In fact, after their prime competition years end, many former athletes, even Olympians, join up to keep in shape and to prolong their careers. **Contortionists**—acrobats able to bend their bodies in dramatic ways—are one example. To be a contortionist, though, you generally need great natural flexibility and usually have to have an extensive gymnastic background.

Trapeze performers, who perform on a short bar hung by two cords suspended from a high support, must have incredible balance, timing, and physical strength and flexibility. In addition to static trapeze, there is also flying trapeze, in which a performer grabs the bar and leaps from a higher platform, working with gravity to create the swing. Happily, this is typically done over a net.

Tightrope walkers need excellent balance and agility to follow a small wire or rope at a great height. Sometimes these performers use a pole to aid in balancing; sometimes they even work without a safety net! If you're an experienced gymnast, swimmer, synchronized swimmer, diver, or the like, check out the Web sites of the circuses in which you're interested; most big circuses hold auditions periodically. Better yet, apply by sending a video of you performing your act. If they're interested, you'll be invited to audition.

Live for Danger—or Not

If it's danger you live for, consider training to be the **human cannonball**, launched into the air by a spring or compressed air. These personal projectiles can go as fast as sixty miles per hour, (hopefully) landing on a net. You can also train in **knife throwing**, an art that is extremely difficult to master, as knives tend to rotate as they fly (a warning if a would-be knife thrower asks you to stand in for him or her!).

Keep in mind that circus talent isn't limited to those willing to eat fire or walk tightropes hundreds of feet above the ground. Singers, musicians, dancers, and actors are constantly in demand as well, and the same audition process generally applies for these positions. Less-glamorous but always-needed positions include lighting technicians, costume designers, and makeup artists. To find which circuses are hiring, look at their Web sites; most circuses now have such sites and use them to advertise job openings as well as upcoming shows.

If these jobs sound like they entail too much commitment, keep in mind that some people do become very successful in the circus by starting with much more menial tasks such as cleaning up after animals or selling candy. The turnover for these jobs tends to be quite high (go figure!), so the next time the circus is in town, stop in and apply. But have your bags packed, because if something's available, they'll most likely need you to start right away. To land entry-level positions like this, check out *The Circus Report,* an industry magazine. (Can't find it at the local bookstore? You can order it for $48 a year at *http://www.amazon.com.*)

BEFORE YOU RUN OFF . . .

So, you've honed your skills and your suitcase is packed. Before you leave behind friends and family, though, consider a few of the not-so-positive aspects of circus life. If you are hired to work for a circus, you'll be on the move much of the year, perhaps living in somewhat rustic housing—or maybe a notch below that. You may not get wealthy as a circus performer, and the benefits may not amount to much; but if you love to perform, love to travel, and want a lifestyle that's radically different from most people's, go for it. You can make that dream you had as a ten-year-old come true.

Be a Teacher

8

Want to mold impressionable minds, have people listen to you all day long, or simply have your summers off? Become a teacher and you'll have the opportunity to make a real difference in the lives of others while enjoying a rewarding profession.

If you were lucky enough to have a teacher who changed your life, you already know what an effect a good one can have. But teaching isn't for the faint-hearted. It takes commitment, patience, and flexibility—in addition to some smarts.

DO YOU HAVE THE TALENT TO TEACH?

If you think you want to teach, consider why. Sure, having summers and all those school holidays off is cool, but don't forget you are expected to actually teach the little buggers, whether they're in second grade or sixth.

The good news, though, is that the United States is going to need a lot of teachers in the near future—we're talking in the range of two million more. That means if you decide on teaching as a career, your job should be relatively secure (assuming you're decent at it, anyway!). And hey! You'll be doing society a favor. How cool is that?

And when it comes to bucks, the salary for a typical teacher is higher than you might think. According to the U.S. Bureau of Labor Statistics, the average salary for an elementary, middle-, or high-school teacher is in the $40,000 to $44,000 range.

In addition to job security and decent pay, teachers have the satisfaction of working with kids to help them learn about the world. If you're so inclined, you can also become more involved by taking on extracurricular activities, so if you've dreamed of coaching basketball, you may have a chance to do it—albeit at the junior-high level.

And when you teach, you have the opportunity to use your brain and keep adding to your knowledge every year. Just as a researcher is continually developing her expertise, a teacher stays mentally engaged in the process of educating. If you love to learn, you'll probably enjoy teaching as well.

WHAT YOU NEED TO PASS MUSTER

While many schools need teachers, you can't simply show up and apply for a job. First, you have to be licensed by the state you teach in, and licensing requirements vary from state to state. Check out *http://www.uky.edu/Education/TEP/usacert.html* for more info about each state's requirements. However, most states require that teachers:

- *Have a bachelor's degree (and, in some states, a master's degree).* If you want to teach elementary school, you usually need to major or minor in education.

- *Have a degree in the area in which they want to teach—* at least if they want to teach secondary subjects, or those taught to students in grades seven through twelve.

- *Complete an accredited, approved education program that includes student teaching.* (Hey, look at it as good practice.)

- *Pass a state test or licensing exam.*

In some states, you must demonstrate a strong liberal-arts foundation by taking a variety of courses in basic subject areas like language, English, math, science, and social studies.

Because of the demand to attract more teachers, especially in geographic areas that have shortages, some states now offer "nontraditional" routes to teaching. With a nontraditional or alternative route, you'll usually need to have a bachelor's degree in the subject area you'll be teaching, take and pass state-required exams, and complete an intensive teacher prep program. You may also have to complete a teaching internship before you receive a teaching credential. Visit *http://www.teach-now.org/* for information about alternative certification programs.

While you should teach subjects that you care about (it helps make you a better teacher, after all), there is a definite shortage of teachers in some specific areas, including: bilingual education, computer science, English as a second language, foreign languages, mathematics, science, and special education. And if you're not lily-white, that's a good thing—teachers "of color" are also in demand.

Already got a four-year degree? You can enter a post-collegiate program to become a teacher; these programs usually last a year. Or check whether there are alternative programs in your area that combine intensive teacher training and graduate school courses with practical teaching experience. Some programs allow you to apply your credits toward a master's degree if you're interested in one.

READY TO TEACH? WHAT'S NEXT?

Because of the demand for teachers, there are several programs that can help place you in an area where teachers are most needed. Teach for America (*http://www.teachforamerica.org*) is a national teacher corps program that places recent grads in two-year positions with urban and rural public schools.

The National Teaching Academy in Washington, D.C. (*http://www.nationalteachingacademy.org/*) recruits wannabe teachers, who then participate in a one-year program that prepares them to become effective teachers in an urban environment. Upon completion of the program, participants receive their teacher certification and a master's degree in education. There are also regional programs throughout the country; check out your options at *http://www.teacherscount.org/wannateach/how/pathways.shtml*.

However, most teachers still find their jobs by applying directly to a school district. Don't overlook private or independent schools, which may have their own criteria for hiring teachers. In many cases, you needn't be certified to teach in an independent school.

ON THE FENCE? WHAT TO DO

Maybe you're considering teaching, but you're not sure whether it's a good fit for you. The best thing to do is try it out for a while to see if you like it. There are a number of things you can do to get involved teaching in a classroom with kids or teens in the age group you'd like to work.

Teachers work in one of three basic age ranges: early childhood, elementary, or secondary school. But first-graders are way different than fifth graders, which is why it's smart to actually spend time with kids of the age you'd like to teach, before you commit to doing it.

Your teaching responsibilities will vary, depending on the age of your students. For example, if you work with preschool kids, you'll be with the same group of children day after day, doing basic things like helping them learn to write their names, recognize letters, identify colors and shapes, and learn basic number skills like counting to ten. At this stage, your main job is helping them learn through play and getting them ready for kindergarten; your students may still be sucking their thumbs and learning basic social skills like sharing toys and cooperation.

If you teach at the elementary level, you'll usually work with the same group of kids day after day, but you'll be responsible for teaching them a variety of subjects, including reading, math, and social studies. The older the students, the more detail you'll go into, but it can be just as challenging to teach third-graders their multiplication tables as it is to cover the Declaration of Independence with your sixth-grade class. There's a big difference between teaching younger children and older ones, especially by the time hormones get involved (around sixth or seventh grade), so consider which ages you're drawn to.

At the secondary-school level, you'll probably specialize in one subject, say science or history, and teach it all day to different groups of kids. On one hand, you don't have to teach as many subjects; on the other, you may not develop the close relationships with your students you can develop at the early-childhood or elementary levels. High-school students can be the most challenging to work with, but they're nearing adulthood and you may be able to have the most dramatic impact on their lives.

Check with your local schools for volunteer opportunities like tutoring or mentoring children, or look into other programs like the ones listed in this chapter.

More than 1,000 universities and colleges participate in America Reads, a national campaign to help children read well by the end of elementary school. Approximately 300 colleges participate in America Counts, a similar program that helps students master challenging mathematics. If you're a college student, visit *http://www.teacherscount.org/wannateach/how/pathways. shtml* for more info, or ask whether your school participates in this program.

If you're considering a career change, you may want to look into Power Lunch, a lunchtime literacy and mentoring program in which elementary-school students are matched one-on-one with volunteers to share conversations, good books, and lunch. The program currently operates in forty-three cities; visit *http://www.everybodywins.org/* for more information.

And if you're in New York City, you can participate in Learning Leaders (*http://www.learningleaders.org/*), which helps public-school students; volunteers work with children from pre-K to high school with subjects ranging from reading to math.

TEACHING GROWN-UPS

But what if you want to teach adults rather than kids? If you have a skill or talent you'd like to share, you can teach noncredit or community education classes. This is a great way to make a few extra bucks, expand your repertoire, and experience the thrill of people listening to what you have to say.

Come up with an Idea

First, you have to come up with the idea for your class. Maybe you weave the most extraordinary baskets. Or you design cool jewelry. Or you've become an expert at designing Web pages. Figure out what you want to teach, and how long you need to teach it. Will the class be a one-time, three-hour session? A two-hour class that meets for six weeks?

Look at the catalog for the classes offered by your local adult education program, park district, or community college; that will give you an idea of what's offered and how long the classes typically last.

Make Your Pitch

Next, contact the place where you'd like to teach. Ask for the person who's in charge of noncredit or adult education classes, and pitch your idea by phone. Explain what people will get out of the class, what your relevant background is, and what kind of teaching experience you have, if any. Expect to follow up by e-mail or regular mail with a formal class proposal before you get the go-ahead.

The Actual Teaching Process

It's a good idea to plan out your class before the first time it meets. You'll feel more prepared and will be able to better organize the material as well. Some colleges will want you to have an overview or outline prepared that you share with your students.

If you're nervous before your class, that's normal. There are several things you can do to ensure that your class is a hit among your students:

- *Get people talking.* Poll the students on the first day of class. Have them share their names, their backgrounds, and what they hope to get out of the class. They'll feel more comfortable with each other.

- *Give plenty of specific examples.* Students remember stories and examples much more easily than general rules.

- *Listen to your students.* Ask for feedback and be willing to adapt the class to what your students want and need, not just what you think is important.

- *Give them breaks.* It's a good idea to give a bathroom break every hour or so. If you notice people spacing out, fidgeting, or squirming in their seats, it's time for a breather.

- *Finish your classes on time.* Nothing drives students battier than a teacher who makes them late.

- *Be accessible.* Share your e-mail address and phone number, and encourage students to contact you with questions. Even if they don't take you up on it, they'll appreciate the gesture.

Teaching adults can be draining, especially when you've already put in a full day before teaching an evening class. But the rewards are more than just monetary. And the same is true for teaching children. Most teachers say they get as much out of their students as their students do from them, which makes for a stimulating, satisfying career if you love kids and want to make a difference in the world.

Explore the Great Outdoors

9

Isn't it time you got off the couch? If your idea of exploring the outdoors is the stroll from your car to your house, or a quick walk to the subway, think again. Mother Nature's got a world of wonders out there. All you have to do is leave the house—even just for a hike. Other outdoor activities require equipment, but they can help you make the most of your time outside. You'll get some fresh air, get in better shape, and may even unleash your inner Mountain Man or Mountain Babe.

EASY EXPLORING

Don't let your couch potato status keep you from participating. Give these activities a try:

Camping

If you're never camped before, hook up with a friend who knows the ropes. Inexperienced campers can rent a site at a state or national park, which typically include ready-made fire pits and barbecues. They often also offer bathroom facilities for those who don't want to rough it all the way.

<u>What You'll Need</u>

The whole idea of camping is to eat, sleep, and live outside, but you'll still need a few supplies. Your needs will vary depending on the time of year and location, but generally you should plan to bring the following:

- *tent and rain cover*
- *portable light*
- *cook stove* (unless your campsite has cooking facilities)
- *dry firewood and matches* (the former can often be gathered at the campsite)
- *sleeping bag(s)*
- *waterproof bag for matches and other supplies*
- *bottled water (unless there's a water source on-site) and food* (don't forget the marshmallows!)

Canoeing

Check out the outdoors from the water for a different perspective. You can canoe on a lake or other open water (easier, but slower going) or on moving water such as a creek or river. Skip the roaring rapids unless you're with an experienced guide or you have some technical experience.

Lake, or flat-water, canoeing doesn't require a whole lot of technical experience. The most difficult part is the portage, or having to carry your canoe and gear from one body of water to another. While this gives you a chance to stretch your legs, the monotony can get to you. Paddling a canoe requires repeating the same motion for long periods of time. You'll be paddling with a partner, and getting in sync with this person can be a challenge. Once you get the hang of it, though, it feels natural and you can enjoy your surroundings.

The most basic stroke in a canoer's repertoire is the **J-stroke**. This requires a subtle flick of the wrist at exactly the right paddle position, which can be tough to do depending on the headwind, waves, or current. After the J-stroke comes the C-stroke, which is an easier stroke that moves the boat in the opposite direction of the J. Have an experienced canoer show you how to perform each stroke, and note how your wrist and arms move the blades of the paddle. Then you're ready to hit the water.

What You'll Need

- *canoe (duh!)*
- *some water to float on*
- *paddles*
- *flotation device (e.g., a life jacket)*
- *watertight pack*
- *extra shoes and clothes in a watertight bag*
- *bug spray*
- *sun hat*
- *water and snacks*

Hiking

All you need to do is find the nearest forest preserve, state park, national park, or hill, and start walking! Easy enough, right? Visit the ranger's station for maps of the area and info about the park and weather. Most forest preserves and state and national parks now offer online maps as well.

What You'll Need

- *hiking boots or athletic shoes with good support*
- *layered clothing* (so you can remove or add layers, depending on the weather)
- *sunscreen and sunglasses*
- *water*

Road Biking

Pedal through your local forest preserve or state park for an easy adventure. The terrain will be mostly flat and suitable for beginners, and it's a great way to spend time with friends.

If you're new to biking, practice balance, steering, using the brakes, and changing gears in a place without cars or other bikes. Once you've brushed up on these skills, try riding single-handed so that you can make hand signals. Practice making turns, riding over uneven surfaces, and looking over your shoulder without swerving or wobbling. Then you're ready to hit the roads.

What You'll Need

- *a road or mountain bike*
- *a helmet to protect your noggin*
- *elbow guards* (optional)
- *water bottle*

MORE ADVANCED EXPLORING

Fit and healthy enough to try an activity that's a little more demanding? Here are a couple of cool options:

Mountain Biking

If you've mastered road biking and are looking for a bigger challenge, try mountain biking, which presents additional challenges and obstacles.

Pedaling

It's easy enough on flat ground, but when you're biking up and down hills, you'll have to remove your feet from the pedals frequently. If you use pedals with toe clips, which help keep your feet on the pedals, make sure that you can pop your feet out of them quickly. This ability may save you from a nasty spill.

Before heading out, sit and spin the pedals to find the proper riding position. Your arms should be slightly bent to reach the handlebars, and your seat height should be adjusted so that your legs are extended about 75 percent at the bottom of each pedal stroke. Your body should remain loose and relaxed as you ride; never lock your knees or elbows.

Another skill you'll need in order to mountain bike is the ability to pedal while standing. Lift yourself off the seat, stand on your pedals, and crank them around. Practice using high gears on flat ground before you tackle the hills; on hills, you'll use low gears.

Shifting Gears

Speaking of shifting gears, this skill is particularly important for mountain biking. Higher gears make it harder to pedal but allow you to go faster, while lower gears make it easier to pedal and help you get up steep hills. Using a moderately steep hill, try to get comfortable with the gears you'll use for hills of different pitches. As the hill gets steeper, it's best to shift before you get to the highest incline instead of while you're on it. That lets you gain some momentum to tackle the hill.

Tackling Bumps

Practice going over bumps in the road before you tackle the big bumps that trails will throw your way. Start off using a curb in the street. Stand and coast on your bike at a moderate speed straight off the curb from the upper level to the lower level; absorb the drop, or bump, with your arms and legs. Do this at different speeds until you're comfortable.

Like climbing stairs, going up the bump is a little tougher. Approach the curb at a slow to moderate speed, standing on the pedals of the bike. Right before you reach the curb, push your body down toward the handlebars to get some spring in the front tire; then quickly push your body up from your hands and pull the handlebars up, lifting the front wheel up just in time to clear the curb. Then lighten your weight on the pedals, allowing your rear wheel to pop up to the top of the curb, letting your legs absorb any bump.

Sound easy? It is, once you get the hang of it—but give yourself plenty of time to practice these skills before you head out for the trails.

What You'll Need

- *a helmet* (No bones about it—it may save your life. Make sure it fits properly, too.)

- *cycling gloves*

- *sunglasses or goggles*

- *padded shorts* (your butt will thank you)

- *elbow guards* (optional)

- *water bottle*

Cross-Country Skiing

This popular winter sport involves using your arms and legs simultaneously on skis. You've got to be in decent cardiovascular shape to try it; in fact, it's got the rep as the world's best aerobic exercise. But if you are just beginning, don't be intimidated! Once you get the hang of it, it's fun—albeit a lot of work.

Most newbies learn the "classical" style of cross-country skiing first. You slide one ski forward and reach forward with the opposite arm to plant the pole in the snow in front of you, then pull on the pole to move forward; as you lift the pole out of the snow, you repeat the process sliding the opposite ski forward and shifting to the pole on the other side of your body. It sounds complicated, but once you get into the "flow," it feels natural and smooth. Have a friend show you how the motion works, or take a how-to lesson from your local park district or YMCA. They'll often have equipment available for rental as well.

While you can cross-country ski pretty much anywhere there's snow, starting out you may want to stick to places with groomed trails. Groomed trails make it easier to get around. They're packed and not as rough as fresh snow; the packed, groomed surface requires less energy to slide your skis, which means it takes less effort to move forward.

On the other hand, **off-track skiing** can let you explore fresh snow and get off the beaten path—literally. Just keep in mind that it is hard work, especially if you're skiing in deep snow on hilly terrain. Master the basics before you go off-track, and for the best experience, match the difficulty of the trail to your level of interest and fitness.

<u>What You'll Need</u>

- *cross-country skis, with bindings attached, and boots* (Start with waxless skis at first, which don't slide as quickly, giving you time to master the equipment and skiing technique.)

- *ski poles*

- *waterproof pants and coat*

- *warm socks* (Cold tootsies will make you miserable.)

- *warm gloves*

- *a water pack, sunscreen, and sunglasses* (On a sunny day, the glare from the snow can give you a terrific headache.)

Snowshoeing

If you want a winter activity but the idea of skiing is too intimidating, try snowshoeing. Snowshoeing is similar to hiking, but you use a wider stride. It can feel a little awkward until you get the hang of it, but beginners usually pick it up pretty quickly. And few things are more beautiful than walking through a silent forest in the winter and watching for deer.

You can snowshoe pretty much anywhere you have a wide open space—and snow, of course. Better yet, you don't have to search for groomed trails—you can get through anything on these things! In the beginning, though, you may want to stick to places where the snow isn't really deep, as it takes a certain amount of effort just to move your snowshoes through it. The snow shouldn't be too shallow, though, as you can trip on rocks or uneven terrain.

<u>What You'll Need</u>

- *hiking boots that fit inside your snowshoes—and warm socks*

- *snowshoes* (rent them if you've never tried them before—many parks offer rental equipment in the winter)

- *waterproof pants and ski jacket*

- *gloves and hat*

- *sunglasses and sunscreen*

- *ski poles, if you want them* (they can help you navigate up steep hills)

GET OUT THERE!

Regardless of the activity you choose, spending more time in the outdoors pays off—with benefits ranging from rosy cheeks to a fitter bod. Develop a closer relationship with Mother Nature and you'll appreciate all those natural wonders more—plus develop those hearty, healthy Eddie Bauer-type looks. Even if you eschew the more active choices to spend most of your time sitting by the campfire telling ghost stories, you've made it off the couch! And that's something to be proud of.

10 Contribute to a Cause

There's little in life that feels as good as helping someone else—and you don't have to channel Mother Teresa to do it. Contribute your time, money, or worldly possessions you're no longer using to a worthy charity, and you'll get that warmhearted feeling—and often a tax deduction as well. And you'll make a difference in someone's life on top of it.

THEY WANT YOU—AND YOUR MONEY

So, you've decided to support a charity. Awesome. Now comes the hard part—choosing one.

There are so many worthy charities (and lots of not-so-worthy ones—more about that in a bit) out there, it's a good idea to think about what types of organizations you'd like to support before you start your research. Otherwise you'll be overwhelmed by the number of organizations that want and need your money, and you may feel like you can't possibly help all of them, so why help any?

What types of organizations do you want to support? Consider questions like these:

- *Who does the charity help?* Is it people in a particular geographic region, for example, or those of a particular race or religious group? Does it assist children, or old people, or those who are fighting a disease? Remember, too, that charities don't just work on behalf of people—you can help animals, or protect the environment, or support national parks, or work to preserve historic buildings.

- *How does the charity help?* Do they hand out monetary donations, or do they offer job training, shelter for the homeless, or social support to people in need? For example, a home for unwed teenage mothers may frown on giving out cash to recipients, but may offer food, shelter, parenting classes, and baby supplies to moms. Other charities, like Habitat for Humanity, work to build homes for deserving families, who are expected to donate their own "sweat equity," and disease-specific charities may raise money for research for a cure.

- *Is the charity local?* Some people prefer to "give at home," knowing that their money will help their neighbors or improve their own community. Others want to give where people need it most, or choose to do both.

- *What's the mission of the charity?* If you feel strongly about animal rights, you may want to support a no-kill animal shelter that doesn't euthanize healthy animals, for example. On the other hand, some charities may have a mission that clashes with your own—and while they sound good, they may support a cause you don't. In that case, you may want to seek an organization that has views similar to your own.

- *How long has the charity been around?* Just because a charity is established doesn't mean it deserves your support, but brand-new charities may not be legit—and even if they are, they may not have the funding or infrastructure to last very long. You want your money to be used to help your chosen cause, not to save a struggling organization.

- *What personal involvement or connection do you have with the charity?* If you lost a friend or family member to a disease, you may want to support organizations designed to help people with that condition. Or maybe the Red Cross came to your family's aid after a natural disaster. You'll probably want to support organizations that you have personal experience with—after all, you know the difference they can make.

- *What's your budget?* It would be great if you could help every deserving charity out there, but even Michael Dell and Oprah have to decide who will (and won't) benefit when they give money. Consider your income and your various responsibilities, and set a charity budget for yourself so you don't overreach in the name of doing good. And remember that you're not limited to giving money. In many instances, giving your time is just as valuable—or even more so. Sure, donating to a charity can mean forking over the green stuff, but it can also mean that you show up and help the charity accomplish its mission. (Many charities also accept donations of stuff—clothing, household goods, furniture, computer equipment, even cars—so check to see what yours needs.)

BE A CHARITABLE SUPPORTER, NOT A SUCKER

In 2004, people, corporations, and foundations gave 250 billion dollars to charities. The biggest recipients were religious organizations (e.g., churches), schools, and health agencies. And you may be surprised to know that more than 80 percent of the money raised in the United States comes not from companies but from individuals.

While there are many worthy charities, there are some that aren't so worthy—or are outright frauds. Don't be taken in by heartfelt pleas. Do your research first and you'll feel better about the donations you're making. Get smart about giving by following these guidelines:

- *Donate by check or credit card.* Giving cash may seem easier, but a cancelled check is the best type of receipt for tax purposes, and cash is all too easy to steal or misuse. After all, how do you know that the person collecting donations won't just keep it?

- *Make sure that you know who you're giving to.* Some organizations have names that intentionally sound like the names of other, better-known (or better-respected) charities. If someone claims to be from the Red Crosses, for example, that should be a red flag. Ask for the specific name of the charity before you give, and for its address, phone number, and Web site. A legit charity will be happy to share this information.

- *Confirm that your gift is tax-deductible, if that's important to you.* Donations to 501(c)(3) organizations can be taken as tax deductions, but others—even those made to tax-exempt organizations—may not be deductible. Organizations that qualify under section 501(c)(3) have filed documents with the Internal Revenue Service to prove that they're operated for charitable purposes under the Internal Revenue Code. If the IRS agrees, it sends a Letter of Determination, which means that contributions to the organization are tax-deductible. A legit charity will be willing to give you a copy of this letter to prove its tax-deductible status.

- *Don't fall victim to face-to-face pressure.* Sure, it's hard to turn down someone standing at your door, but you'll feel better about making a donation once you have all the facts. Ask for identification and for more information about the charity the person is collecting for. There's nothing wrong with saying that you'll consider donating, or that you've already selected the charities you want to support. (Of course, "get the hell off my front porch!" is also effective.)

- *Keep records of any donations you make.* If you donate throughout the year, keep a folder or file where you record your donations and keep copies of receipts, cancelled checks, and credit card statements. If you volunteer your time to a charity, you can also take out-of-pocket expenses, including transportation costs, as deductions. The charitable mileage deduction you can take is determined by the Internal Revenue Service; check *http://www.irs.gov* for the current figure.

- *Check out any pledge "invoices" you receive.* Some fly-by-night "charities" will send an invoice or pledge confirmation when you haven't agreed to make a donation. If you don't remember committing to giving, double-check your records. You may want to be wary, too, about charities that send you "gifts" like pens, holiday cards, and address labels with a plea for funds. Legally, you're not required to pay for items you didn't purchase, nor do you have to return them—or give a donation. But the charities hope you'll feel grateful (or guilty—probably both) and send money.

- *Consider the "costs" of donating.* If you buy tickets to a fund-raising dinner, for example, the entire cost of your ticket may not be tax-deductible. Rather, you'll have to sub- tract the value of your rubber-chicken dinner from the amount of your donation. (So, if you spend $100 on a ticket for a dinner that the IRS would value at $40, you've only made a $60 tax-deductible donation.) Same goes for buying candy from those adorable tots who show up at your front door. If you spend $20 on candy worth $8, your tax deduction would only be $12.

- *Ask how your money will be spent.* Will it support a partic- ular program, or simply be used to satisfy the charity's most pressing needs? Most charities will let you earmark donations if you want your money to be spent to support something specific. If someone tells you that your money will support a particular hospital, police department, or fire department and you're skeptical about it, double-check with the organization before you donate.

- *Check out the charity's financial information.* Raising money is all well and good, but how does the charity actu- ally spend it? There are several watchdog organizations that rank charities based on how effectively they spend their money—i.e., what percentage actually is spent on the charity's mission versus operating and administrative costs. Check out these organizations to learn how charities are spending their money:

American Institute of Philanthropy
3450 Lake Shore Dr., Suite 2802 E
Chicago, IL 60657
(773) 529-2300
http://www.charitywatch.org

BBB Wise Giving Alliance
4200 Wilson Boulevard, Suite 800
Arlington, VA 22203
(703) 276-0100
http://www.give.org

Charity Navigator
1200 MacArthur Boulevard, Second Floor
Mahwah, New Jersey 07430
(201) 818-1288
http://www.charitynavigator.org

GuideStar
427 Scotland Street
Williamsburg, VA 23185
(757) 229-4631
http://www.guidestar.org

Keep in mind that, while you can find most major charities on these lists, smaller or local groups may not be listed. These Web sites are also good places to review if you're looking for a charity to support; or check out http://www.justgive.org or http://www.volunteermatch.org for more ideas.

- **Stick to your guns.** Once you've decided which charities you'll support, don't feel badly about not donating to all the other groups who now want your money. They realize that most of the people they approach won't donate. (And ask charities that you do support not to share your address and contact information with others. That will reduce the amount of mail and phone pleas you receive.)

- **Watch out for misleading statements.** A fund-raiser that claims that "all proceeds will go to charity" sounds enticing. But the reality is that the group could spend $50,000 on a fund-raiser that produces $50,005 in donations, leaving a whopping $5 for charity. Make sure that the charity's expenses don't outstrip the amount of actual donations.

- **Don't stand for high-pressure tactics.** No one should threaten or intimidate you or continually harass you in an attempt to get your money. Report such incidents to your Better Business Bureau or to the appropriate division of your state's attorney general's office, which is usually responsible for investigating such complaints. Phone solicitors who harass you or refuse to put you on a do-not-call list when you request it can be reported to the Federal Trade Commission (FTC) at *http://www.ftc.gov.*

- **Don't give out personal information, especially to door-to-door or telephone solicitors.** No one needs your bank account or Social Security number. It's safer to give directly to a charity than over the phone or to a stranger who shows up at your door.

- **Ask for a copy of the charity's annual report.** This will give you specific information about how much money the charity raises, who is involved with it, how funds are distributed, what programs it operates, and how much is spent on fund-raising and administrative costs. The annual report should reveal income and expenses so you can determine who the major donors are and how the funds are used; this may tell you whether you want to support the organization or not.

Finally, consider how you want to give. Some people like to donate small amounts throughout the year—for example, by giving when they attend church every week. Others prefer to write checks once or twice a year, or when they're motivated by a natural disaster like Hurricane Katrina. How you give isn't important—it's that you care enough to help someone else. Whether you choose to give money, time, or valuable stuff, you'll get something amazing in return—the warm fuzzy feeling that comes from caring enough to help someone else.

Get in Great Shape

11

Okay, you noticed your body's gotten a little bit . . . flabby. Or maybe you used to be "all that" and now you're more than all that—and not in a good way. You've decided you're going to get in great shape or get back in shape. Either way, you're ready to sweat and strain your way to a buff, beautiful bod.

Fortunately, you don't have to dedicate your life to getting into shape, but you do have to make it a priority. The bad news? You're pretty much stuck with your genetics. Does your family have a tendency toward chunky thighs? There's nothing you can do about that. But you can make the most of your genes by adopting a regular fitness program, and it's easier than you might think.

FIRST THINGS FIRST: GET YOUR MIND IN THE GAME

We know you're tempted. You just saw a thirty-minute infomercial, or your best friend swears by the latest gadget. Don't fall for it. Getting into shape takes more than a simple seven-minute workout you do three times a week. It takes time and commitment. But you needn't train for a marathon or spend hours pumping iron to get in great shape. A realistic but challenging program will give you the body you want without sacrificing the rest of your life.

First off, get clear on your goals. After all, you can't get where you're going unless you know where you want to be. Do you want to lose weight? If so, how many pounds? Do you want Brad Pitt's *Troy* triceps and all the rest, or a butt that rivals J.Lo's? (Um, if so—time to get real. Remember your genetics? If your parents bear no resemblance to Brad or Jen, chances are you won't, either.)

Seriously, identify your fitness goals. They should be specific, measurable, and realistic. Losing ten pounds in three days is not realistic. Losing ten pounds in three months—that's more doable.

Once you know what you want to achieve, consider how you'll do it. This is key. If you've exercised before, think about what you've enjoyed—and what you've detested. (Chances are, gym class dodgeball ranks somewhere in the latter category.) Do you prefer working out alone or with others? Do you like team sports? Do you enjoy higher-intensity activities or are lower-key ones more your style?

Ponder these questions before you begin your workout program, and you'll be more likely to stick with it once you start. But simply deciding to sculpt a new bod isn't enough. You need to create a strategy to get you there.

Think about how you'll achieve your goals. Will you eliminate desserts? Exercise four mornings a week? Lift weights at the gym on Tuesday and Thursday nights? You also need to determine how you'll handle obstacles as they arise—and they will arise. If you travel frequently for work, you might plan on taking exercise bands and workout gear along, or staying at hotels with gyms. If you tend to snack when you're anxious, make a list of other activities you can do instead. Remember, you need a plan.

And while long-term goals are valuable, you should have

lesser goals as well, like exercising three times this week. It's important to have a big-picture goal, but by focusing on these smaller (and more doable!) benchmarks, you'll stay mindful of what you're doing and increase your chances of success in the long run.

Say you want to lose twenty pounds. If you make short-term goals—such as eating less than thirty-five grams of fat a day and working out for half an hour five days a week—you may not achieve your overall objective immediately. But if you keep it up and continue to meet those behavioral goals, everything else will fall into place.

THE PHYSICAL COMPONENT: YEAH, YOU HAVE TO EXERCISE

OK, your mind is ready. Now you've actually got to do it. If you're new to the fitness scene, don't get sidetracked wondering about the difference between aerobic and anaerobic exercise, or whether you're supposed to lift weights before cardio or after. Right now you want to get in shape. You can always tweak your program later.

There are just a few things to keep in mind as you develop your fitness plan. You want a program that incorporates aerobic exercise, strength training, and stretching. **Aerobic exercise** is activity that uses the large muscle groups of the body and raises your heart rate for a certain period of time—say, twenty or thirty minutes. Running, biking, Rollerblading™, and swimming all qualify as aerobic exercise.

Strength training, or **resistance training**, involves challenging a muscle or group of muscles beyond its normal day-to-day activity. It includes things like lifting free weights, using Nautilus™ machines, and doing calisthenics like push-ups and sit-ups, which use your body weight as resistance.

Flexibility, or **stretching**, includes exercises that are designed to maintain muscle and joint flexibility. Simple stretches, yoga, and Pilates™ (a total body-sculpting system) all help maintain and improve flexibility.

According to the College of Sports Medicine, you should aim for the following balance:

- *three to five days a week of twenty to sixty minutes of cardiovascular exercise*

- *two to three days a week of strength training that includes at least one set of eight to ten exercises targeting the major muscle groups*

- *two to three days a week of flexibility exercises that stretch the major muscle groups*

THE GET-YOUR-BUTT-IN-SHAPE WORKOUT

Yikes! Sound like too much? Don't worry—you can start off slowly and improve from there. I've made it easy for you with the workout below. It will target your major muscle groups, provide both cardiovascular and strength-training benefits, and boost your metabolism in the process. Make time for some simple stretches post-workout or at the end of your day, and you'll notice a difference in six weeks.

Mondays/Thursdays: Intensity Training

Select the cardio machine of your choice—treadmill, bicycle, stair stepper, or elliptical trainer. (By the way, don't worry about doing the "perfect" cardio workout. The key is choosing something that—duh—you'll actually do. Sure, running burns more calories per minute than biking, but if you hate to run, how likely are you to stick with it?)

Warm up for five to eight minutes and then run, pedal, or step at near-maximum effort for one minute; then recover at a comfortable pace for three minutes. Repeat this cycle for thirty minutes. (If you like, you can use longer or shorter intervals, but your rest periods should be three times longer than your intensity periods.) This type of training forces your body to work much harder than usual, providing it with a new challenge, and demanding additional calories. Cool down for five minutes, and you're finished.

Tuesdays/Fridays: Strength Training

For the strength training component, aim for two to three sets of between eight and twelve reps each. Warm up for at least five to eight minutes before you start your weight routine. Then do the following strength moves in this order:

Squats. Stand with your feet slightly wider than hip-width apart. Holding dumbbells at your sides, bend your knees and slowly move your hips back until your knees go no deeper than parallel to the floor; return to original position and repeat.

Push-ups. Lie face-down on the floor. Place your hands flat, just outside your shoulders at about chest level, and push up so that your weight is on your hands and your toes. Keeping your body straight and your abs tight, bend your elbows and lower your body toward the floor and then push back up. (Too difficult? Then let your weight rest on your knees instead of your toes.)

Rows. Bend forward at the waist, keeping your abs tight, so that your back is nearly parallel to the ground, and hold dumbbells in both hands. Keeping your abs tight and your torso stable, pull your arms up toward your shoulders and return to your original position.

Lunges. Stand with your feet under your shoulders. Step forward with your right foot, making a large enough step so that your shin stays perpendicular to the ground when you lower your body; push back up and return to your original position.

Biceps curls. Stand upright with a dumbbell in each hand. Bend your elbows and slowly curl your arms toward your chest and then return to your original position.

Triceps kickbacks. Step forward with your right foot so that it's about two feet in front of you (like you're doing a lunge) and lean forward. Hold a dumbbell in your left hand with your arm bent, near your hip; keeping your left arm close to your body, straighten it and then return your arm to its original position. Do all reps and then repeat on opposite side.

Lateral raises. Stand with your knees and hips slightly bent, feet shoulder-width apart, dumbbells in hands. With your elbows slightly bent, move your elbows out to the sides of your body, keeping your wrists straight. Raise your arms until they are about parallel to the floor and return to original position; repeat.

Bicycles. Lie on your back, legs lifted off the floor, knees slightly bent, hands behind your head. Lower your legs toward the floor one at a time; as you do so, lift your head and shoulders off the ground and twist your right shoulder toward your left knee as the right leg lowers toward the floor, and vice versa.

Wednesdays/Saturdays: Endurance Training

On Wednesdays and Saturdays, you'll perform an hour of cardio on the machine of your choice. You want to choose a pace that you can maintain for an hour to ensure that your body used a mixture of glycogen and fatty acids. You burn more fat during endurance activity than shorter-intensity exercise.

Sundays: Rest/Easy Day

Sundays, you should relax and let your body recover. Do some yoga or perform some gentle stretches or other light exercise.

STRETCH IT OUT

Stretching needn't be done at the gym; you can do it anywhere. Try these simple moves to relieve tension and improve flexibility:

Simple forward bend. Sit on the edge of a chair, feet flat on the ground, arms folded across your chest. Gently roll your chin toward your chest, then roll your body slowly forward until you're resting your folded arms over your knees, or let your arms drop toward the floor; finally, let your head slowly drop forward. Hold for ten to thirty seconds; then slowly return to your original position.

Neck stretch. Gently grasp the right side of your head, between the crown of your head and your ear, with your left hand. Place your other hand behind your back at waist level, and gently pull your head away from your right shoulder with your left hand. Repeat five times, holding for ten seconds each time, and then switch to the other side.

Scapular squeeze. Sit up straight. With arms bent at a 90-degree angle, take your elbows and draw them behind your back as if to touch your elbows behind your back. You'll feel the stretch in your chest; hold it for ten seconds and repeat five times.

Knee-to-chest stretch. Lie flat on a bed or floor and use your hands to pull your bent knees toward you. One at a time, bring each knee up to your chest and then hold it there until you feel a stretch in your lower back. Keep your head and neck relaxed, and do not arch your back. Hold for ten seconds and repeat five times.

THE NEXT STEP

Hey, if getting in shape was easy, we'd all be sporting six-packs of the abdominal variety. But for most people, simply getting off the couch and getting moving is the biggest challenge. Keep these tips in mind to become a lifetime exerciser:

A day or two off won't hurt your routine. Sure, it's important to commit to regular exercise. But too many people give up on their routines simply because they're forced to miss a few days. Don't let that be you. Simply start up your program again and move forward.

Every little bit helps. Recent research has shown that discontinuous exercise—taking three ten-minute walks during the day instead of one thirty-minute walk—is as good for you as continuous exercise. Little chunks of physical activity—such as walking three flights of stairs instead of taking the elevator, or spending fifteen minutes tending your flower bed—all burn calories and help you stay fit.

Calories really do count. You exercised today? That's great. It's not, however, carte blanche to polish off seconds at dinner, especially considering that the average person only burns 200 to 300 calories per workout.

Fatigue means you need exercise! "I'm too tired" is one of the most common excuses people give for not exercising. Scratch it off your list for good. It may seem counterintuitive, but exercise boosts your energy levels. When you first begin a workout program, you may feel more tired because you're not used to it. As your body adjusts, however, you'll feel peppier, more alert, and have more energy, even when you're not exercising.

The more muscle you have, the more calories you burn. Aerobic exercise is great for strengthening your heart and reducing stress. But to up your body's metabolism, you need to strength-train. Muscles are more metabolically active than fat, which means that they burn more calories and can help you lose or maintain your weight, even when you are being a couch spud.

12 Practice Feng Shui

Feeling stuck in your career? Can't find lasting love? Want more money and success? Maybe it's not your fault your life isn't going so well. Maybe your chi is blocked—and the principles of feng shui (pronounced "fung shway") can save the day.

The basic idea of feng shui is that the placement of objects in your home can have a dramatic effect on your life—both negative and positive. You can always hire a feng shui expert to come in and overhaul your home, but in the meantime, why not employ some basic techniques to enhance your life?

FENG SHUI: THE ART OF PLACEMENT

So what is feng shui, anyway? It's sort of a blend between art and science that originated thousands of years ago in China. **Feng shui**, which literally means "wind" and "water," isn't a religion (although its adherents can be pretty fervent about not having a water feature in the wrong place); it's more a philosophy of decorating. The idea is that every object has **chi** (pronounced "chee"), a positive energy source. Good enough—until chi gets blocked. That's bad. That's why one of the fundamentals of feng shui is removing barriers that would interfere with the flow of chi.

But feng shui goes beyond simply making sure that chi is flowing freely. It embraces the idea that, by balancing the forces of time, space, and the chi of objects, you're more likely to improve your relationships, your health, and your financial situation.

However, we have to fess up. True feng shui isn't as simple as hanging a wind chime in the right corner of your house. In fact, many practitioners of traditional feng shui spend years learning the art, and treat the practice of it very seriously. To them, it's not nearly as simple as taking a quick look at your floor plan and scattering some water or metal elements in the right locations.

Traditional feng shui practitioners use something called a Chinese compass to ascertain specific details, such as the direction a house faces. They also consider such factors as the location of the front and back doors, as well as when it was built and the age of the owner, when making feng shui recommendations. The idea of you practicing feng shui on your own would make them laugh—or even offend them. If you want the real thing, consult a certified feng shui expert for a comprehensive analysis. I'm not going to turn you into a feng shui expert in the next few pages, but I can introduce to some of the basic elements of feng shui and give you some technique to try in your own home and office.

MORE THAN ONE WAY TO FENG SHUI

Over time, practitioners of feng shui have split into a number of different schools. The three primary ones are the **Form** or **Land Form school**, the **Compass school**, and the **Black Hat Tantric Sect**, which is also called the **Western school**. All use a rough map called the **ba'gua**, which is an eight-sided compass that refers to eight aspects of life. The idea behind quick-and-dirty feng shui is that, by mentally placing the ba'gua over a room, a house, or a building, you can determine which areas correlate to the different parts of your life—such as family, career, and money. Or you can take a compass reading to determine which direction is north, and divide your floor plan into compass sections to determine what direction each section of your home falls.

The eight directions and their aspects, or areas of influence, are:

NORTHWEST: mentors/people who can help you
NORTH: career and business prospects
NORTHEAST: education and knowledge
EAST: health and relationships
SOUTHEAST: prosperity and wealth
SOUTH: fame and recognition
SOUTHWEST: marriage
WEST: children and creativity

Keep in mind that it's not only where you place objects, but also what objects you place that has an effect. With feng shui, you can use the **five elements**, and the symbols of those elements, to help make changes in your life. The five elements include water, wood, metal, earth, and fire. Each has different properties:

- *Earth:* associated with the color yellow; enhances stability and security, particularly in the home.

- *Fire:* associated with the color red; enhances action, passion, and motivation.

- *Metal:* associated with the color white; enhances vision, riches, and abundance.

- **Water:** associated with the color black; enhances clarity and emotional health and provides focus.

- **Wood:** associated with the color green; enhances growth, beginnings, and activity.

Finally, feng shui also seeks to balance **yin and yang**, the two elements that comprise the universe. Everything contains yin and yang, and there is always a flow between the two. In general, yang is associated with the masculine, and with light, warmth, and activity; yin is associated with the feminine, and with dark, coldness, and passivity. A balance of the two is optimal; if one is more pronounced than the other, there will be disharmony.

EVERYBODY FENG SHUI TONIGHT

OK, you're ready to harness the power of feng shui. Where do you begin? Number one, clear the clutter. Stuff—even stuff you love—blocks the flow of chi. Whether it's unread magazines, unfolded clothes, or piles of CDs, clutter traps energy and can make you feel tired and confused—not to mention disorganized! Remember that every object has chi, and mounds of stuff loaded with chi can affect you emotionally, physically, mentally, and even spiritually.

Number two, keep your home and office in good physical shape. Broken, cracked, or dirty windows can affect your clarity. Chi symbolically enters your home at its main entrance, so this area should be clear, open, and well-lit. (If the pizza guy has trouble finding your doorbell, that's a bad sign.) Make sure that your home's plumbing and electrical systems are also in good repair; chi can get caught in a clogged drain or in mounds of wires around your PC.

Number three, choose wisely. If your home is cluttered with huge furniture, chi is going to have a hard time circulating. A more minimalist approach is preferable to rooms filled with massive furniture. Lighter colors rather than dark ones and simple furnishings also help attract and move chi.

OK, you've got the basics down. Now, look for ways to draw more chi into your home or work space, and to improve the chi that is already there.

Feng Shui at Work

- *In your office, you should sit with your back to a wall and be able to see the door from your desk.* If that's impossible, hang a mirror so you can see the door from your usual position. You want to be able to see anyone who comes in.

- *Your desk should be placed against a wall to provide stability and support.* It shouldn't be at an angle to the walls of the room (or cubicle).

- *According to the principles of feng shui, even the direction in which you sit can affect your concentration and productivity.* At work, use a compass to determine the direction in which you usually sit, and consider changing your office layout, or at least your position, depending on what you're working on:
  FACING EAST: good for concentration, focus, and ambition, especially if you're starting a new job or a new project.
  FACING SOUTHEAST: good for brainstorming and creative ideas, or working through tricky problems.
  FACING SOUTH: good for self-promotion and getting noticed.

FACING SOUTHWEST: good for methodical tasks and improving the quality of your work.

FACING WEST: good for completing projects and for increasing profits.

FACING NORTHWEST: good for organization and control, especially with long-term projects.

FACING NORTH: good when you need to be flexible and objective.

FACING NORTHEAST: good when you need to be more focused, decisive, and motivated.

Feng Shui at Home

- *Don't put your bed in the corner—you'll block chi.* You should be able to climb out on either side. Because chi flows in and out through doors and windows, your bed shouldn't face the door or be under a window—it will disrupt sleep. And your bed should be against a wall, not at an angle to it, for more security and stability.

- *When you decorate, choose pairs of objects, such as two candlesticks, two prints, or two pillows.* (While two is considered a good number, four is not, and is thought to trap chi.) If you only have one of an object, place it in front of a mirror so the reflection makes a second, giving the illusion of two objects without extra clutter.

- *Aim for a balance of light and dark colors, as well as straight angles and curves, for a blend of yin and yang.* Colors like pale blue, pale green, pink, and pale yellow are considered yin; bright red, bright yellow, bright green, and bright blue are more yang. In a similar vein, fabrics and furniture made from wood are considered more yin; furniture made from stone, metal, and glass is more yang.

- **Wind chimes are commonly used in feng shui to spread chi.** They add natural sound to rooms, and should be hung where they will chime frequently. While metal wind chimes are the most common, wood chimes are most effective in the northern, eastern, southeastern, and southern parts of your home.

- **Want to get rid of bad energy in a room?** Sprinkle sea salt on the floor and leave it overnight; then vacuum it up and dispose of it outside your home.

- **Use fresh flowers to bring more chi into your home, but once they begin to die, make sure you throw them out.** The same goes for living plants, which can be used throughout your home. Just be sure to remove dying or dead plants immediately.

- **If you're looking for a financial boost, put a collection of coins on red cloth in the western part of your home to help draw more money to you.**

- **The backs of chairs and couches shouldn't face the entrance to a room.** In fact, couches, like beds and dressers, should always be placed against walls for maximum stability.

- **Water features are popular and bring more energy to a room.** For calming energy, use still water; for vibrant energy, look for a waterfall or fountain. Water features are most helpful in the eastern or southeastern parts of your home; just make sure the water is kept clean and fresh.

- *Use mirrors to change the direction of chi, but avoid them in the bedroom where they can interfere with sleep.* If possible, keep them away from the foot of your bed, or cover them with a blanket at night. A good place for a mirror is to the right or left of your front door; it shouldn't face the front door, as it will reflect chi back out of your home. Also, never position a mirror so that the top of your head is cut off in your reflection.

- *Feeling agitated?* Close your drapes, or use heavier window dressings. To draw more energy into your home when you want to feel more active and alert, do the opposite—open your blinds or drapes as far as they will go.

- *If you tend to gulp your meals or suffer from heartburn, use softer colors in your kitchen and dining room.* Bright red, yellow, and orange are stimulating (that's why fast-food places employ these shades in their décor); instead, use paler shades of blue, green, and cream.

- *To enhance a relationship, place a photograph of you and the other person in a frame, and put in the western part of your home. Add fresh flowers or a plant to draw extra energy to the room.*

- *To bring more energy into your home or office, use more lighting.* A spotlight on your desk, for example, can help you focus. Up-lights encourage upward flow of chi and make rooms look larger.

- *To relax at the end of a stressful day, get close to the ground.* Lie on the floor with some comfortable pillows. On the other hand, if you need energy, stand up or sit on a stool to make yourself taller.

Remember, feng shui isn't magic or a cure-all, but why not give it a try? It may give you the boost your career or love life or creativity needs—and give you a reason to de-clutter your clutter. And, in the meantime, mentioning the "bad feng shui" of a room is a great conversation opener—now that you know enough to sound like you know what you're talking about!

Become a Pilot

13

What's that in the sky? It's a bird! No, it's a plane—and you're flying it! You could soar over the house you grew up in, fly to your next business meeting, and impress your next date, all with one license—your pilot's license. If you're willing to invest the time and money, you could join the more than 700,000 licensed pilots in the United States—and fly for fun or launch a career as a pilot.

WHY FLY?

To become a pilot, you have to go to flight school and get your private pilot's license. After you obtain that, you can get additional training and licenses, such as an **instrument rating** (where you prove you can fly using instruments alone), **commercial pilot's license** (which lets you fly for pay), and a **flight instructor certificate** (which lets you teach others to fly).

And what will you learn? For one thing, you'll learn the three motions of aircraft: **pitch**, or rotation about the lateral axis (through the wings); **yaw**, or rotation about the vertical axis; and **roll**, or rotation about the longitudinal axis (through the nose and tail). You'll be trained to scan your instruments, focusing on the "T" comprising the **airspeed indicator** (which, no surprise, shows your speed through the air), **artificial horizon indicator** (which indicates aircraft position relative to the horizon), **altimeter** (which indicates your altitude above sea level), and **heading indicator** (which shows the direction in which you are flying). You'll learn the anatomy of spirals, stalls, and spins, and how to recover from them.

Before you even choose your flight school, consider your aviation goals. Are you learning to fly to take up a fascinating hobby, or do you want a career in aviation? Are you fortunate (and rich!) enough to purchase your own aircraft, or will you be renting when you fly? Will your flying be centered around one airport or small region, or do you plan to fly long distances or for travel?

Also decide whether you'll train full- or part-time. There is a variety of options for training full-time, even if you're only pursuing your license as a hobby. Answering the questions listed above will help you select your ground school and instructor.

FLIGHT SCHOOL BREAKDOWNS

Let's talk flight schools. The **Federal Aviation Regulations** (FARs) are the rules that govern all aspects of aviation; you'll purchase the most recent edition of the FARs when you begin your flight training. Flight schools fall into two FAR categories: **Part 61** and **Part 141**. The most important difference between these types of schools is the structure of their training programs and the periodic audits by the Federal Aviation Administration (FAA) that they undergo. Check out the FAA's Web site, *http://www.faa.gov*, for info about the latest regulations and policies. For example, Part 141 schools must have FAA-approved course outlines and meet student performance standards. Because the FAA regulates their instructional programs, Part 141 schools enjoy far less flexibility in designing training schedules than do Part 61 schools, which have fewer accountability requirements.

This doesn't mean, though, that a Part 61 school will provide poor training or be a cakewalk. The **check ride** (the flight you take for your license, during which you prove you know how to fly) is the same regardless of the type of school you attend. At a Part 141 school, you're required to have at least thirty-five hours of flight time to obtain your private pilot certificate; at a Part 61 school, the requirement is forty hours. Regardless, though, plan to spend about sixty to seventy hours of flight time to get your private certificate.

Flight lessons typically cost around $100 an hour, three-fourths of which goes toward aircraft rental and the rest of which goes toward the instructor's hourly rate. Obviously, classroom time is much cheaper, especially in classroom settings versus one-on-one instruction. All totaled, a private pilot's certificate will generally run between $4,000 and $7,000, so ask your potential flight schools what their average cost is for a license.

If you're learning to fly for fun and can't devote a lot of time to your training, a Part 61 school is probably your best bet. These schools can adjust lesson content and scheduling to fit your busy life. (Keep in mind that several Part 141 schools train some students under Part 61 rules. If you really like a particular Part 141 school but you need the flexibility, contact the school to find out whether it offers Part 61 programs.)

On the other hand, if you want to pursue a career in aviation, you should enroll at a Part 141 school. The minimum flight time requirements for a commercial license differ; at Part 61 schools you need at least 250 hours, compared to 190 in Part 141 programs. Because the FAA approves the training at Part 141 schools, potential employers may prefer pilots who train there. Check out *http://www.aopa.org/learntofly/school/index.cfm* for a list of flight schools near you.

Future career pilots should also attend a nationally accredited training institution (which means the flight school has met high standards in all aspects of its operation), so ask the schools you contact if they've received accreditation.

COLLEGE OR NO COLLEGE

Several aviation schools across the country are located at four- and two-year colleges and universities. Deciding whether to attend a college and pursue a degree with your training depends on whether you want a career in aviation. If you do, you should seriously consider this option.

Ninety-five percent of civilian pilots who fly for a living have four-year college degrees. The aviation industry is very competitive, especially for pilot positions. Military pilots traditionally have the first crack at jobs, but the number of pilots coming out of the military is shrinking, and civilian pilots are taking up the slack. Airlines and other aviation companies prefer military pilots because they are confident about their training, experience, and knowledge of aircraft. For you to compete, you must have the same kind of confidence, and that starts with the school you choose and the education and training you receive from it. You'll also get valuable connections and resources by attending college: career guidance, placement opportunities, and internships are priceless when it comes to looking for work.

With a degree in an aviation field, you will know more about the engineering and avionics behind aircraft, and the more you know about the industry, the better off you'll be. As a pilot you must always be prepared for worst-case-scenario situations, and the knowledge you learn in school may save your life—and the lives of your passengers and crew.

Remember, too, that airline and professional pilots must comply with strict medical requirements. If you develop a health condition and fail a medical exam, your flying career is over. Like many industries, the aviation industry is subject to booms and busts. Airlines go under, crews get laid off. A degree can help you find another job if you're forced out of the industry—at least in theory.

MONEY, COSTS, AND FEES—OH, MY!

Flight lessons are expensive. College is expensive. What do you get when you combine the two? A great motivation to visit your school's financial-aid office. Don't forget that by attending college you may be eligible for financial aid, student loans, and scholarships. Check out what different colleges offer before you pick one.

If you have to work full-time and want a career in aviation, there are options for you as well. There are several junior colleges with excellent aviation programs. Traditionally, the tuition at these schools is cheaper than at a four-year university, and you still may be eligible for the financial-aid options listed above. These schools are also more likely to offer night and weekend classes to fit your schedule.

After receiving your two-year degree, you can transfer to you a four-year institution and continue your education. If that's the plan, choose the four-year school you plan to transfer to at the same time you choose your junior college. That way you can be sure that all the classes you enroll for will transfer to your next school.

Some two-year-program schools focus almost entirely on the aviation portion of your education. This can be advantageous because you may earn several ratings, including that of flight instructor, by the time you transfer. Then you may be able to make some money on the side training other students, and enroll for more advanced ratings at your new school. The downside is the lack of general education courses—you'll probably have to spend more than two years at your next program to obtain a four-year degree.

CHOOSE YOUR FLIGHT SCHOOL, COLLEGE, AND INSTRUCTOR

Enough about all your educational options. Let's make a decision! Make a list of potential flight schools by checking your local yellow pages, or by looking online at sites like *http://www.aopa. org*, the Web site of the Aircraft Owners and Pilots Association (AOPA). AOPA is a valuable resource regardless of how far along you are in your training. If you do a Web search for flight schools, be leery about those that are willing to set up training for you. It's always best to contact a school directly before you decide to enroll there.

Once you've compiled your list, contact the schools and ask them to send you all available material about the school and its training. You can use this material to narrow your decision, but a final choice should only be made after a visit. Consider your overall flying goals as you make your decision. For example, if you want to become instrument-rated, does the flight school's airport have instrument approaches to train on or will you have to fly somewhere else? What type of aircraft does the school use? Is this the same type of plane you'll rent once you're certified? If you want more advanced ratings, do they have the aircraft to facilitate your needs? Consider talking to other students to ask about their experiences, and meet with the instructors.

Your flight instructor is the most important element of your training. He or she should make your flight training both exciting and challenging. The AOPA has a database of instructors on its Web site, and if you're going to attend a flight school, choose your instructor before you commit to it. Most instructors will offer to take you up on an introductory flight. These flights are typically cheap and allow you to see how the instructor flies and teaches. Don't be afraid to ask for references, either—good flight instructors have students who are happy to put in a good word for them.

If you're taking flight classes at colleges, you may not have as many choices when it comes to flight instructors, but you're not powerless either. When you know who your instructor is, ask other students about the person. You can always ask to be reassigned even after your training has started. At many colleges, you're assigned a new instructor every semester. This helps you learn new techniques because you're flying with a variety of experienced pilots.

When choosing an aviation college, consider what degrees are available with your flight training. You may want to contact the school's aviation department for additional information. Check out the AOPA's list of aviation colleges and universities online to help make a list of options. When you visit the school, make sure you let them know you're interested in aviation. Narrow your list to your top three or five choices and send off your applications.

BEFORE YOU LEAVE THE GROUND

Learning to fly is more than training in an aircraft. The information you learn on the ground (at what is called **ground school**) is vital to your training. Before you can even take a check ride, you must pass an FAA **airman knowledge test** at a computer testing site. If you don't plan on attending a flight college, several ground school options exist. Instructor-taught classes are one option; if you're highly self-motivated, a home study system is available at some schools. And some community colleges and independent ground schools offer courses even if they don't have flight training programs.

The method you choose is up to you and your instructor, but remember that this training is needed not only to obtain your certificate but for your safety as well. Find out about your ground school options when touring a school and take a peek to see if it has on-site classrooms. Many colleges have dedicated classrooms to ground school study, so your campus visit should include these areas.

TAKE OFF!

Once you've decided whether you want to fly for pleasure or pay, you're ready to take the leap and sign up for flight school. In a matter of weeks, you can be a pilot—and your license can provide you a lifetime of enjoyment or a fabulous career. In fact, the sky's the limit!

Make Your Own Movie

14

Want to make your mark on the big screen, or add your own film to your DVD collection? The size of the film you make (think Hollywood blockbuster versus small independents) may be directly related to the size of the available budget, but bigger isn't always better. If you want to make your own movie, then it's time to become an independent filmmaker.

BE (AN) INDEPENDENT

Let's talk terms first. An **independent film** is usually any film made outside of the major film studios. The term is very general and includes a wide array of movies. Independent films can be any genre, any-size budget, shot anywhere (yes, even in Hollywood), and can have any amount of success. Most important of all, anyone (even you!) can make one.

The common denominator for these films, however, is money. No matter what the scale of your film, the money it costs to create that film has to come from somewhere. Raising funds for these films is difficult because independent films are typically a very poor financial investment. Lots of people dream of their "indie" picture making it big like *The Blair Witch Project*, which was made for an estimated $35,000 (a tiny budget for a feature-length film), yet grossed over $140 million in the United States alone. Sure, that's possible, but countless independent films fail to get distributed and have poor showings at film festivals. Until you become the next Quentin Tarantino, the bigger your film is and the more money it needs, the harder it will be to finance.

START SMALL, START SMART

If you want to make your own movie just for fun, you're in luck. There are affordable ways to see yourself or your friends on your home television. Sure, true film buffs may consider such films nothing more than home movies, but you can give these projects a professional feel.

The first step is to get your hands on a mini DV (digital video) camera, one smaller than a standard camera. Mini DV is the most common format for consumer cameras on the market. Most mini DVs have the ability to capture TV-quality images. They won't look as good as the big cameras you see news teams using, because the image chips aren't as large or crisp and the lenses are of lesser quality. But some TV stations use mini DV cameras for their small projects or for extra and backup footage, called **B roll**.

Lights Before Camera and Action

If you want your film to look more professional, follow the same guidelines as the big boys. Even if you have the best camera on the market and the sharpest set of lenses, your film could still look bad. Film sets are covered with lights, stands, reflective surfaces, cable, and several other pieces of equipment to create, modify, or cut light. Cameras are very sensitive instruments, and if you want a shot to look good, the lighting has to be just right. For the best results, try to get your hands on a simple light kit. You can see examples of kits and other equipment made by Lowell and Arri on their Web sites, *http://www.lowell.com* and *http://www.arri.com*.

Can you use lights from your house? For this sort of project the answer is "yes," but you should be aware that practical lighting has flaws. The color temperature of household lights is likely to vary. This means that each section of a shot lit by a different light will have a slightly different color. This is avoided by using film lights that have two consistent color temperatures, one to match white light and one to match daylight. (Yes, daylight has a different color temperature than the lights inside your house!) Your camera will have settings to switch from white light to daylight.

Pick up a how-to book for cinematography like *The Five C's of Cinematography: Motion Picture Filming Techniques* by Joseph Mascelli (Silman-James Press, 1998) or *Cinematography: Image Making for Cinematographers, Directors, and Videographers* by Blain Brow (Focal Press, 2002). It won't replace film school or on-set experience, but it can take your film from silly-looking to authentic-appearing.

The most basic lighting setup is called **three-point lighting**. Here you have a **key light**, which illuminates an actor's face from the direction of the light source in the shot. Next you have the **fill light** to illuminate the side of her face so the camera doesn't "read" it as unusually dark. Finally, the **backlight** illuminates the person from behind. This light helps actors stand out from their backgrounds and lights the tops of their heads.

But lighting the actors themselves isn't your only concern; the entire set must be lit as well. Your book on cinematography will provide guidelines about lighting and help you understand how to communicate to an audience visually, such as how to show viewers that it's nighttime or raining.

The Camera's Ear

Almost all consumer-level cameras have built-in microphones. These devices record sound poorly and lack the ability to focus their reception areas. Professionals use a variety of wireless and wired microphones that can attach to actors or to long boom poles that float across the action. The cables from these mics run into a device called a **sound mixer**. The person operating the mixer, also called a sound mixer, ensures that all the sound is well-received and balanced.

Sound-mixing equipment is quite expensive, so take a look at products made by Sennheiser, maker of some of the finest microphones, to get some idea of prices, at *http://www.sennheiserusa.com*. Professional-level cameras have the ability to mix sound. Microphones are wired directly into the camera with XLR cables, and mixer settings can be reached through menus or switches on the side. While this won't provide you with as high-quality audio as a sound mixer, using such a camera and microphone will be a step up from consumer mini DV.

Cutting and Editing

Once you have your film on tape, it's time to edit. Sure you can edit it yourself, but you'll need a pretty swanky computer to do it—a setup with lots of RAM, lots of hard-drive space, and a nice video card. Many computers come with video-editing software, but if you want a solid program with cool bells and whistles, you'll have to fork out some cash. Two of the most commonly used programs are Final Cut Pro, *http://www.apple.com/finalcutstudio/*

finalcutpro/ and Premiere, *http://www.adobe.com/products/premiere/ main.html.* These programs help you manage your video files as you capture them from your camera, and give you a professional-looking final edit. They are expensive, but if you take the time to learn their features you can take your video projects to the next level.

Get the Words Down

Even the smallest of films requires a script. If you're going to shoot your own film mini DV-style, you might as well write it too. Screenwriting format is quite a bit different than you might expect. Here is a simple script excerpt as an example:

INT. OFFICE—NIGHT
A WRITER sits alone in front of his computer.

WRITER (*whispers*): I can't think of a thing to write.

The first line is a scene heading. "INT." indicates the intro, and simply means "interior" as opposed to "EXT.," which means "exterior." OFFICE is the location and NIGHT is the time of day. The next line describes the action. Character's names are capitalized when they first appear. The remainder of the excerpt illustrates the proper formatting for character dialogue. Names in the dialogue portion of the script are always capitalized, and the parenthetical portion (e.g., *whispers*) may be omitted.

There's more to screenwriting than simply planning out different scenes. One terrific resource is Syd Field, the author of some of the most famous and well-respected screenwriting books. His Web site, *http://www.sydfield.com*, lists his work and upcoming workshops and contains several other helpful tools. Syd partnered with Final Draft software, *http://www.finaldraft.*

com, which makes the seemingly complicated task of screenplay formatting quite simple. You can see examples of finished scripts, some of which are completed movies you have probably seen, at *http://www.dailyscript.com/* or *http://www.simplyscripts.com/*.

You can also buy a script or hire a writer to create one, but this may not be a feasible option if you're planning on shooting mini DV-style film. However, if you're looking to go a little more big time, several options exist. Visit *http://www.mandy.com*. Here you can post your need for a script, browse through listings of screenwriters, and even read summaries of completed products.

HIRING HELP FOR THE BEST FILM POSSIBLE

Forget home movies. You want to make a film that could play at the theaters or make the rounds at the film festivals? It's no easy task, but if you surround yourself with the right people, you can do it. The first thing to establish is what you want your role in the film to be. Most people who say "I want to make a movie" mean that they want to direct. The director's job is to take the script and turn those words into his or her vision of the story. Everyone else involved in the film aids that metamorphosis. However, the role of director is not the only "upper crust" film position.

Producers are in charge of the logistical aspects of the production. They secure locations, allocate funding, rent equipment, and carry out many other essential tasks. The **director of photography**, or DP, is in charge of making the film look like the director wants it to look. He or she is responsible for the camera, grip, and electrical departments, along with their crews. The **assistant director**, or AD, is basically the on-set manager. This person deals with problems and attempts to keep the production on schedule. As a rookie in the industry, it will be difficult to find quality people to fill these vital positions.

Production Companies to Help You Produce Your Movie

Fortunately, there is help. For your first film, your best bet is to hire a production company. These businesses specialize in overseeing productions from beginning to end. They have connections with people in the industry and can make recommendations about which DP to hire. All directors of photography have **reels**, or clips from their films, to demonstrate their lighting and shooting abilities; they're usually hired on the quality of their reels.

Production companies can take the budget you have available and present you with a variety of options, such as how long you can shoot with a certain type of equipment package. For example, you could shoot on 35mm film and have the highest-quality product at the highest cost, shoot on 16mm and save money, or even shoot on high-definition video, or HD, and save money in the editing room because HD video is already in a digital format. (Film has to be transferred to digital format to be edited, which takes more time and is more expensive.) These are the types of decisions a production house can guide you through.

Your focus as a director should be to ensure that what you are seeing through the lens of the camera is what you envisioned. Trying to take on all of these other responsibilities can only take away from your much-needed attention. Check out http://www.mandy.com under "services" for production companies, and be sure to ask your potential candidates for their own reels so you can see the quality of products they have produced.

If you're a complete film novice, get on a few movie sets to acclimate yourself to the general process of filmmaking. Call up the production houses you've contacted and ask if you can visit their sets to observe. Or look for a position as a production assistant, or PA, where you'll gain experience on the job.

Keep in mind that production houses will not help you raise money, and you may find this to be the most tedious task of making your film. Many filmmakers seek investors who are looking for a return once the film sells. Unfortunately, such money is hard to come by, despite the fact that many independent films have sold and turned a profit for their investors—probably because many more have not.

A Few More Monetary Musings

Other filmmakers are willing to stake their family's money on their projects. If your film is sympathetic to a cause, hit up organizations that share your film's values. Check out the Independent Feature Project (IFP) "Make your Movie" page at *http://www. ifp.org/nav/makeyourmovie.php* for forums and articles about directors, writers, and producers. You'll find articles about how to raise funding for your film and advice about how to sell the finished product.

FINDING YOUR PLACE IN THE FILM BIZ

Staying on top of what's happening in the world of film can also give you a leg up in the movie business. Check out the Internet Movie Database at *http://www.imdb.com/* for information about all types of film in all stages of production. Stay up-to-date on the industry and visit its independent page, *http://indie.imdb.com/ index.indie*, to read up on the indie scene and visit links to major film festivals like Sundance.

The Association of Independent Video and Filmmakers, at *http://www.aivf.org/index.html*, supplies its readers with helpful information on getting started in the industry and compelling stories about those filmmakers who are realizing their dreams. It also has message boards where you can exchange ideas.

Whether you make movies for yourself or for the world, you'll find filmmaking is both a skill and an art. If you're ready to yell "Lights! Camera! Action!", go for it!

15

Go Skydiving

Want to jump out of a plane with nothing between you and the ground but 10,000 feet of air—and live to brag about it? When you skydive, the only thing to slow you down is strapped to your back—either a parachute or a skydiving instructor. Whichever path you choose, you're in for an experience you'll never forget.

YOUR FIRST STEP

First, locate where you'll skydive, or "jump." Your local yellow pages will probably have a list of **drop zones**, or skydiving centers, under "skydiving'" or "parachuting." Your best bet is to look for those affiliated with the United States Parachute Association (USPA). The USPA is the know-it-all of skydiving in this country. This nonprofit organization of skydivers and group member drop zones represents skydivers to the government, is recognized by the Federal Aviation Administration (FAA), and issues internationally recognized skydiving licenses through the International Parachuting Commission of the Fédération Aeronautique Internationale, which is in charge of all air sports.

While there is currently no organization providing safety ratings for skydiving schools, USPA group member drop zones have committed to following the USPA basic safety requirements. That includes training only with USPA-rated instructors and using USPA-required equipment. The USPA Web site, *http://www.uspa.org*, includes a list of member drop zones organized by state. The list includes information about aircraft used, types of training available, on-site services, and, of course, directions.

Most areas of the country are located close to more than one drop zone. To choose the right one for you, compile a list of nearby schools and call each one. Ask them to confirm the equipment used, the training available, instructor qualifications, and price. (Expect to spend $100 to $300, possibly more, depending on the class you choose.) It's a great idea to spend some time at each school; have a look around and talk to the instructors and other students before you register.

One word of caution: There are several Internet sites that have, or claim to have, networks of skydiving schools that offer lower prices. The USPA has issued a consumer alert warning about these sites because the organization has received a number of complaints about the shady activities of these services. Instead of directing you to the closest school, for example, they may only tell you of the schools that have signed up with them, which may be farther away or more expensive than others.

YOUR FIRST DAY AT SCHOOL

Once you've chosen a school, you'll be required to fill out some paperwork. You'll need to fill out a registration form and a liability release. There is risk involved in skydiving (um, you are jumping out of a plane, after all!), so the liability form will ask you to acknowledge the risk and agree to take it. You also have to agree not to sue the school or any persons if you are injured.

Skydivers are expected to be in good physical condition and to meet the USPA's basic safety requirements. If you're worried you may not be able to make the cut, check out the info on how to meet these requirements in the Skydivers Information Manual (SIM) or on the USPA Web site at *http://www.uspa.org/shop/coursemat.htm*.

Be aware that jumpers cannot be taking any medication that can affect their judgment. Most medical conditions are controllable if the instructors are aware they exist, so be honest. People who have recently been scuba diving or donated blood must take a few days off before jumping.

Most schools require jumpers to be at least eighteen years old. Some schools will allow a minor of at least sixteen to take part in some of the training activities with a parent's or guardian's consent, and the consenting person may be required to sit in for ground school training. State law may also limit or restrict minors from jumping, so double-check your own state's requirements if age is an issue.

Ground school, or in-class instruction, will be required no matter what form of training you choose. Expect to spend thirty minutes to several hours in ground school, and you'll take written, oral, and practical tests before you jump. The tests are designed to reflect and develop your understanding of the skydiving process, as well as your decision-making and hands-on skills.

TYPES OF TRAINING

Tandem

This is the most common method for people making their first jump. The instructor and student are strapped together and connected to the same parachute system; both face the same direction, with the instructor on top. The **free fall**, or period before the parachute is activated, will last somewhere between thirty and fifty seconds. It varies depending on the jumping altitude, normally between 10,000 and 13,000 feet. The tandem parachute is larger than average because of the additional weight; the system also has dual controls that allow the student to maneuver after the parachute has been deployed.

The ground school portion of this type of training is generally thirty minutes or less, and the entire jump process can be completed in half a day. Many schools use this method as an intro to a student's solo free-fall career. It's also a great way to experience skydiving if you're not interested in going through the licensing program and just want to try a jump. Many schools also offer in-air video of you jumping, falling, and landing so you have proof to show disbelieving friends that you really did it.

Static Line

The **static-line method**, or **Instructor-Assisted Deployment** (IAD), is a tamer version of skydiving. While it is done solo, the instructor helps the student during **climb-out**, or the process of getting ready to leave the plane, and with the **leap-out**, or actual jump, from the aircraft. The catch is that the parachute deploys immediately after exiting the aircraft; the student then glides down to the landing area. Because the parachute deploys right away, the jumps take place around 3,500 feet.

The ground school program covers: climb-out, exiting the aircraft, free fall, canopy flight, landing, and emergency procedures. Often an IAD ground school and jump can be completed on the first day; again, several schools offer video services so you can record your experience for posterity.

Accelerated Free Fall (AFF)

This is the "real thing"—jumping out of the plane, free falling, and opening the chute all by yourself. But you're not alone. The AFF-method ground school will cover all the topics listed above for static-line jumping and, again, the first jump can normally be accomplished on the same day.

With this method, the student jumps from the aircraft with two AFF instructors. The free fall lasts from thirty to sixty seconds and is done at the same altitudes as a tandem jump. The instructors hold onto the student's harness during free fall and provide instruction and stability. The student opens his or her chute at about 4,000 feet and glides to the landing area alone. Instructors on the ground can guide the student in by radio. And yup, wouldn't you know it? Once again, schools can videotape the jump for you.

Wind Tunnels

If you want to work on your parachuting skills without climbing into a plane, look for a vertical wind tunnel. These tunnels have large fans that are strong enough to simulate the wind in free fall. The current of air can suspend a person or even a small group of people in air. Wind tunnels can be a great tool for instructors to teach students stability and maneuvering during free fall, but they're relatively rare. The USPA currently only has two group members with wind tunnels—one in Perris, California, and the other in Orlando, Florida.

KEEPING TRACK OF YOUR JUMPS—AND GETTING LICENSED

Logging

If you're going to pursue skydiving more than once, it's a good idea to get a logbook for your jumps. This book will qualify as evidence of your skydiving experience, as long as the jumps were made in accordance with the USPA requirements at the time. Your log must also be legible, in chronological order, and include the following information about each jump: jump number, date, location, exit altitude, free-fall time, type of jump (i.e., tandem or solo), landing distance from target, equipment used, and a verifying signature.

When a skydiver is jumping to obtain license or rating qualifications, the person who signs the book must be another skydiver, a pilot, or a USPA or FAI judge. If you're jumping to meet skill requirements, the signature must come from a USPA instructor, instructor examiner, safety and training advisor, or member of the USPA board of directors. Fortunately, if you are jumping for your first license, an instructor will always be supervising you and can sign your logbook.

Licenses

The USPA offers four basic types of licenses: A, B, C, and D. A is the first while D is the level that is most complicated and requires the highest experience level. Until you have a license, you're considered a student, but after receiving your A license you can make jumps without supervision, pack your own main parachute, participate in basic group jumps, and participate in water jump training.

Currently the requirements for the USPA A license are:

- *completion of twenty-five jumps*

- *completion of all the requirements for the USPA A License Proficiency Card*

- *completion of five group free falls with at least two participants*

- *the stamp and signature of a USPA instructor or instructor/examiner on the USPA Proficiency Card or USPA A License Progression Card*

The USPA A License Proficiency Card requires six categories of different skills. It's essentially a checklist that outlines the abilities you must have to become licensed, and these include:

- *Exit and free-fall skills.* You have to prove your competence in the air. This means control over your body, both when you are alone and when other jumpers are present. For example, you are required to show control by completing a back loop, a front loop, and a barrel roll. You must be able to dock with other free fallers and be able to create separation, or distance, from them under your own power.

- *Canopy skills.* This portion documents your skills after your parachute has been deployed. You'll have to demonstrate mastery of things like flying in a landing pattern, sticking a stand-up landing (as opposed to landing on your butt), and landing within 20 meters (about 65 feet) of a target.

- *Equipment knowledge.* You're required to prove your knowledge about skydiving gear. You'll be expected to inspect, maintain, and use equipment for jumps, demonstrate an understanding of skydiving devices, such as an automatic activation device, and pack a main chute without assistance.

- *Aircraft and spotting.* These skills include everything from knowing how to handle yourself on an aircraft, identifying local runways and aircraft patterns, spotting aircraft, and using aviation weather reports to plan your jump.

- *Emergency review.* This category includes all the things you don't want to think about, but for which you must prepare just in case. Skills you must learn include responding to parachute failures; avoiding objects like power lines, trees, buildings, and water; and memorizing aircraft emergency procedures.

- *License examination.* This is the section where your instructor verifies your completion of the license examination. It's a two-part test: The first part is an oral examination and the second an actual jump, called a **check dive**, in which you're required to demonstrate a set of maneuvers and knowledge.

Keep in mind that the requirements for this license and others may change. To ensure that you know the most recent information about all skydiving procedures, purchase the most recent SIM available. You should be able to get it at your flight school; otherwise, USPA has it available online.

Each new license level allows the skydiver more liberties. For example, with a B license a diver can perform night jumps. A C-level diver is eligible for an instructor rating, but not a tandem one, and a D-level is eligible for all available ratings.

The USPA can also issue restricted licenses to those who qualify for one. These are designed for people who are unable to meet all the requirements for a license, such as those with a physical handicap. To qualify, a student must submit a petition to the Safety and Training Committee detailing the type of license requested, requirements that he or she is unable to meet, the reason these cannot be met, and a completed application. Before sending the petition, the student must complete all the requirements for the license that he or she is able to complete. The committee then evaluates each application individually. If the license request is approved, the license number will be followed by the letter "R."

GET GOING!

Now that you know the basics, you can strap yourself to an expert for a joyride or go through the license process and become an expert yourself. Go find your school, slap down your money, and start your free fall!

Patent Your Own Invention

16

Forget the Clapper™ and the Chia Pet™. You've come up with something better—a cool new invention that everyone will want. You've never seen anything like it, and you're hoping this is your big break. But to be safe, you need to patent your invention in order to keep some unscrupulous opportunity seeker from running off with it (and all the money you stand to make).

WHAT IS A PATENT, ANYWAY?

Let's start with the basics. A **patent** is a sort of a legal monopoly. It lets its owner prevent others from selling the patented invention—or from making or using it—throughout the United States and its territories. You can obtain a patent for an invention or product itself (a **design patent**), or you can obtain a patent for the process used to make the product, called a **utility patent**. (In manufacturing, for example, a streamlined or enhanced process for creating a product may be just as valuable, or more so, than the product itself!) There's even a third kind of patent that protects you if you develop a "distinct and new" kind of plant—called, you guessed it, a **plant patent**. In some cases, when you invent a product that also involves a different manufacturing process, you may file for both utility and design patents on different aspects of the same invention.

Whether your idea is a whole new invention or a modification of an existing product or process, you may be surprised to learn that more than 5 million patents have been granted by the U.S. government. Patents cover everything from gaming software to inflatable rugs to toe puppets to motorized ice cream cones for when you're too lazy to turn your head to lick your butter pecan. Those patents protect their owners from having someone else infringe on their rights—in other words, from letting someone make money off work that isn't theirs.

Once you have a patent, it's good for twenty years. And it's solid protection. With a patent, you can seek royalties from **infringers**, those who use your invention without permission. You may also be able to prevent them from unauthorized use by going to court. There are other legal remedies available as well. For example, if you're in business and your competitor steals your patented invention, you may be able to recoup your lost profits. In other situations, you may get extra bucks if you can prove that someone deliberately copied your patented invention. Keep in mind, though, that your patent only protects your own invention. It doesn't mean you can use other people's patented inventions without permission.

APPLY YOURSELF

OK. You've got your invention, process, or kooky new plant. How do you know if it's patentable? Ask yourself these questions:

- **Is it new?** This is a biggie. If your invention is already out there, you're too late.

- **Is it an abstract idea?** Ideas can't be patented. Nor can physical phenomena—like the fact that when you flush a toilet in the United States, the water drains in a counterclockwise fashion. (Down under, it's the opposite!)

- **Is it useful?** Granted, a toe puppet doesn't sound like it meets this particular test. But if it will work, it's generally considered useful.

- **Is it obvious?** You can't just change the color on something and seek a patent for it, for example. Your invention will have to pass the "nonobvious" test—more about that in a bit.

- **Has it already been patented?** Then you're out of luck. And how do you know if your invention is already patented in the United States? Search the records of the U.S. Patent and Trademark Office at *http://www.uspto.gov/patft/index.html*. There are also private companies who will perform patent searches for you—for a price.

- **Can you adequately describe your invention?** In your application, you'll have to be able to explain what your invention is, what it does, and how to make it. If your invention is something only you can create, you can't patent it—which means that unique works of art aren't patentable.

- **Finally, can you describe exactly how your invention is different from anything similar?** This is what you'll be seeking patent protection using descriptions that the

Patent Office calls **claims**, so you'd better be able to answer this question.

If you're ready to apply for a patent, plan on it taking a while. Check out the U.S. Patent and Trademark Office's Web site at *http://www.uspto.gov/* or call **800-786-9199** or **571-272-1000** if you have specific questions about how to apply. There's an excellent "Frequently Asked Questions" section at *http://www.uspto.gov/main/faq/*.

In the meantime, plan on having to provide the following in your application:

- *A specification.* This is a written document that includes a technical description of the invention, process, or plant, and of how it is made and used.

- *One or more claims.* These are statements that specify the subject matter you believe is original and therefore patentable.

- *An oath or declaration that you're the inventor.*

- *A drawing or drawings of the invention, if necessary.*

- *Filing, search, and examination fees.* The basic filing fee for a U.S. patent application is $150 to $300, depending on the type of patent you're applying for and whether you're an individual or part of a larger company; other search and examination fees vary. You'll find a detailed list of them at *http://www.uspto.gov/go/fees/fee2005oct01.htm*.

Sounds easy enough, right? Maybe not. For example, the claims you make in your patent application must be extremely precise and describe what exactly is being protected. You want to make sure that you're protecting your invention—not just now, but for twenty years in the future—and that can be tricky. That's why most inventors hire a registered patent attorney or a **patent agent** (someone who is qualified to prepare patent applications) to fill out the paperwork.

What's the difference between an attorney and a patent agent? For application processes, there really isn't one. However, a patent agent can't sue on your behalf or represent you in court the way an attorney can. In addition to doing a Google search or looking in the yellow pages, you can also visit the Web site of the National Association of Patent Practitioners to search for both patent agents and patent attorneys by state and practice area, at *http://www.napp.org/*. The Association of Patent Law Firms lists its members, as well as law firms throughout the country that concentrate their practice in patent law, at *http://www.aplf.org*.

Whether you choose a patent attorney or patent agent, you want to choose someone whose engineering background is related to the field your invention is in. Other questions to ask include:

- *How long have you been a patent agent or attorney?*

- *What kind of background do you have?*

- *How many patents have you drafted?*

- *What types of inventions have you patented?*

- *How much will you charge to file the patent application?*

- *What will you need from me to complete the patent application?*

You can expect to spend between $3,000 and $10,000 for an agent or attorney to file for a patent application; ask whether that includes the filing fees that accompany the application. Instead of applying for a regular patent, you can also apply for a **provisional patent**. With a provisional patent, you don't have to make any formal patent claims, oath, or declaration the way you do with a regular patent application. Instead, you fill out parts of the application and include a **provisional cover sheet** with your paperwork. A provisional application for patent only lasts for a year; to protect your patent, you have to file an application for a patent within that time period. And your additional application must contain or refer to the original provisional patent.

Once your patent application is on file, you're not done. It has to be accepted by the patent examiner. Remember those questions you were supposed to ask yourself about your invention? Well, they had a purpose. Here's the test for patentability:

1. *Your invention must be useful!* That means it must work. Think about it—an invention that looks amazing but doesn't actually function isn't exactly useful, is it?

2. *Your invention has to be new to the public; it can't have been available before.* The inventor of the bird diaper (just what you need for that pet parakeet with the runs) must have known no one had seen anything like it before.

3. *Your invention must be "sufficiently different" from anything that has been used or described before.* This is often the trickiest part. The standard used is the "not obvious" one. That means that your invention has to be different enough from what's been used before that it's not obvious to a person with ordinary skill in that particular area of technology. Get it? So, if

your invention is a glaringly obvious "tweak" of another invention, forget it. Meeting this standard can take quite a while—it's not unusual for a couple of years to elapse between the filing of a patent application and the granting of one.

After considering your application, the patent examiner—who has expertise in whatever area of technology you're seeking a patent—will grant you a patent or reject your application. This alone may take more than a year. You'll then receive an **office action** that lists previous patents and documents relating to your invention. If the examiner rejects any of your claims or finds that you're missing necessary documents, you can still try to meet the criteria for patentability.

If the patent examiner still rejects your desired claims, you can appeal the decision to the Board of Patent Appeals within the Patent Office. If the board agrees with the patent examiner's finding, then you can appeal to the U.S. Court of Appeals . . . but this process can take years and be very expensive. The bottom line? From the time you file an application to the time a patent is issued is usually two to three years. Once it's issued, you have twenty years of protection. But if you want to protect your invention in other countries, you must patent your invention there as well.

One more thing. You know that your invention or process must be new. Make sure you don't disclose or develop it too early before you apply for a patent. (In other words, keep your big mouth shut.) Under the law, you have a one-year grace period before you file for a patent; you can disclose or commercialize your invention any way you want. But if you disclose your invention more than a year before you apply for a patent, the law says your application should be denied. Don't go public with your invention until you're ready to file for patent protection.

Keep in mind, too, that usually once a patent is issued, it's valid. But if it turns out that the patented invention was already developed by someone else, and the existing invention wasn't discovered in the search for identical patents, your patent may be invalidated. When the patent examiner reviews your application, he or she will look to make sure that your invention is patentable; hopefully your bright new idea is all that and a bag of chips.

TAKING THE NEXT STEP

Once you have your patent, the next question is, what will you do with it? You may want to sell your patent outright to a company who wants to buy the rights to it. You may want to license it to someone else; in that case, you're still the patent owner, but someone else pays you for the right to make, use, or sell your invention. Or you may want to produce and sell your invention yourself. Deciding what to do depends on the potential value of your invention and what you hope to get from it. Once you have a patent, though, you leap from being a dreamer to an honest-to-God inventor. Who knows—you may be the next Thomas Edison, or at least the next Stan Mason, a Connecticut inventor who holds more than one hundred patents on inventions ranging from squeezable ketchup bottles to shaped disposable diapers.

Publish a Book

17

"You should write a book!" So your friends tell you, and you've decided they're right. You're ready to add "published author" to your résumé. But how do you do it?

First off—yup, you've got to write the book.

Then you have to find a publisher—or self-publish. The right option for you will depend on your goals and experience, but the good news is, if you're willing to put in the time to write the book, you can publish one, too.

WRITING THE BOOK

Remember that old kid's joke? "How do you eat an elephant? One bite at a time." The same applies here.

First, take a deep breath. A big project like a novel or a non-fiction book can seem like a daunting task at the outset. To make it seem more manageable, break it down into smaller chunks. For example, divide it into chapters. Or, if you're writing a book proposal (more about that in a bit), approach the sections as separate pieces.

Next, set some deadlines for yourself. Without deadlines, it's all too easy for a project like this to keep slipping to the bottom of your to-do list. Make a deadline for when you'll have the book done—say, a year from today—and then work backward to set deadlines for each chapter. Then take a look at your calendar and figure out when you'll work on your book—and write it down. Schedule an hour or two each day, or whatever you need to get the work done, and treat it like you would any other responsibility. Meet those "mini-deadlines" for each chapter, and you'll complete the entire book.

Next, you have to decide whether you want to work with a traditional publisher or go the self-publishing route. The primary difference is that, with a traditional publisher you're paid money—called an **advance**—for your manuscript. Then, if your book **earns out**, or makes back the money the publisher put into it, you also earn **royalties**. (Some publishers, however, will ask to buy your book on a work-for-hire basis, meaning that you're paid a set amount of money regardless of how well the book sells.)

Before self-publishing came along, authors who didn't want to pursue traditional publishers or couldn't sell their work to them had to rely on so-called vanity publishers, whom you pay money to publish your book rather than a publisher paying you. Today, however, self-publishing is far more common—it's less expensive and easier than ever to get your baby into print.

PITCHING YOUR MANUSCRIPT

If you're writing fiction, you'll have to complete your entire manuscript before you move on to publishing it. But if you are writing nonfiction and want to work with a traditional publisher, you may not want to write your book—yet. The reason has to do with the way the publishing world works. To interest a publisher in your nonfiction book, you typically send a query letter and/or book proposal to the applicable editor. If the editor likes it, he or she makes an offer on it—and you write the rest of the manuscript pursuant to a book contract.

The advantage is that you don't spend a year of your life (or more) working on a manuscript that no one wants to buy. The drawback is that writing a book proposal takes some extra time.

Proposals differ in length and format, but the typical one sets out the premise of the book, provides an outline of the material that will be covered, lists competing titles and explains how your book differs from the competition, offers marketing and promotion ideas, describes your relevant background and experience, and includes one or more sample chapters. The purpose of the proposal is to convince the publisher that the book will sell enough copies for it to make a profit. It will also help you research and organize your material before you begin the book itself.

There are several excellent books to help guide you through the process, including:

- Book Proposals That Sell: 21 Secrets to Speed Your Success, *by Terry Whalin (Write Now Publications, 2005)*

- How to Write a Book Proposal, *by Michael Larsen (Writer's Digest Books, 2004)*

- Nonfiction Book Proposals Anybody Can Write: How to Get a Contract and Advance Before Writing Your Book, *by Elizabeth Lyon (Perigree, 2002.)*

Before you start on the proposal itself, research the market to see what other titles are available on your subject; for a speedy search, type in some keywords at *http://www.amazon.com* or *http://www.barnesandnoble.com* to see how many books you find.

While this will give you a general idea of what's out there, you'll want to read the titles that seem closest to yours. That way you can briefly describe them and explain how your book is better than/different from these titles; this "competition analysis" is important. Another critical part of the proposal is the marketing/promotion section. What will you, as the author, do to promote and publicize the book once it comes out? Think beyond author signings and media interviews; the more creative you are here, the better. In addition to an outline of the book itself, the proposal should include chapter summaries and at least one complete chapter. The proposal should also have a brief "about the author" section that highlights your relevant experience, and a paragraph describing the format of the book: the number of pages, possible appendixes, and the like. If this is your first book, you may also want to include clips, or published articles, with the proposal.

Before you send a proposal, though, you'll usually send a query letter to interest an agent or editor. For a nonfiction book, the query letter should describe what makes your book unique, demonstrate that there's a market for it, and mention your relevant qualifications, regardless of whether you're sending it to an agent or an editor. If you can, demonstrate familiarity with the agent or editor's work. Mentioning a book he or she has published or represented or using a referral (if you have one) is a good way to start. If the agent or editor is interested, you'll be asked to submit your proposal. If you've written a novel, give a brief overview of the book, your writing background, and why you're contacting this person.

ATTRACTING AN AGENT

Let's talk about agents for a bit. While you can pitch your book to publishers on your own, a literary agent represents your manuscript and probably has a better chance than you do of selling it. In exchange, your agent receives 15 percent of whatever you make on the book. If you decide to pursue an agent, you'll still need a book proposal, which the agent will submit to publishers on your behalf.

But how do you find one—and who do you choose? There are thousands of agents out there, after all, and it can be hard to select the one who will be the best fit. Start with a guide like Jeff Herman's *Guide to Book Publishers, Editors, and Literary Agents* or *Writer's Market*, both of which are updated annually, and make a master list of possibilities. Consider factors including the following:

- *What types of books does this agent represent?*

- *How long has the agent been in business?* In general, the more experience, the better.

- *Is the agent located in New York?* No, an agent doesn't have to live in NYC, but it's probably a plus when it comes to face-to-face meetings and keeping tabs on the publishing industry.

- *Is the agent a member of AAR, the Association of Author's Representatives?* Members of AAR are expected to adhere to its Canon of Ethics, which provides, among other things, that agents will not charge reading fees for potential clients. (Many writers have been duped by less than reputable "agents" who agree to evaluate and/or market a manuscript—for a fee of hundreds, even thousands, of dollars.)

- *How many clients does the agent represent?* (And do you prefer working with a small agency or one with hundreds of clients?)

- *What's the agent's philosophy toward his or her business?* Did the agent sound like someone you'd like to work with?

- *Have you heard anything else about this agent?* Positive or negative?

Considering these factors, make your initial list of possibilities. Then head to the bookstore to look at the books that are similar to yours. Check the Acknowledgments section of those titles—authors almost always thank their agents, and book editors, by name—and add them to your list.

After reviewing the list and considering the factors that are most important to you, start contacting your top choices. If they turn down your project, continue down the list until you've found the perfect agent for you—or have decided either to pitch your work to publishers on your own or to self-publish.

GOING ON YOUR OWN: SELF-PUBLISHING

If you strike out with traditional publishers or simply want to see your book in print much more quickly, your other option is to self-publish. When you self-publish, you're responsible for doing much of what a traditional publisher does, such as cover design, page layout, and marketing and promotion—and that's a lot of work.

But there are a variety of self-publishers who offer package deals: All you submit is the manuscript; they help with layout, design, and book production. Self-publishing companies offer a menu of services that range from editorial services to formatting and indexing, so consider your options carefully and choose the right self-publisher—and the right package—for you. The least you'll need is layout, formatting, and an ISBN number; many also list your book in distributor's databases and provide an e-book format in addition to the traditional book. They may list your book on their Web sites for sales, and offer volume discounts to authors.

Self-publishing companies include:

- http://www.authorhouse.com

- http://www.booksurge.com

- http://www.infinitypublishing.com

- http://www.iuniverse.com

- http://www.virtualbookworm.com

- http://www.xlibris.com

To self-publish on your own (without a self-publishing company), you'll have to tackle the following tasks:

- *Edit your manuscript.* Yes, you can use what you have. But consider hiring an editor to do a read-through—or at least seek out a trusted friend with a good grasp of spelling and grammar. When you self-publish, there's no one overseeing the actual copy, or words, in your book, and you don't want a slew of typos making you look like a moron.

- *Proofread the manuscript.* This task is similar to editing, but this is the read-through aimed at catching every little boo-boo—before your book is printed.

- *Secure an international standard book number, commonly called an "ISBN."* In the United States, the company

R. R. Bowker handles ISBN applications; you'll find information and an application at *http://www.isbn.org/standards/home/isbn/us/printable/isbn.asp*.

- *Design the book cover.* The cover is critical—after all, it's what invites a would-be reader (and buyer!) to pick it up. Don't skimp on the cover. Many self-publishing companies offer cover designers, or hire an artist to develop an eye-catching design. Also, make sure that the ISBN and bar code appear on your book's cover.

- *Format the manuscript.* You may need special software for this, or you can work with a printer.

- *Print the manuscript.* Again, a self-publisher will tackle this for you; otherwise, you have to find a printer for the book. In general, the more copies you print (the number of copies in print is a book's **print run**), the less expensive each copy becomes, because there's an initial setup charge.

- *Deal with every unexpected headache, hassle, and glitch in the process.* That's why a self-publishing company can save your sanity. They publish books every day. You don't.

SELL THAT SUCKER!

Once your book is in print, your job isn't over. Even if you work with a traditional publisher, you still have to market and promote your book to let potential readers know about it. If you've self-published, you may have to work with a distributor to get your book into stores; ask your self-publishing company how it handles distribution. You can also sell copies on your own, or through a Web site developed for that purpose.

In general, you want to get the word out about the book to as many people as possible through book reviews, press releases, and as much related media exposure as you can get. The more people who know about your book, the more people there are to buy it. With more than 150,000 books published every year by traditional publishers—and thousands more by self-publishers—the chances are slim that you'll have a best seller on your hands. But once you've got your baby in print, you can join the ranks of published authors. And won't that feel good?

18

Join the Peace Corps

So, you want to make a difference—and see the world. Why not join the Peace Corps? There are currently almost 8,000 people in the Peace Corps, and you may be surprised to find that, as a member of the Peace Corps, you can do a lot more than simply help people in a third-world country learn to grow crops. Today's Peace Corps volunteers work in diverse fields ranging from information technology to business development to education to agriculture. It takes more than a willingness to serve to be a Peace Corps volunteer. But if you've got the chops, it may be a once-in-a-lifetime experience.

IS IT FOR YOU?

The Peace Corps doesn't take any sucker off the street. Nope, you need more than an altruistic bent to serve. Basically, the qualifications to serve include:

Citizenship. And you have to be a citizen of the good old United States of America. If you're not a legal U.S. citizen, you won't be considered.

Commitment. The Peace Corps isn't a short-term thing, so it's not for the flighty. You commit to more than two years of training and service—twenty-seven months in all. If you're not sure where you want to be six months from now, you're better off considering another volunteer opportunity.

Flexibility. When you apply, you can indicate your countries of preference, but you don't get to choose where you will be sent. And while you receive a living allowance while you serve, you won't get rich serving in the Peace Corps. (Your medical and dental care is covered, as are transportation costs, and you receive about $6,000 at the end of service to spend as you like.)

If you have student loans, you can apply to have them deferred during your time of service; if you've taken Perkins loans (federal financial aid through the U.S. Department of Education), you can also apply to have part of your loan balance canceled based on the amount of time you serve.

Good health. But you needn't be a perfect specimen. Minor health problems or chronic problems that can be treated won't keep you out of the corps.

DON'T LET THIS STOP YOU . . .

In addition to the above-mentioned factors, your motivation and willingness to serve in the Peace Corps are paramount. Regardless of what you've heard, don't let these factors deter you:

Your age. You have to be at least eighteen to join the Peace Corps, but there's no age cutoff. While you may assume that Peace Corps volunteers are recent college grads, people of all ages—including retirees—participate.

Your lack of knowledge of foreign tongues. You needn't speak a foreign language to join the Peace Corps, although it doesn't hurt. (If you speak French or Spanish, however, that will be taken into consideration for certain positions.)

Your lack of a college degree. Some positions require a four-year degree; for others, your work experience and background are just as important.

Your marital status. If you're married, you and your spouse can serve in the Peace Corps together. However, there's no guarantee that you will be able to serve with another friend or family member.

WHAT WILL I BE DOING?

You might picture a typical Peace Corps volunteer helping to dig an irrigation canal in the middle of nowhere, but Peace Corps volunteers do far more than that. The Peace Corps classifies six areas for volunteers to work in, including:

- *Agriculture.* These positions include working with farmers to help produce more crops, conserve natural resources, and produce higher-quality food.

- *Business development.* You might be training entrepreneurs, improving the business environment, or helping local businesses find new markets for their products.

- *Education, youth outreach, and community development.* For example, you might be teaching English, math, or science, or training teachers in English or academic subjects; working with at-risk kids and young adults from ages ten to twenty-five; or leading adult education classes or working with community organizations.

- *Environment.* These volunteer positions include efforts to help protect the environment, including recycling and providing clean water to communities.

- *Health and HIV/AIDS.* These volunteers work to improve basic health care; they may also educate people about HIV/AIDS to help prevent the spread of the disease, and support families affected by the disease.

- *Information technology.* Yes, the Peace Corps needs geeks, too! These volunteers educate people about technology and help communities take advantage of it.

THE APPLICATION PROCESS

While applications are accepted year-round, the entire application process takes longer than you might think. From the time you apply to the time you actually leave to join the Corps takes about nine months, sometimes longer.

Here's the drill, in short. After you submit your initial application, a Peace Corps recruiter will contact you. After a personal interview, you must have a medical exam that confirms you're in good health, and that you're legally able to travel to another country. If the Peace Corps administration determines that you qualify to serve based on your skills, an appropriate position and country are chosen for you. You're then notified of your placement and will have several weeks before you leave.

If you want to serve in the Peace Corps, the application process is critical. Here are some tips to make it through—and to let them know you're PC material:

The Initial Application: Get Everything Down

You can apply online at *http://www.peacecorps.com* or through regular mail by printing out an application from the Web site. Either way, the process is similar. You submit the following forms:

- *a completed volunteer application form*
- *a completed health status review form*
- *a copy of your college transcripts (an unofficial copy is fine)*
- *a copy of your résumé*
- *the names of three references*

While the application includes basic questions about your education, work background, and volunteer experience, it also includes essay questions. Don't freak out! Use these questions to explain more about why you want to join the Peace Corps and what you want to get out of the experience. Be honest. Don't just try to give a model answer or what you think they're looking for. Double-check the form to be sure that you've filled in all of the necessary information.

The health status review form isn't designed to weed you out if you have a health problem; on the contrary, it's to help the Peace Corps determine what regions would be appropriate for you based on your current health and any medical problems. Again, don't lie or omit any relevant information. Be honest about your health situation to avoid problems in the future.

Include a copy of your résumé and college transcripts, along with the names of three references who can speak to your personal and professional abilities. (Just as with other job applications, your references should be people who know you well enough to speak about your personal and professional abilities. Former employers or those who oversaw your work in volunteer positions are good choices.) If you have any questions, visit the Web site or call the Peace Corps at 1-800-424-8580; they'll hook you up with a recruiter in your area.

Personal Interview: Let Them See You Shine

So, your application has been turned in. Good enough. If it's missing any information, your recruiter will call to clarify it; otherwise, you'll receive forms for your references to fill out and return. Make sure your references complete the forms, or your application will be stalled. In the meantime, you can monitor your application process online and submit address changes or additional information as needed.

Now for the nerve-wracking part—the face-to-face interview. This is usually scheduled after you've turned in all of your application materials. Expect to spend an hour answering some potentially personal questions. You'll most likely be asked about:

- *Why you want to serve in the Peace Corps.* (Well, duh! You expected that, right?)

- *Any concerns you may have about living and working overseas for two years.* They expect you to have some concerns or questions, after all. And this is the time to ask any questions you may have about what it's really like to serve in the Peace Corps.

- *The work, both paid and unpaid, you've done in the past.* This includes part-time jobs, full-time positions, and volunteer stuff.

- *How much experience you have living and working with people who are different from you.* And they don't just mean people with a different hair color!

- *Any preferences you have in terms of type of assignment and where you'll actually be serving.* Remember, there's no guarantee you'll wind up with one of your choices.

- *Your current romantic status, your life philosophy, and other personal questions you wouldn't be asked in a typical job interview.*

After the interview, if you pass muster, the recruiter will select a program that requires your particular skills and nominate you to it. Once you're nominated, you'll be told the general program in which you'll be working, the geographic area, and your approximate departure date.

Doing the Doctor Thing

But you're not there yet—you need a formal invitation, and that only happens after you get medical and legal clearance, and are deemed qualified for service by the Peace Corps' placement office. First, the medical screening. You'll receive a packet with instructions about the exams you'll need, including physical, dental, and eye exams, all of which can be conducted by local doctors. Again, don't try to hide anything. Your health information is kept confidential, but it's important to be open and honest so that any health needs can be addressed in your new location.

The Legalities

Depending on your situation, you may have to provide the Peace Corps with additional information about your financial obligations, marital status, and other legal issues that could affect your ability to be accepted. You'll also have to have a background check through the Federal Bureau of Investigation; among other things, it will confirm your U.S. citizenship.

OH, MY GOSH . . . YOU'RE GOING!

Once all these hurdles are cleared, you'll receive a formal invite in the mail, and you have ten days to review it and decide whether you want to accept the invitation to serve in the Peace Corps. The invitation packet will include information about your job description, departure date, passport and visa applications, and a handbook to help you prepare to leave.

Finally, when you accept the invitation, you receive another packet. This is the one (at last!) that tells you where you'll be going, what to bring, and what type of training you'll receive once there. Then you'll have a few days or weeks to round up your friends and family, plan your good-bye parties, and get ready for the adventure of a lifetime. Peace Corps volunteers say the experience is all that—and more.

19

Change Your Identity

So you don't like your name. Your last name is Butts, and your parents thought it would be funny to name you Seymour. Or, with a handle like "Candi Kane," you're sick of all the snide jokes about your "film career."

If you're tired of being teased, maybe it's time to consider changing your name and launching a whole new identity. The process takes some time and effort, but there's no more-public way to announce a shift in your life than changing the name you go by.

WHY CHANGE IT?

People change their names for all kinds of reasons. They get married. They get divorced and want to reassume their maiden name. They adopt a child and want to change his or her last name to theirs.

But your reasons for wanting to change your name may have nothing to do with your marital or family status. Maybe you want to resume the ethnicity of a name your great grandparents had (such as by putting back the "o" they took out of "O'Callahan" at Ellis Island.) On the other hand, maybe you want to streamline a long, complicated name for something shorter, simpler, and more memorable. Actors do it all the time. Never heard of Thomas Mapother? Try Tom Cruise—a bit more catchy, right? The Jon Stewart we know and love from *The Daily Show* was born as Jonathan Stuart Leibowitz, and if Jennifer Anastassakis doesn't ring a bell, think of Jennifer Aniston. Maybe you've got dreams of fame and fortune but think your name is weird, or too offbeat, or too hard to pronounce.

There are all sorts of different reasons people change their names. When you get down to it, your name is one of the most personal things you have. Disliking yours is the only reason you need to change it!

A ROSE BY ANY OTHER NAME . . .

There are a couple of ways to change your name. Many people do it through usage—meaning if your name is Bartholomew and you would rather be named Tom, stop answering to Bartholomew. Have people call you Tom, or Dick, or Harry, or Matthew, or whatever you want.

Of course, the best time to do this is at a significant junction in your life, like when you're moving to a new city, starting college or a new job, or meeting people for the first time. Otherwise there will be a lot of confusion between Bartholomew and Harry, and people may think you're a bit odd. If you don't like your name and prefer to be called something else, changing it through usage works pretty well. It won't cost anything, and it's easier than going through the courts. In some states, altering your name through usage is legally valid as a name change.

However, not all states recognize usage as a valid means of name change. (Check the law in yours to be sure.) If you have an official court document that recognizes your name change (such as a divorce decree or other court order), everyone must legally recognize your name change. You'll also be able to get new forms of identification, such as a passport and an attachment to your birth certificate (necessary to officially change your birth certificate), if you change your name through the court. A court order also links your old name to your new one, and this kind of record can be used to prove your identity.

Before You Become the Next Jesus Christ . . . or Someone Else

Even though this is America, there are restrictions on changing your name. The courts won't let you change your name to just any old name you want, unfortunately. For example, you'll have a difficult time changing your name to that of someone famous. It's going to be difficult to change your name to that of best-selling legal author John Grisham unless you can convince the courts that you don't look like him, are not a writer, have no interest in becoming one, and have no intent to capitalize on his name to make money. This may be quite difficult to prove, and your request to change your name to his may be denied.

Trademarked names (brand names that are registered with the Library of Congress) are also difficult to get approved. So you love Coca-Cola. Do you really want that to be your signature for the rest of your life? You might want to think that through pretty well. Even if you're set on it, chances are the company won't agree. Coca-Cola owns the name, which means that you'll need its consent to change your name to the company's name. And the chance of that happening is pretty slim.

It's also going to be tough to change your name to !, *, or @. It doesn't matter that you'd love to be known as "the at symbol," but it's tougher to get approved than you might think (unless you're The Artist Formerly Known As Prince). In some states you can have one letter or a symbol and a letter as your name, but it's typically more difficult to get the court to OK such names.

Skip names that would be intentionally confusing or involve racial slurs, obscenities, or threats. The court probably won't agree to them anyway. And you can't change your name to try to avoid debts or lawsuits against you. If you're running from the IRS, keep running, because the marathon won't stop here.

The Legal Way

Once you've chosen your un-trademarked, non-slur, unconfusing new name, it's time to change it legally. In most states, the first thing you do is visit the court in the county you live in to fill out a **name change petition** (or a document with a similar title) and pay a small filing fee to cover court costs. Many states also require you to publish a notice in the local paper that covers the county in which the name change would take place. This notice states that you've filed a petition to change your name. The idea is to let potential creditors know what's going on. In some states, you must also personally notify people who will be affected by the name change, such as your spouse, parents, or a minor you're legally responsible for—like your child.

The court may want you to appear at a hearing (don't worry—this just means you must appear in front of a judge) before it will grant your name change. This is the time when anyone who objects to, or feels he or she may be defrauded by, your name change may come forward. Keep in mind that courts do consider objections by others to your name change and are allowed to deny the change on the basis of such objections. If there are no real objections and the judge feels the name isn't inappropriate, he or she will issue a judgment or court order officially changing your name.

After the formal order changing your name has been issued, you'll need to let others know about it. Pretty much any agency or person who dealt with you under your old name will need to be informed. Such agencies include your employer, the Department of Motor Vehicles, the Social Security Administration, the post office, credit bureaus, the IRS, insurance companies, the state tax authority, your bank . . . the list goes on and on. Don't forget about changing your will, power of attorney, and trust, if you have them.

Some states will require you to return to the courthouse to file forms proving that you have informed all the necessary persons and agencies of your name change as required by the court. You may be able to prove this by publishing a notice in the local paper about your name change, and then presenting an affidavit supplied by the newspaper showing the court the date(s) on which the notice ran.

The Cost of a New Identity

Taking the legal steps to change your name does cost some green, and the amount depends on the state you live in. All courts require that you pay a filing fee, but you may be able to get it waived depending on your financial situation—say, if your former husband ran off and left you completely broke. While the fee varies from state to state, expect to spend between $50 and $165 for court costs. (Check out *http://www.namechangelaw. com* for info about what your state requires.)

That's if you represent yourself. If you hire a lawyer, you may spend quite a bit more, especially considering that higher-end lawyers can make a couple hundred bucks an hour. In some states, you don't need a lawyer—paralegals can walk you though the procedure. Good news for you, as they don't charge as much as their lawyer counterparts.

There are also Web sites that offer name-changing services, and their fees vary considerably. Now there are also Web-based kits you can buy to change your name. Be very wary about using one of these services. You'll have to disclose a lot of personal information, such as your Social Security number and credit card number to do so and you don't want to have your identity stolen in the process.

But Wait! I'm Getting Married!

Good news—if you're getting married, it's a bit easier to change your name, especially if you're a woman. The reason? Marriage certificates usually have a space on them for the wife's new name, but may not have a space for a name change for the husband. It's assumed that the woman may change her name, but that's not the case for most men. Because of this gender inequity, if you're a man who changes his name when he marries, you may still have to go to court to do it legally. Sorry!

If you're changing your name through marriage, though, simply obtain certified (that is, official) copies of your marriage certificate to present to agencies—such as the DMV—that will need to see it before allowing you to change your name. Request a new Social Security card with your new name by contacting the Social Security Administration, get a new driver's license, and change your car registration and insurance information. If you have a passport and will need a new one with your new name, contact the local passport agency and ask for a **passport amendment/validation application**. Submitting this application, your current passport, a certified marriage certificate, and a fee will get you a passport with your new and improved name.

Just as with any other name change, inform your bank, employer, and any other agency of your new name. Once your new legal name is official, the only thing you'll have to do is practice your new signature!

20

Be a Movie Extra

"Lights, camera, action!" Looking for a way to get into showbiz? Wanna see the stars up close and personal (well, maybe not so personal, but you might catch a glimpse) and make some money doing it? Whether you are a college student looking to make extra cash on your days off from class, or just want part-time work that's relatively undemanding, becoming a movie extra may be just the ticket—pun intended.

EXTRA, EXTRA: READ ALL ABOUT IT

Clueless about extras? Well, TV and movie extras are the people you see in the backgrounds of your favorite weekly shows and blockbuster movies. On *ER*, Cook County Hospital would look a little funny with no patients and only the main-character doctors. Extras fill up the background of a movie or show, and make scenes look realistic while the cameras are shooting. Although they rarely have speaking roles, extras are quite important to assistant directors. After all, it wouldn't be very believable if Rachel were at Central Perk serving coffee only to her five other Friends, would it?

While acting talent isn't required to be an extra, you do have to figure out how to get gigs. The most time-efficient way, if you live in a large city (or anywhere in the L.A. or New York City areas) is to find a casting agency and register with it. Look for casting companies that specialize in extras. Registration usually involves going in for an appointment and paying a nominal fee. This may cover anything from posting your photo in a directory to actually calling around to find work for you. If you have multiple agencies to choose from, call around to see which gives you the most for your money.

Treat this appointment like you would any other job interview. Impress the interviewer with your acting experience or knowledge of how movies and television shows are filmed (if you have it); special skills you have, from water-skiing to bartending to mountain climbing; and how extremely available you are. Let the interviewer know that you understand what's expected of an extra: to show up on time, be quiet, and follow directions.

If you register with a casting company, you'll be given a number to call to check where and when to show up if you want to work that day. Call early in the morning and the agency will let you know whether they need you. Obviously, it doesn't hurt to build some rapport with the people who answer the phone. And don't be afraid to call them—it shows initiative, after all.

What if you live in a place without a casting agency? You may be able to secure work as an extra by registering online to receive info on extra jobs as they become available. Some Web sites may request personal information to create a profile about you; again, make sure you highlight special skills that may give you a leg up on the rest of the extras.

Check out the following Web sites:

- **http://www.extrasearcher.com/** This site lets you post information about your background and experience as well as photos; producers can then search for the kinds of extras they're looking for.

- **http://www.moviex.com** This site offers the chance to create a profile or personal Web page that can include a detailed description of you, contact information, résumé and description of skills, and up to five photographs. Talent managers, casting directors, and potential employers can find you, while you try to find them. You can also check the site's members' area for casting notices and audition schedules, or visit the message board to read messages from past actors about auditioning or acting experiences. You'll also find acting guides and instructions to pick up pointers, as well as listings of acting coaches and schools.

- **http://www.showbizltd.com** This site claims to work with such companies as HBO, Showtime, NBC, Disney, and Paramount Studios, among others. The site is updated daily and there's a special section to check for movie extra parts.

- **http://www.talentrock.com** This company sponsors talent search events; it also lets you set up a personalized entertainment Web site with a bio page and résumé.

I'D RATHER SKIP IT

Registering sound like too much work? You can take the more casual approach and simply show up at filming locations and hope to be cast as an extra. Keep your ear to the ground—often you'll hear about casting calls on the radio, TV, or Internet (particularly if you live in or near a big city), in which case you can go to the location and try to get in as an extra on speculation (**on spec**). Sure it's a bit more difficult to get work, because you have to show up and find someone who is in charge of the extras and convey your interest. But the flip side is that you can choose to show up only on the days that work for your schedule.

Keep in mind that you'll probably only get hired if someone else doesn't show up, or if you have some talent or "look" that catches an assistant director's eye. (The **assistant director**, or **AD**, is usually the crew member in charge of dealing with extras—and that means you.) Worst case scenario? You show up, and don't get hired—but hey, you get the cachet of hanging out "on set" (well, at least close to it).

BEAUTY AND THE BEAST

You don't have to look like Angelina or Brad to score extra roles. (In fact, looking too good—good enough to show up the stars—may hurt your chances.) But just as in life, it doesn't hurt to be attractive. More important is whether you "fit" into the scenes being shot.

There's a need for almost every look in this business, not just "beautiful" people. Suppose the scene takes place in a prison. They'll be looking for people a little (or a lot) rough around the edges, so to speak. So feel free to show us those tattoos of bloody daggers on your belly or your jailhouse biceps. Try to picture what an assistant director is looking for when he or she envisions the people in the background of the scene, and then see what you have in your wardrobe (or laundry basket) to match it.

If you're constantly being carded, that's good news in the world of Tinseltown, or anywhere movies and shows are filming. A youthful appearance comes in handy with shows that involve high-school kids (think *The OC!*) or other minors. It's much easier to work with an adult (that's you) who looks young than to deal with kids on the set, who come equipped with parents and are subject to strict labor laws. In fact, nearly every "high school student" on *Beverly Hills, 90210* was an actor or actress in his or her mid-twenties when filming started.

Remember to mention your "special talents" when you fill out your initial paperwork. If you can operate espresso machines from all those years slinging coffee during college, put it on the application. That's how Gunther on *Friends* got his role: he was the only extra who could operate the coffee machine. He ended up landing a role on TV's most successful sitcom. Have experience driving police cars and operating the sirens? You could land a part in *Police Academy #987*.

KEEP YOUR LIP ZIPPED

The biggest thing you have to do as an extra is show up on time. In other words, if you have accepted work that day, be there or be square. The AD won't care if your head is pounding or you have cramps. Dose yourself with some over-the-counter meds and get there. If you miss a gig, you may get cut from the agency's roster. The last thing you want is a black mark against you in this business. People talk, and it can be hard to find work with a different agency if it hears negative reports on you, such as that you fail to show up for work. When you leave the set, "sign out" so the AD knows you're done.

While you're on the set, act like the kid you maybe weren't. Be quiet, and behave. The being-quiet part may be the most important (along with not being a starstruck freak). Assistant directors have enough to do trying to get the scene right and people placed correctly to make it all work. If you are talking to other extras or making noise, you might tick off the directors.

Remember, extras are practically a dime a dozen. ADs can and do always find new ones, so make sure you behave. Behaving includes:

- *being quiet on set*

- *making sure you hit your mark (where you're supposed to stand when the cameras are rolling), if you have one*

- *remembering not to look directly at the camera (You're supposed to act as if everything is normal.)*

- *not doing anything to call attention to yourself as an extra* (Like the extra in a scene from *Teen Wolf* who revealed his, um, special friend while the cameras were rolling—and it made it into the movie!)

- *not talking to the actors* (Remember, you're just an extra. Though if an actor talks to you, yes, you can respond.)

- *not acting starstruck* (That means no asking for autographs, no taking pictures of the stars with your cell phone or camera, and no kissing up in hopes that you'll be the next wife of Tom Cruise . . . or husband of J.Lo.)

- *entertaining yourself while you wait* (And you will wait. Bring something to amuse yourself on long days, such as something to read or your iPod. Just make sure it's something quiet! Eat before you show up on the set so your stomach does not suddenly start to growl, or bring a snack just in case.).

DON'T BE A SUCKER

Unfortunately, as with almost any other business, there are those who will be taken advantage of simply because they are new and don't know the ropes. Would-be extras may be particularly vulnerable because they're so desperate to get into the biz.

For instance, beware of casting companies who insist that you use their photographers to have **head shots** (8 x 10 photographs used in the industry) taken. The "photog" may not have any talent, and may be getting a kickback from the casting company. Besides, a head shot isn't necessary for extra work. Most agencies will just take a picture of you when you go to register and keep it for future reference.

The résumé can be another way for agencies to get you to pay more than is necessary. Some agencies will tell you that you need a résumé on some special or expensive paper they will provide to you at a "big discount." This can be another scam. Again, if you plan on going into acting as a full-time thing—not just extra work—head shots and a résumé are a must. Not so for the somewhat lowly extras.

Finally, run away from agencies that ask you to front money for an upcoming project in exchange for your being able to work on the film. Forget that! As an extra, you should never be expected to fund a film; that's not your job and you don't want to be working for an agency that is obviously not well-funded— which is clearly true of any agency that's asking the extras for money! You only want to work for financially sound projects.

WHAT'S YOUR FACE WORTH?

Finally, let's talk bucks. You probably won't make a fortune in this business as an extra. The pay can range from as little as $50 a day to as much as $300, depending on the budget of the film, and what you are required to do—it may be higher if you use special skills like Irish dancing or ice-skating.

You might consider joining the Screen Actors Guild (SAG), a union for actors, because SAG actors typically get paid more and are better respected on the set than non-SAG actors. The fact is, though, that nonunion extras get more work. Also, bear in mind that SAG has the highest unemployment rate of any union in the United States. Over 73 percent of SAG members had earnings of less than $5,000 last year. One-quarter of the members earned between $1 and $1,000; 30 percent of the membership had no earnings at all. Only 12 percent of SAG members earned more than $20,000. In other words, acting—as an extra or as the "real thing"—can be one hell of a hard way to make a living. So you better not quit your day job just yet.

But hey, it's not all about money. Being an extra can be a fun way to get introduced to the movie and television business and make a little money on the side. And who knows, you may even get lucky—and be discovered in the meantime!

21

Donate Eggs or Sperm

Guess what? You've got valuable body parts and you may not even know it. And I'm not talking about donating organs once you're gone, although that's a selfless way to leave a legacy. I'm talking about donating eggs if you're a woman, and sperm if you're a guy. The process is less involved if you're male, but either sex can turn its reproductive organs into moneymakers. And in the process, you may actually help someone's dream of becoming a parent come true.

GRADE-A-QUALITY EGGS FOR SALE!

Egg donation is more common than you think. Some women are unable to conceive because of poor egg quality, which tends to decline as one gets older. But other women simply have a hard time getting pregnant with their own eggs. In that case, they often look for a donor. The donor may be someone they know—say a relative or close friend—or they may look for a donor through a fertility clinic.

If you're considering becoming an egg donor, you probably have one of two major incentives: helping out someone you know, or making money. If you're smart, attractive, and talented, your eggs may be in high demand. In fact, many clinics advertise on acclaimed college campuses looking for the "crème de la crème" of eggs. Typically, clinics pay $2,500 to $5,000 for one cycle of egg donation, but some people will pay tens of thousands of dollars for a specific type of donor (think stunningly gorgeous, outstanding SAT scores, Olympic-caliber athletic abilities, etc.).

Whether you're doing it for money or love, however, the process is similar. I'll focus on doing it for the money and cover all the basics so you know what to expect.

First things first. Not everyone who wants to donate eggs can do so. First, you've got to be healthy and within a certain age range, usually twenty-one to thirty-five. Some programs prefer to use donors who have either donated in the past or who have already given birth to "prove" that they're fertile. Some programs prefer that you not smoke. But each program has different limitations and standards, so it's important to look into them carefully.

How do you find a clinic? Look for newspaper ads and online, or contact local fertility clinics. Check out *http://www.ihr.com/infertility/provider/* or *http://www.sart.org/find_frm.html* for clinics near you.

Keep in mind that ads for egg donors may be placed by egg brokers, fertility clinics, or couples themselves who want specific qualities in their future children. Once you've contacted the person, you'll probably have a brief phone interview or fill out an application to make sure you're healthy and of the right age, and that you sound like a good candidate.

The Donation Process

If you meet the basic requirements for donation, you can expect to spend some time in the gynecological stirrups. First off, you've got to have physical and gynecological exams and blood and urine tests. You're going to be tested for about every sexually transmitted disease, or STD, you can imagine, and you may be asked personal questions like how much you drink, how often you have sex (and with whom), and whether you use drugs. (They may check for drugs with all those blood tests, so you're better off being honest.)

In addition, you'll complete a family medical history and probably take a psychological exam to make sure that you're compos mentis (of sound mind). You'll have an interview of sorts with someone at the fertility clinic to make sure that you understand the health risks involved and that you're willing and able to make the commitment to become a donor.

If you're donating eggs to someone you know, you needn't worry about being selected—obviously someone already chose you. But if you are a donor working for a fertility clinic or "egg broker," you may be asked to wait to donate until a prospective parent chooses you. Wannabe parents may be looking for egg donors with certain physical characteristics, academic ability, religious or ethnic backgrounds, or even talents. If you fit the bill, great; if not, you basically wait until someone chooses you.

Once you've passed medical and psychological muster and have been chosen as a potential donor, the fun begins. Here's a brief overview of the process.

- *First, you need to stop your regular menstrual cycle.* You'll be given a drug that temporarily stops your ovaries from functioning; this makes it easier to control your response to the ovary-stimulating drugs you'll take. This medication may be injected by a nurse or doctor, or you may be able to inject yourself at home.

- *Next, your ovaries are stimulated to produce more eggs than they would in a normal cycle.* (In general, the more eggs you produce, the better, as it gives the doctors more chances to produce a healthy embryo.) In a normal cycle, your body produces one mature egg, which is released from its follicle during ovulation. When you donate eggs, you want to produce more than one mature egg, but delay ovulation until the doctor is ready to retrieve the eggs. To stimulate your ovaries, you'll take medications that are injected for about ten days. You'll learn how to inject the medications; if you can't handle it, you'll have to find someone who's willing to do it for you, probably twice a day, twelve hours apart. Depending on the drugs you take and your body type, you may be injecting them into your arms, thighs, stomach, or butt. During stimulation, you can't drink alcohol, smoke, or use any drugs (legal or otherwise) without your doctor's permission—nor have unprotected sex. Your doctor will tell you what you can and can't do.

- **You'll be monitored during the stimulation process to make sure that your hormone levels are normal, and that the eggs are developing the way they should.** Monitoring includes blood draws and vaginal ultrasound examinations, which are usually conducted every couple of days. You're taking pretty potent medication, so you may notice side effects like mood swings, tender breasts, enlarged ovaries (it may feel like you've got a couple of softballs in your abdomen), or fluid retention. Your doctor or nurse will monitor you to make sure you don't develop a condition called **ovarian hyperstimulation syndrome**, or OHSS, which causes severe fluid retention and swelling of the ovaries. With a mild case, you'll probably just have to take it easy for a few days; moderate to severe cases may require treatment or hospitalization. If you start to have OHSS symptoms before retrieval, your doctor may cancel the cycle. In that case, you quit taking the drugs and may let your body get back to normal before you try another cycle.

- ***When there are one or more mature eggs, you'll be given another injectable drug that triggers ovulation, usually about thirty-six hours before retrieval is scheduled.*** The day of the retrieval, you shouldn't eat or drink anything; you'll probably be given a mild sedative during retrieval. The eggs are then retrieved vaginally, using a thin needle that is inserted into each **follicle**, the sac that holds the egg. After as many eggs as possible have been retrieved, you'll need to recover for a couple of hours before you can leave. The retrieval process itself takes less than an hour, but you should plan on taking it easy the rest of the day and maybe for several days thereafter. If you're swollen or sore from the stimulating drugs, you probably won't want to do much anyway. You'll probably take an antibiotic to reduce your risk of infection, and then you may schedule a follow-up appointment.

- Keep in mind that the process isn't without risks, one of which is accidentally becoming pregnant—especially if you ovulate early or the doctor doesn't retrieve all the mature eggs. Make sure you're aware of any restrictions on intercourse during your donation cycle. Another factor is that some studies suggest that using fertility drugs may increase a woman's chance of developing ovarian cancer; the link isn't clear. The retrieval process itself carries some risks, although most procedures proceed without a hitch. If you have no complications, donating eggs shouldn't affect your fertility in the future, but serious problems like infection could make it harder for you to conceive in the future.

What Happens Next?

At this point your responsibilities are over, but that's not all there is to the story. Next, your eggs will be mixed with sperm. If a fertilized egg develops into an embryo, it may be transferred into the recipient's uterus. If she then becomes pregnant, she will be the legal and birth mother of that child even though the child is genetically related to you.

That fact is something to carefully consider before you decide to become an egg donor. How will you feel about creating children you may never meet? It's a good idea to talk about this with your partner or close friend, or even seek professional counseling. Most egg donor programs offer counseling to make sure that you're comfortable with your decision to donate your eggs. Obviously, if you're under a lot of stress or have any concerns about the process or what it means for you in the future, it's not the right choice for you—at least not now.

One other factor to consider is whether you'd want the recipients of your eggs to know who you are. Most egg donor programs keep the identity of donors confidential, which means neither the recipient(s) of your eggs nor any children created as a result would ever know who you are, but some programs may allow you to meet recipients or allow children to contact you after they reach the age of eighteen. Obviously, confidentiality isn't an issue if you donate eggs to someone you already know, but you may want to discuss whether the child will be told about it—and when. You may also want to consider whether you'd feel comfortable being a "friend" or "relative" to your genetic child.

If you're donating your eggs for money, you're usually paid for the cycles you participate in, not for the number of eggs produced. If your cycle is canceled, some programs will provide partial compensation; others only pay if you make it to egg retrieval. Before you sign any agreement, make sure you've had all your questions about the medical procedure, risks, payments, insurance, and legal rights and responsibilities answered—and that you're willing and able to assume the responsibilities of donating.

MILLIONS OF POSSIBILITIES: DONATING SPERM

Compared to donating eggs, donating sperm is a walk in the park. But there are still screening processes to go through and, just as with egg donors, you and your guys may not pass muster. Hard to believe, but not every wannabe sperm donor is chosen to donate. Check your local phone book for sperm bank listings, or check out *http://www.spermcenter.com/* or *http://www.spermbankdirectory.com/* to find one in your area.

Different sperm banks and fertility clinics set different standards for sperm donors, but in general they're looking for young, healthy men. Some programs ask that sperm donors commit to a specific time frame—say, one year—to be considered.

As with egg donors, potential sperm donors usually have to go through an application process. There may be a phone and/or an in-person interview; at that point you may be asked to provide a sperm sample before the rest of the screening process. How do you get it? By masturbating in a private, comfortable room with a stash of porno; most places have everything from magazines to videotapes. No reason to feel embarrassed; this is what you're here for, after all. It's a good idea to abstain for forty-eight hours before your visit to produce a sample with high sperm count.

The screening process includes testing for sexually transmitted diseases like HIV, hepatitis, syphilis, genital herpes, and genital warts, as well as a complete physical and family medical history. After you "pass," you'll be asked to provide ejaculate samples (yeah! The fun part!); you're usually paid for each one that meets the minimum sperm count requirements. (You won't get rich, but expect to get $50 to $100 per sample, maybe more if you've got stellar qualities like great looks, smarts, athletic prowess, you name it.) The number of times you're asked to donate will depend on the program and whether you've been specifically chosen by a potential mom. After your participation ends, you may be asked to take another blood test six months later (to make sure you're still clean and healthy).

Once again, you have no legal rights or responsibilities to any children who are created by the sperm you donate. Most programs allow you to donate anonymously; with some, you can agree to release your identity to children when they reach the age of eighteen. As with donating eggs, before you offer up your sample for cash, carefully consider how you feel about being a father to a kid—maybe more than one—whom you may never know.

Get the idea? The most important thing to consider when donating eggs or sperm is whether you're truly comfortable with the idea before you hand over your genetic material. But if you've carefully pondered the process, advantages, drawbacks, and potential legalities and emotional consequences, the decision to donate can make a difference not only to your pocketbook, but to one or two people out there who are desperate to become parents. That's good karma you can probably never live down.

22

Run a Marathon

Maybe you're already a runner, and you're looking for a new challenge. Or you want a goal that will get you in great shape. Or you want to train for an event just to prove that you can do it. Run a marathon and you'll have bragging rights that will last a lot longer than the inevitable soreness that follows the next day.

GET SMART

First off, people throw around the term **marathon**, but it's not a generic term for any race. Rather, a marathon is a 26.2 mile race, and there are hundreds held throughout the country and the world. In fact, about a million people toe the line at marathons each year. Sure, some are super-fit, but most are everyday people who welcome the marathon challenge. If that sounds like you, we've got a plan to help you meet it.

If you've never run before, attempting a marathon may be a lofty goal. Most experts recommend that you have some running under your belt before you boost your mileage (the amount you run in a typical week) to compete in a marathon. Consider these general guidelines:

- *If you're a complete couch potato, give yourself a year to get in shape for a marathon.* You'll spend about six months just getting used to running; then another six building up your mileage to train for the marathon without overdoing it.

- *If you run several times a week with a weekly mileage of ten to fifteen miles, give yourself six months to train for a marathon.* Your legs are already acclimated to doing some mileage, but, again, you'll want to ramp up your mileage slowly so you don't get injured.

- *If you run four days a week or more, and are regularly running twenty-five miles a week or more, give yourself at least three months to train.*

CHOOSING A RACE

Before you start training for a marathon, you need to pick one. There are hundreds to choose from, so keep these factors in mind:

- *Where is the race held?* If it's a local marathon and you can sleep in your own bed and drive or take public transportation to the starting line, this may be a plus. You'll probably get more people to come and watch you if it's a nearby race, too.

- *How big is it?* Marathons range from a few hundred people or even smaller to massive 30,000-plus crowds like those at Chicago, Los Angeles, and New York. Do you want to run surrounded by others or would you prefer a smaller crowd?

- **What's the course like?** Chicago is known for being "flat and fast"; other marathons cherish their reputation as difficult courses. You may want to skip the hilly or "rolling terrain" course your first time out; no marathon is easy, so there's no sense making it more challenging than it must be.

- **What time of year is the race?** Typically, most marathons fall during the spring or summer to avoid extreme temperatures in either direction. Fall marathons are popular because they let you train during the longer days of summer. If you live in the Midwest, choosing a spring marathon may mean doing a lot of training in the cold and snow, or relying on an indoor track or treadmill to get your miles in.

- **What's the race's reputation?** Some marathons are geared toward first-time runners; others pride themselves on drawing lots of "old pros." Consider, too, what kind of crowds the race draws. Grandma's Marathon in Duluth, Minnesota, limits the field to 9,300 runners but is known for its amazing crowd support.

Check out *http://www.marathonguide.com/* for a complete list of marathons, or do a Google search for "marathon" and the name of the city you want to run in. Once you've chosen your race, you're ready to train for it.

THE TRAINING GAME

Stage One

At the earliest stage of the game, you simply want to get in better shape and spend more time on your feet. Some people use a running/walking program—by running for a certain period of time, and then walking for a minute or two before resuming running again. Once you've been running regularly—say, twenty-five miles a week for three months with no injuries—you should be ready to tackle the marathon.

Stage Two

Now that you've gotten in decent cardiovascular shape, you can start your training program. The easiest way to train for the marathon is to simply add a long run to your weekly schedule. Start with six miles, working up to twenty miles about three weeks before the marathon. Sound overwhelming? Don't worry. You can gradually increase your long run as you get fitter.

Here's what your first week might look like, running three days a week, with a long run on Saturday and a rest/recovery day on Sunday:

DAY:	Mo	Tu	We	Th	Fr	Sa	Su
MILES:	off	3-5	4	3	off	6	off

The next week, you'd increase your long run by a mile or two. This lets you gradually build your endurance. It's also a good idea to drop your run mileage every few weeks so you're not increasing the length of your long run every single week. So, you might do a long run of six miles the first week; eight miles the second week; nine the third; and six again the fourth week. Then you could step up to nine miles, ten miles, eleven miles, then back to eight. The key is to gradually increase your long-run distance while giving your body "rest weeks" during which your long run is a distance you've covered before.

Running two or three days a week in addition to your long run will help your training, but doing more than that may be more than you can handle. Remember, you don't want to get sick or injured. You want to gradually increase your physical and mental endurance so you're ready to tackle the marathon. Long runs also give you a chance to practice drinking and eating on the run, which you'll do during the marathon.

It's the long run that separates would-be marathoners from the real thing. Long runs prepare your body for the challenge of running more than twenty-six miles. They increase your cardio-vascular conditioning and improve your muscles' ability to utilize oxygen, which increases your endurance. They also gradually strengthen the muscles, tendons, joints, and ligaments in your legs and feet so you're ready to tackle a race that will take you three, four, or five hours (or more!) to finish.

Just as important is the psychological effect that long runs produce. Running twenty-six miles is bound to feel a bit daunting. But as you're able to go farther and farther, you become more confident in your abilities. Run ten, fourteen, twenty miles, and you believe that you can run a marathon. In fact, most first-time marathoners don't go farther than twenty miles for their longest training run. If you can finish a twenty-miler in training, you'll be able to run that extra six miles the day of the marathon.

Running Long

But long runs can be tough if you've never gone farther than a quick five-miler. Keep these tips in mind as you plan your long runs:

- *Hook up with a buddy (or two).* Even the most dedicated runners can find spending an hour, or two, or three out on the roads alone a drag. Run with a friend, or join a marathon-training group (most big cities have running clubs that sponsor them, often tied to a local race). Check with a local running shop; they usually have running clubs and may be able to hook you up with other runners.

- **Rest the day before your long run.** Drink plenty of water, and eat well so you'll have energy to run the next day. Don't forget to get enough sleep, too.

- **Take the day after your long run off, too, to speed recovery.** Drink lots of water and have a meal high in carbs to replenish your glycogen stores. Take it easy the rest of the day, and take the next day off. If your legs are sore, an easy walk or bike ride may help.

- **Start early, especially during the summer, to take advantage of cooler temps.** If the weather is scorching, consider bagging your run or push it to the next day.

- **Plan your route in advance.** Look for lightly traveled roads or trails or sidewalks away from traffic. Routes that have water stops along the way are great, or consider doing loops (say, of two or three miles) that bring you back to a water fountain or other water supply.

- **Carry water with you.** Even if you run a route with water stops, you should always carry water. For longer runs, consider taking sports drinks or energy gels for extra calories. There are a variety of water bottle belts that let you carry water and still keep your hands free.

- **Dress for the weather, and don't forget sunscreen.** Wear the clothes you'll race in a couple of times before the big day.

- *Go easy.* You shouldn't worry about how fast you're going during the long run; it's more important to simply be out there doing it. Aim for a comfortable pace and check to make sure you can pass the "talk test" and hold a conversation as you run.

- *Build your distance gradually.* Every few weeks, drop back down in mileage to give your body a break.

- *Feeling tired is normal; feeling exhausted or in pain is not.* Listen to your body, and ditch a long run if you're not up for it. You can make up the distance next week.

The Marathoner's Diet

People often lose weight while training for a big race, but you should be consuming sufficient calories to give you energy for your long runs and help your body recover. A 150-pound person burns about 100 calories per mile, so you need to make sure that you're taking in enough food to fuel your muscles.

Sure, running gives you some latitude when it comes to your diet, but eating healthy is a better idea. In general, you want to eat a lot of carbohydrates during training. Carbs fuel your muscles for both your short and long runs. That includes things like pasta (haven't you noticed runners are obsessed with pasta?), potatoes, bread, rice, and cereal, along with fruits and vegetables. Beans are another carbohydrate source that is also loaded with protein. Eating after a long run is particularly important because the carbs replenish the glycogen stores in your muscles. That glycogen is stored glucose, and it's what your body runs on— pardon the pun.

Drink plenty of water and other fluids—eight eight-ounce glasses isn't nearly enough when you're training hard. Check your pee to make sure you're drinking enough—your urine should be plentiful and straw-colored. Dark-yellow urine is a sign to drink up.

THE BIG DAY

As the morning of your marathon approaches, it's normal to feel nervous. **Taper**, or cut your mileage, the two weeks before the marathon; your last long run should be at least two weeks before marathon day. The last few days before the race, stay off your feet, drink plenty of water, and consume lots of carbs. They'll help store glycogen in your muscles, which you'll need during the race.

Don't worry if you don't sleep well before the race; that's normal. Here are a few tips to keep you (hopefully) cool, calm, and collected before and during the race:

- *Get up a couple of hours before the race.* You want time to drink some water, have a light breakfast (like a banana and bagel), and visit the bathroom before you head to the starting line.

- *Dress for the weather.* If it's cold at the start but supposed to warm up, wear an old long-sleeved T-shirt or jacket you can toss after a mile or two. (A plastic garbage bag works, too.)

- *Position yourself carefully.* Some of the big marathons have estimated-finishing-time signs (3:30, 4:00, 4:30) to help you determine where to start. Don't position yourself near the front when you're planning on a five-hour race. Better to start in the back and pass people than get trampled at the start.

- *Start off slow.* It's normal to run a bit faster when you're nervous. Stick to a comfortable pace. You've got twenty-six miles to go, you know!

- *Drink at every water station.* Every mile or two, you'll have the chance to drink some water. Staying hydrated will reduce your fatigue. At later stations, when they offer Gatorade or energy gels, go for it—as long as you've tried the same thing on a long run.

- *Wear the tried-and-true.* Race morning isn't the time to break in a new pair of running shoes or a new singlet. Run in everything before race day so you know it's comfortable.

- *Walk if you want to.* Walking breaks throughout the race can help you finish. If you feel the need to walk, don't feel bad. Just keep going.

- *Talk to people around you.* Conversation can help distract you from discomfort, and make the miles go by more quickly.

- *Finish strong.* Throw your arms in the air as you cross the finish line! They'll be taking a finisher's photo and you want to look your best . . . or as good as you can with dried sweat caked all over your face. You did it!

- *Drink, drink, drink.* After the race, drink plenty of fluids, and treat yourself to a carb-heavy meal and a relaxing massage. Expect to feel some soreness for a few days. If you have any throbbing or sharp pains, though, get them checked out at the medical tent at the race.

Ahhhh . . . it's over. The first thing you'll probably say after the marathon is, "never again." But after the soreness wears off, you may start thinking about your next marathon. If so, you've been bitten by the bug. Even if you only do one marathon, though, it's a way to prove that you can stretch yourself physically and mentally. And you get a shiny finisher's medal on top of it!

23

Be a Human Guinea Pig

Are you concerned with the welfare of the next generation? Does the fact that there is still no cure for cancer or diabetes keep you up at night? Well, here's your chance to do something about it. Become a medical guinea pig and you'll help save future generations the pain and suffering of ailments big and small while advancing medical knowledge—and pick up some cash while you're at it.

If you're interested, the good news is that there are tons of medical experiments requiring volunteer "guinea pigs" each year. In fact, demand is so great that an estimated 80 percent of studies (clinical trials, to be proper) are postponed due to lack of volunteers. The bad . . . well, you are taking a risk when you donate your body to science, even on a temporary basis. But if you want to join the 2.5 million people who take part in medical research every year, we'll give you the scoop on this unusual way to make money.

GONNA BE A GUINEA?

Researchers need volunteers for their clinical trials to help determine whether new drugs or procedures being tested are more effective than what is currently being used. Keep in mind that every drug or medical procedure must receive FDA (Federal Drug Administration) approval, so there's a big demand for volunteers. Guinea pigs are needed not only for studies involving major diseases like cancer, AIDS, and Parkinson's disease, but also for less-serious problems ranging from headaches to hangnails.

But don't rush out and volunteer your toes to a new fruit-scented antifungal cream for athlete's foot just yet. Keep these things in mind:

Understand What You're Doing

Make sure you know the risks of the trial or experiment. In general, the risks to you are low, but once in a while something serious can happen—like when an otherwise healthy young woman died during an asthma study at Johns Hopkins University in 2001. Fortunately this is a rare occurrence, and so are adverse reactions. The rule of thumb is **one-in-thirty**, meaning that about one person in thirty people may experience some type of adverse reaction (say, a cough or fever) to a medication.

And make sure you know what restrictions, if any, are involved. For example, will you be required to give up caffeine, nicotine, or alcohol during the course of the trial? You don't want to wreak havoc on family, friends, and other drivers on the road because you're restricted from your daily Starbucks™ fix. Please, for the sake of yourself and the rest of us, consider these things.

How Low (or Far) Will You Go?

Another issue to consider is how far you're willing to take a clinical trial. If you're healthy, do you really want to test a drug for a life-threatening illness? Obviously, there's less apparent risk in donating the use of your scalp to test a dandruff shampoo or donating part of your face to test a new acne medication. And it's true that the risks for medical experiments are very low, particularly in the United States, due to extensive regulations. But you should consider how involved you're willing to get from the outset.

Of course there's always a chance you'll receive a **placebo**, a harmless, inactive substance that may resemble "the real thing." Most medical trials include a control group, or people who don't receive the medication or treatment, to help determine the efficacy of the treatment or drug being tested.

Research Your Researcher

It's also not a bad idea to check up on the people conducting the study. Confirm that the trial has the blessing of an institutional review board (IRB). These boards usually consist of a panel of doctors and ethicists, and clinical trials within the United States are generally required to obtain the approval of an IRB, regardless of who or what type of institution is running them. Drug trials usually require the oversight of a data safety committee to prevent or lessen potential risks.

Don't Read It and Weep

When you participate in a clinical trial, you'll be given an **informed-consent document**. Read it as if your life depended on it—after all, it may! Even if you become cross-eyed from reading so closely, you'll know exactly what you are getting into. This document explains the study's purpose, risks, and benefits, in addition to the required visits and duration of the trial. If you have any questions about it, you may want your personal physician to take a look at the document; he or she may catch something you might not.

Take a look, too, at the **study protocol**, which is a detailed description of the trial, and talk to the researcher about any questions you have. For example, you may want to ask what the purpose of the trial is or whether similar research is being conducted in other locations. If you're really nervous, ask if there are other volunteers undergoing this experiment who would be available to talk to you. Finally, ask what happens if you decide in midstream that the trial isn't for you. In theory, this shouldn't present a problem, as your right to withdraw is protected under federal law. But in reality, researchers may try to pressure or guilt-trip you into staying.

WHY TAKE THE PLUNGE?

Given the risks and sometimes invasive procedures involved, you may be wondering about the benefits of participating in medical studies. But there are benefits; it's just that some may be significant to you while others may not matter as much.

Get healthier while helping. In addition to your being a "pioneer" in the quest for necessary medical information, you may also receive actual medical benefits from participating. If you already suffer from some sort of condition, such as heart disease, you could be part of a study that finds the cure and gives you the treatment you need in the meanwhile. For example, the famous Framingham Heart Study has studied more than 10,000 people over the past fifty-five years. (This is the study that enabled scientists to determine the links between smoking and heart disease and other serious conditions.)

The Framingham volunteers are kept under the watchful eye of volunteer researchers, and every two to three years they spend half a day having an echocardiogram and blood workup. Occasionally during these routine checkups, another health problem is detected. For instance, one participant was found to have a blocked coronary artery that could have been fatal had it not been found in time. Because of his participation in the study, though, the blockage was detected and treated in time.

You may, in fact, be desperate for a cure. If you suffer from Type 1, or juvenile, diabetes, and are lucky enough to qualify for a pancreatic islet transplantation study, you might have a chance to rid yourself of diabetes and the daily hassle of insulin shots. To many people, that's worth much more than a check for any amount of money. It's a chance to better your own life while improving the lives of others not fortunate enough to qualify.

Make a difference. There are always the philanthropic folks who see participating as an "if-not-me-then-who?" situation. Think about it. If no healthy volunteers had stepped up to test the first life-prolonging drugs for HIV patients, many people with HIV wouldn't have lived longer than a year or two. If you decide to make this type of commitment, you may be helping thousands or even millions of people due to your courage. To some people, this reason alone makes it worthwhile.

Garner some clams. There's also a chance to make some money, although the amount usually depends on the type of trial and length of time involved. The greater the risk involved or time spent, the more you usually make. A cancer drug study will typically pay more than a sleep study, for example. You don't have to "do" much for a sleep study; typically, participants just sleep under observation in a laboratory for several nights. On the other hand, a cancer drug study may require months (or longer!) of study, time, and possibly pain (think blood draws and other diagnostic tests).

GUINEA PIGS WANTED

So, you're interested. Now it's time to consider the types of studies you want to participate in.

Questionnaires/Interviews

This is about as easy and low-commitment as it gets. Completing questionnaires and participating in interviews doesn't take long, but it generally doesn't pay that well, either. These studies may involve anything from interviews to looking at pictures of blobs and explaining how you feel about them. The going rate tends to be about $5 to $20 total. (The less risk you take, the less you get paid.)

Medical Exams/Interviews

This class of study can be broken down into two main categories. The first category involves mildly invasive studies, such as links between weight and depression or stress and seasonal depression. You usually have to undergo a general physical examination in which your height, weight and blood pressure are taken. Afterward, you may be asked questions about your mental health to get a more thorough idea of your emotional condition. Expect to make roughly $20 to $100.

The second type of study in this category is a little more high-tech, and could involve internal exams like EKGs, MRIs, or blood tests. Because of the possible discomfort involved, the pay scale tends to be a little higher, in the range of $50 to $100. (Many drug trials fall into this category.) There are also rare studies involving alcohol and illegal drugs, but consider the risks of winding up with an addiction—just for a few bucks.

More Involved Studies

If you're ready for bigger bucks and are willing to do extreme things (hmmm . . . like sewing on an experimental limb, perhaps?), you'll get paid more for your time, inconvenience, and suffering. Keep in mind that these experiments generally require multiple visits and possibly extended hospital stays.

Sleep and Get Paid

Sounds good, doesn't it? Before you agree, realize that you may also have to undergo electric shocks or other such pleasant treatments. A psychiatrist will probably want to conduct an interview and have you fill out a questionnaire before a sleep study, and researchers may also videotape you while you sleep or take an EKG to study your sleep habits. As studies go, this type isn't too bad—as long as you don't mind sleeping away from home in a place that might not necessarily be comfortable. (On the flip side, you might have to stay awake as long as possible—not fun!) Usually you can get about $100 per night for one to three nights.

SUSS OUT THE STUDIES

Finally, if you're going to volunteer, you need to know who needs you.

Surf the Web. Take a look at the following Web sites to find clinical trials:

- **http://www.clinicaltrials.gov** The National Institute of Health makes it easy for you to search ongoing clinical trials by location, treatment, or disease.

- **http://www.nccam.nih.gov** The National Center for Complementary and Alternative Medicine at the National Institute of Health may be more your speed; the Web site contains information on alternative medicine research that may not be available in other government databases. It focuses on trials using alternative forms of medicine such as massage, Reiki (a form of spiritual healing which uses touch to strengthen the body's energy fields), and electromagnetism.

Drug companies. Pharmaceutical companies are constantly running clinical trials, so you can call or e-mail them to join their databases for upcoming trials.

College campuses. Researchers know college students are often hard up for cash, long on time, and willing to volunteer. Check the student center for study postings. Most major universities have research hospitals nearby; you can opt into their databases for future reference if nothing is available at that moment.

Classified ads. The classifieds, both in print and online, can also offer opportunities for medical guinea pigs. Once the ads for these studies are posted or in print, they fill almost immediately, so call as soon as you see an ad.

Hey, chances are that you won't get rich as a medical guinea pig. But it can be a relatively easy way to make some extra cash, make a difference in the world, and maybe even protect your own health in the process. And besides, it's probably the only legal way to "sell your body," or at least the parts of it you choose.

24

Explore Buddhism

It's not just Richard Gere who's spouting the virtues of a Buddhist lifestyle anymore, and for good reason. Learning more about Buddhism gives you an opportunity to achieve inner enlightenment or simply drop terms like "karma," "dharma," and "nirvana" into a conversation and actually sound like you know what you're talking about. Even if you never make it to bodhisattva status (that's the term for a Buddhist who has reached nirvana, or enlightenment, and helps others find their way), you may find that adopting a more Zen-like mindset makes you a more content, less stressed, and overall happier person.

WHAT IS BUDDHISM, ANYWAY?

While many people think of Buddhism as a religion, it really isn't one. In fact, you can be a Buddhist and also be a Catholic or a Jew, or even an atheist. Buddhism doesn't recognize a particular god (the original Buddha isn't considered a deity), and while it does prescribe an Eightfold Path for people to follow, it's not as strict or rigid as some religions.

While Buddhism is still taking hold in the United States, claiming one to five million Americans as practitioners (depending on whose estimates you believe), it's big across the globe. In fact, more than 300 million people worldwide call themselves Buddhists.

So if Buddhism isn't a religion, then what is it? Good question, and one that can be challenging to answer. Think of it as a belief system that's designed to end your suffering and bring inner peace.

Sound like a tall order? Well, Buddhism teaches that true happiness comes from wanting what you already have and not wanting what you don't. In other words, Buddhism encourages the opposite of a materialistic existence or trying to keep up with the Smiths or the Joneses or the Andersons in a never-ending quest for the latest toy or tool or designer outfit. With Buddhism, you're concerned not about the external world but about the interior world of your mind.

But practicing Buddhism means more than just giving up the desire for material things. A central part of Buddhism is an idea called **mindfulness**: the ability to be completely present in every moment, whether you're eating a meal or brushing your teeth or toiling away at a project at work. When you're mindful, you're not thinking about what's going to happen tomorrow or feeling angry at having to work late or worried that your girlfriend's cheating on you. You're caught up in the task at hand—even if it's simply breathing—no more, no less. Think of it as being "in the flow," Buddhist-style.

Buddhists believe that each of us has an inner all-knowing Buddha. Your job is to figure out how to get in touch with it. A big part of that is regular meditation practice (more about that in a bit). Meditation and following the Eightfold Path help you reach enlightenment, when you uncover your inner Buddha. In fact, the word "Buddha" means "one who has awakened."

The Real Buddha

Buddhism is older than Christianity, having been around for more than 2,500 years. The original Buddha was a man named Siddhartha Gautama, who grew up in India as a rich prince with a sheltered life. His life was so sheltered, in fact, that it wasn't until he was in his late twenties and married with a child that he was first exposed to suffering and death.

Gautama was so affected by this (hey, he was a sensitive guy!) that he left his family and fortune behind to wander India as a holy man. He achieved enlightenment under a bodhi tree (that's where the term "bodhisattva" came from) and formulated what Buddhists call the **Four Noble Truths**. The Four Noble Truths basically say that life is full of suffering; that most suffering, including fear of death, is due to craving and attachment (called **trishna**); that this craving and attachment can be transcended, which eventually leads to full enlightenment, called **nirvana**; and that the way you achieve nirvana is by following the **Eightfold Path**. The Eightfold Path encompasses:

- *Right view or understanding.* This means that you understand and accept the legitimacy of the Four Noble Truths, and that you're aware of the impermanent nature of both thoughts and things.

- *Right thought or intention.* Having the right intention means being committed to improving yourself, and to giving up your old selfish attitudes. Buddha described three types of right intentions: being willing to stop thinking about what you want; resisting negative feelings like anger; and developing compassion instead of thinking cruel or violent thoughts.

- *Right speech.* In addition to your actions, the words you say can have a powerful effect on others. Buddha said that right speech meant abstaining from false speech; from words that hurt or could harm others; from words that could offend others; and from chatter that has no purpose. In other words, you should tell the truth, avoid lies, speak with kindness and compassion, and, finally, speak only when necessary.

- *Right action.* Your speech shouldn't harm others; neither should your actions. This means abstaining from harming or killing others; abstaining from taking what is not given (i.e., not stealing, robbing, or defrauding people); and abstaining from "sexual misconduct." In other words, you should treat others compassionately, respect their possessions, and not harm anyone through a sexual relationship.

- *Right livelihood.* No, you don't have to work for a charity, but your dealings with others should be kind and honest no matter what your job is. Buddha, however, did specify four particular occupations that should be avoided: dealing in weapons; dealing in living beings (such as hog farming— or pimping); working in meat production; and selling poisons and intoxicants. Your job also should allow you to practice right speech and right action, so a job where you're swindling little old ladies out of their nest eggs wouldn't fit the bill.

- *Right effort.* Right effort means that you make an effort— a concerted one—with regard to your spiritual practices. In other words, you try—you don't just wait for things to happen. You can't be a lazy Buddhist.

- *Right mindfulness.* This means always keeping your attention focused on the present instead of worrying about the future or obsessing over the past. Ideally, you should be mindful in everything you do. Meditation is an example of focused mindfulness.

- *Right concentration.* Right concentration means being able to focus your mind and clear it of distractions. It's one of the abilities you develop through meditation.

To attain the Eightfold Path, Buddhists practice meditation and also follow the five precepts, whereby they agree to:

1. *refrain from harming living creatures*—Obviously, this applies to humans, but some types of Buddhism also interpret this as commanding vegetarianism; others do not.

2. *refrain from taking something that is not freely given*—In other words, thou shall not steal—or defraud someone out of something.

3. *refrain from sexual misconduct*—Pretty obvious, huh?

4. *refrain from "incorrect speech"*—This precept includes everything from lies to idle gossip. If you love to dish the latest dirt, this may be difficult for you!

5. *refrain from intoxicants*—They lead to loss of mindfulness. Again, some Buddhists drink alcohol, but you're not supposed to get drunk.

According to Buddhist belief, we are reborn over and over in a cycle called **samsara**; our current life depends on what we did in our previous ones, a principle called **karma**. Once you attain enlightenment, you achieve a state of oneness with the cosmos.

As a reward, you get to step off the treadmill of reincarnation, unless you choose to be reborn on Earth as a bodhisattva.

Buddha's teachings are sometimes referred to as the **dharma**; the word can also mean a Buddhist's duty to follow these teachings until he or she reaches enlightenment. The primary tool used to get there is meditation, although other techniques can be employed as well.

What's Your Buddhist Style?

Buddhism is divided into three major schools:

- *Theravada (or Hinayana).* This school is the closest to the "original" Buddhism in its teachings; it focuses on awareness achieved through meditation.

- *Mahayana.* This school maintains the importance of the Four Noble Truths but sees Buddha as a god. Mahayana Buddhists particularly revere bodhisattvas—fully enlightened, Buddha-like beings who could enter nirvana but choose to be reborn to help others. One well-known type of Buddhism, Zen Buddhism, grew out of Mahayana Buddhism. Zen practitioners use a rigorous meditation practice called **kazen**, and often employ **koans**, or unanswerable questions (such as "what is the sound of one hand clapping?") to aid in meditation.

- *Vijrayana.* With this form, Tibetan monks claimed to be able to achieve enlightenment in just one lifetime (instead of many). Rather than only using meditation, breath control, and chanting, they also employ techniques ranging from visualization to yoga to tantric sex to reach enlightenment. Upon the death of the ranking monk, surviving monks locate his next incarnation; in Tibet, the ranking monk is called the **Dalai Lama**, who is also considered the head of state.

MEDITATION: THE WAY TO ENLIGHTENMENT

If you want to be a Buddhist, you pretty much have to meditate. But don't worry. You don't have to sit cross-legged on the floor, burning incense and chanting "om." If sitting doesn't appeal to you, you can choose to do walking or standing meditations; in fact, Buddhists believe that any activity performed mindfully is a form of meditation.

Meditation basically means focusing and quieting your mind so that you're not troubled by pesky thoughts that intrude on your meditation. (Buddhists sometimes call this "monkey mind.") Sitting quietly and focusing on a word or concentrating on your breathing is the easiest way to learn to meditate—and it's easy to try.

Choose a place free from noise and other distractions, and sit in a comfortable position. Loosen any uncomfortable clothing; you want to focus on your breathing, not your tight pants. Inhale slowly through your nose and exhale slowly; count one. Inhale and exhale again and count two. Count up to four, and then start over at one.

If you lose count (or, we should say, when you lose count—because it will happen), don't get annoyed or frustrated. Just start over and focus on thinking of nothing but counting your breaths. When thoughts pop into your head, don't let them distract you. (Again, weird thoughts of all sorts will intrude, including things along the lines of, "You look like an idiot! You'll never be able to meditate! Give it up!") Meditation is much harder than it looks, especially when you haven't tried it before. Start off slow with five or ten minutes. Over time you can gradually work your way up to the forty-five minutes to an hour a day that most Buddhist teachers suggest.

Want to do more? Consider a meditation retreat over a weekend; most Buddhist centers sponsor these kinds of retreats regularly. Keep in mind that it's not for beginners—you may be expected to take a vow of Noble Silence the entire time you're there, which means no talking, writing, reading, watching television, or listening to music. You spend your days chanting, doing yoga, or taking contemplative walks. Other retreats focus on meditation instruction. Check out the Buddhist centers nearest you or their Web sites for more information.

FOLLOWING THE PATH: LEARNING MORE ABOUT BUDDHISM

There are hundreds of books about Buddhism out there, but make things easy for yourself and start by surfing. Check out the following resources for everything you ever wanted to know about Buddhism—and then some:

- http://www.buddhanet.net/ BuddhaNet includes everything from a worldwide directory to information about Buddhist studies, an enormous resource library, and a comprehensive e-store where you can buy books and CDs about Buddhism.

- http://www.ciolek.com/WWWVL-Buddhism.html Serious about Buddhism? The Buddhist Studies Virtual Library tracks the leading information facilities in the fields of Buddhism and Buddhist studies.

- **http://www.dharmanet.org/** DharmaNet's Gateways to Buddhism includes a variety of Buddhist study and practice resources. It includes DharmaNet's own in-house databases and collections, as well as links to a variety of online Buddhist resources.

Buddhism is more than a passing fad, and it attracts people from all walks of life. If you've been searching for something more in your life, it may hold the answers for you. Perhaps it's your karma in this life to discover your inner Buddha.

Give Spellbinding Speeches

25

A widely cited survey once revealed that Americans' number-one fear wasn't death or disasters or even the dentist. It was (gasp!) public speaking.

If that sounds like you, take heart. While getting up in front of a group of people (their beady little eyes boring into you, ready to find fault with the tiniest little mistake) strikes fear into most of us, you can learn to be a better public speaker and give a great speech. And who knows? In the process, you may discover you have more to say than you thought.

WHO'S LISTENING?

Inexperienced speakers make a lot of mistakes. But one of the biggest is that they forget that speaking is a two-part process. One person is speaking . . . the other is listening. Right? Get it? Yet many speakers ignore the fact that the reason they're talking is because other people are (hopefully) listening to them.

To give a great speech, the first thing you need to do (after you get past your initial freak-out about having to do it) is to figure out who your audience is. Ask the person who's requesting that you give the speech for more info about your listeners.

Factors to consider when analyzing your audience include:

- *Are they captive?* In other words, if you're giving a presentation to the rest of the sales team at your office, people have to attend. If you're teaching a class on jewelry-making at the community college, however, people are there because they want to be. Bet you can guess which is considered the "easier" audience.

- *How large will the audience be?* Speaking to a half dozen people is different than speaking to 100—or 500. Knowing the size of your audience may not affect the message you deliver, but it will help you prepare. For example, dramatic gestures might look silly in a small conference room but be appropriate for a room of hundreds of people.

- *Is the audience men, women, or a mix of both?*

- *How old is your audience?* In many situations, the ages will vary, but a group of college students has a different vibe than baby boomers in their forties and fifties.

- *What is your audience interested in?* Obviously, if this is a work-related presentation, you can assume that your listeners care (or at least pretend to care) about their jobs and work performance. If you're speaking to a more general audience, try to figure out its primary concerns. It will help you give a more compelling speech.

- *How receptive will your audience be to what you have to say?* Again, this has something to do with whether it's "captive" and something to do with the subject matter you'll be discussing.

- *How much does the audience know about the subject you'll be talking about?*

- *What are they expecting to hear from you?* You should know the answer to this one—without it, you can't expect to give a decent speech.

Make sure that you ask, too, about the actual location of your speech. Will you be in a boardroom, a large conference hall, or a ballroom? Will you have a microphone? (In a room bigger than a boardroom, you'd better hope so.) Will it be a lavaliere, a mic that you can attach to your lapel, or a stationary mike mounted on the podium? If so, consider whether you'll feel more comfortable standing behind the podium or picking up the microphone and holding it while you present.

It's good to know where you fall in the order of the day. If you're the opening speaker at an event, you can expect to have plenty of late-shows trickling in. If you have the dreaded job of speaking after lunch, your audience may be in a carb coma. And if you're the final speaker out of four, consider how you can make your presentation "ear-worthy" after your audience has already heard a bunch of people before you.

WRITE BEFORE YOU TALK

Now that you have some idea of the lay of the land, both in terms of your audience and the speaking location, it's time to actually figure out what you're going to say. (No, you can't just get up there and wing it. Believe me.)

Probably the easiest speeches to write are those that concern a subject you actually care about. But at work, this might be a luxury you don't have. In that case, you'd better fake some enthusiasm. (Just picture yourself out of work, looking for a job . . . there you go. Feel excited now?)

As you write your speech, you should consider what your basic job is. Are you trying to inform your audience about something? Convince or persuade them to do something? Entertain them? Motivate them? Inspire them? Once you have your purpose firmly in mind, sketch out an outline of what you plan to cover.

While your outline may vary, it's a good idea to have no more than three to five basic points—people can't remember much more than that anyway. You may have heard the old adage, "tell them what you're going to tell them; tell them; and tell them what you told them," but that's a little simplistic. You might find it easier to use a basic outline like this:

- *Opening*
- *Overview* (in which you give the audience an idea of what to expect)
- *Main point #1* (with supporting points, if applicable)
- *Main point #2* (with supporting points, if applicable)
- *Main point #3* (with supporting points, if applicable)
- *Conclusion/call to action*

Let's look at each part of your outline. Your opening should be brief. If humor comes naturally to you, you can open with something funny, but don't take any chances. A joke that falls flat is worse than just about anything else.

Segue into the overview, which may be only a few lines. This is the "tell them what you're going to tell them" portion. Why is the audience there? What will you be talking about? The overview is sort of a capsule of your entire speech, and gives listeners a road map of where you'll be taking them.

Your main points are simply that, with supporting data where appropriate. For example, if you're speaking about how to give a great speech, your outline might look something like this:

- *Opening.* Brief remarks about public speaking being the number-one fear—but the good news is that it doesn't have to be.

- *Overview.* Giving a great speech is easier than you might think; it takes audience analysis, thoughtful writing, and enthusiastic delivery (your three main points).

- *Main points.* Under each main point, show listeners how to do what you're describing, using examples, anecdotes, statistics, or whatever information you care to include.

- *Conclusion/call to action.* Finally, to wrap up your speech, give a brief overview of what you covered ("tell them what you told them") and give listeners a call to action—in other words, invite them to do something. An example "So, the next time your boss is desperate for a speaker, shock her and yourself by volunteering to do it. Just because you open your mouth doesn't mean you have to put your foot in it." (This will work if you can pull off humor; otherwise, stick to something simple yet motivating.)

SWEATY PALMS AND NERVOUS SWALLOWS

After you've written your speech, practice it. A few run-throughs will make you more comfortable with your material, and give you an idea of how long it will take you to deliver the speech. You may want to present in front of a trusted friend; ask if you're talking too fast (common with nervous speakers), fidgeting (again, a common problem), or mumbling your words.

A great speech sounds natural, even if it's been practiced a hundred times. Make sure your speech sounds like you. Don't use "show-off" words when smaller ones will work just fine. Use specifics whenever you can, and vary the pace of your delivery. Also make sure you're not using any jargon or other words your audience won't understand. If you make them feel stupid, they'll blame you.

Maybe you've decided that, rather than outlining your speech, you're going to write it out word by word. That's fine in theory, but in practice reading a speech makes you sound monotone. If you absolutely can't face the idea of speaking without a word-for-word written-out draft, at least make it a point to look up from your notes occasionally to make eye contact with members of your audience.

Remember, even the most polished speakers get nervous before giving a speech. Anxiety is a good sign; it means you care! But to keep your nerves at bay, and deliver the strongest message you can, use these speech-giving strategies:

- *Practice ahead of time!* Yeah, we said it already. But without practice, you'll be ten times more nervous—and more likely to screw up, too. (Sorry, but it's true.) Practicing will make you sound more comfortable and familiar with the material—and may alert you to possible problems (difficult-to-pronounce names or words, for example).

- *Arrive early at the place you'll be speaking.* Check out the facilities and the microphone or public-address system if you can. Look for any hazards (such as power cords) on the way up to the podium or table so you don't trip on them. Drink some cool water, and keep a glass of water (no ice, which is noisy) at your side when you present.

- **Never open a speech with an apology (e.g., "I've got a bad cold, so I sound terrible . . ." or "I don't give many speeches, but here goes . . .").** You'll create a negative impression with the audience from the moment you open your mouth!

- **Remember not to read your speech word for word.** You'll put people to sleep. If you read a speech, look up every paragraph or two to connect with your audience by making eye contact with them.

- **Share anecdotes, or real-life stories, whenever appropriate.** Listeners love "war stories" and are more likely to remember examples like these than the main points of your speech, so look for stories that encompass those points.

- **Open and close your speech as strongly as you can.** People tend to remember the first thing and last thing you say, so the beginning and end of your speech should be the parts you work on the most. Remember that the ending of your speech should be powerful, specific, and (hopefully) should inspire the audience to do something in its "call to action."

- **Be selective with visual aids.** There's nothing wrong with using PowerPoint, slides, or handouts as long as they don't detract from your speech. If you're using PowerPoint or slides, keep the material on display to a minimum—ten to twelve words per frame, max.

- *Write your own introduction.* If you're presenting to an audience that has no idea of who you are, this is an opportunity to prove you're an expert about the subject, and have something in common with them. (Keep your audience in mind as you write your intro, too. What would they want to know about you?)

- *Stand up straight, with your head held up.* Nervous speakers tend to bow their heads, which looks subservient and weak. Smile at your audience when it's appropriate—people will smile back.

- *Watch your audience.* Are they paying attention? If they're fidgeting, chatting, yawning, or, God forbid, sleeping, it may be time to wrap it up—or at least add a little fire into your presentation.

- *End your speech within the time allotted.* Or, better yet, end five minutes early. This is a proven way of making people think you're an incredible speaker!

It's guaranteed that you'll feel nervous the first few times you give a speech. You may even lose your lunch. But as you gain confidence and experience, you may uncover a hidden ability for saying just the right thing—or at least do such a great job that people just assume you're a natural, which is almost as good.

Drive Cross-Country

26

Nothing but you and the open highway, the wind blowing in your hair, your favorite tune cranking out a bass beat on the car stereo. Dreamed of seeing the world from your car window, or taking the time to explore the U.S. of A? All you need is a car that works, gas money, some spare time—and an idea of where you'll go.

CHOOSING YOUR TRIP

First question. Where are you driving, and when? Maybe you're relocating from sunny California to the East Coast. Or you're traveling for a wedding and have decided to make a vacation out of it. Or you simply want to drive a famous highway—say, Route 66, which meanders from Chicago to L.A.—or U.S. Highway 101, which winds down the Pacific Coast. Before you decide to leave, you've got to decide where you're going—or at least have a general idea. Mapping out a route ahead of time doesn't mean you can't deviate from the plan if the spirit moves you, but it does make it easier to figure out how much time, money, and snacks you'll need for your travels.

Estimate the length of time you'll be traveling so you have an idea of when you'll arrive at different places along your route. Having a destination (or more than one) to reach each day can make the driving go faster, and make the trip overall more fun. It can also help you avoid hitting rush hour when driving in or near a big city.

Decide, too, whether you want to use the interstate, back roads, or a combination of both. Traveling by interstate is usually faster and safer (the highways tend to be in good condition), but you may sacrifice sightseeing opportunities. The stops along the interstate are likely to be more homogenous—an endless stream of Marathon™ stations, Best Westerns™, and McDonalds™. Opting for the less-traveled roads can be a more enriching and interesting experience, but it will add more time to your trip.

Check out the following Web sites to help you plan your journey:

- http://www.byways.org Want a more gorgeous journey? The National Scenic Byways Web site shows you which roads offer natural eye candy.

- http://www.historyplace.com/tourism/usa.htm Turn your trip into a learning experience and check out historic attractions throughout the United States.

- http://www.roadtripamerica.com Includes travel resources and North American road trip information.

- http://www.roadsideamerica.com Unique, offbeat, interesting, and just-plain-weird things to do on your trip.

- http://www.seeamerica.org Lots of info about routes to take, national parks, and other attractions.

When to Take Your Trek

Once you've chosen your destination and figured out your basic route, the next question is when you'll travel. Do you really want to drive through the Rockies in January or across Death Valley in mid-July? Doubtful. Maybe you can't control when you'll be traveling but, if you can, choose a time of year that falls between temperature and weather extremes—unless you're up for doing some storm chasing in Kansas, for example.

Give yourself plenty of time to get where you're going. You can't assume you're going to be going 65 mph, or faster. And you will need to stop occasionally for food, drink, gas, and bathroom breaks—and to stretch your legs and de-numb your butt. Traffic, weather, and road conditions may slow you down much more than you originally planned, and you don't want the pressure of falling behind schedule—or having to drive 90 mph to make up for lost time.

Besides, half the fun of your trip is having the time to get off the road and explore all that great Americana stuff, whether it's the World's Largest Ball of Twine in Cawker City, Kansas, or the World's Largest Peanut in Ashburn, Georgia.

Considering a Copilot?

Consider this rule of thumb: The more people you're traveling with, the more time it will take to stop to eat, drink, and pretty much do anything. But traveling companions make it fun—most of the time. Should you take a copilot or travel solo? As with anything, there are pros and cons to each option.

Pros:
- *A traveling companion can share the driving, which is easier on you.* You may even catch some shut-eye along the way.

- *A traveling companion can be great company.* You'll have someone to talk to during your trip.

- *A long trip together can cement your relationship.* Or at least it can give you a chance to share a unique experience with someone you care about.

- *It's cheaper to travel this way, especially if your buddy kicks in for gas and other expenses.* (On the other hand, a freeloading friend who eats all your snacks may cost you instead of saving you bucks.)

- *You may have more fun on your side trip adventures with a friend along.* Hey, you need someone to appreciate the glory of that giant ball of twine, don't you?

Cons:
- *A car is a small place to be cooped up with another human being for hours or days on end.* (Important consideration: Does your traveling companion have good basic hygiene habits?)

- *If you're not a big talker and bring along a chatterbox, the constant noise can get annoying.*

- *Backseat-driving tendencies in a passenger can bring out the worst in any driver.*

- *When you're traveling solo, all decisions are up to you.* Bring along a pal, and now you've got to think about what he or she wants, too (or risk losing the friendship).

Preparing Your Chariot

Driving cross-country means you're relying on your car to get you there safely, so make sure your vehicle is in good working condition. If you get all the required oil changes, tire rotations, and regular tune-ups recommended in your owner's manual, your car is probably already in great shape. But if you're like most of us, you'd better take your car in for a quick checkup instead of discovering a problem hundreds of miles down the road.

At the least, you should check on the following:

- *that the car's oil has been changed recently*

- *that the engine has the proper levels of oil, transmission fluid, brake fluid, window washer fluid, and coolant*

- *that the car's tires are in good shape, and have been rotated recently, if necessary.* (If you can swing it money-wise, there are tires—called **extended-mobility** and **self-sealing** tires—that will stay inflated even after they've been punctured; they're more expensive but may be worth it.)

- *that your wiper blades are in good condition and work properly*

- *that your brake lights, turn signals, headlights, and horn are all in good working order*

- *that the belts, hoses, and cables in the engine are all in good condition and properly attached*

- *that there is no other problem with the engine or the rest of your vehicle* (e.g., holes in the floorboards, missing doors, and the like)

A quick checkup at your local oil-and-lube place is well worth the peace of mind it will bring. And clean your car before you go—you'll likely accumulate lots of wrappers, souvenirs, and empty soda cans along the way.

If the worst happens—say, if your car breaks down—it helps to be prepared. An emergency kit for your auto is well worth the expense. Your kit can contain anything from flashers or reflective cones to let other drivers know you're stranded; jumper cables; a flashlight; and, of course, a spare tire. If you're traveling in cold weather, don't forget a couple of blankets. If you're a member of the American Automobile Association (AAA) or your car insurance has a roadside assistance plan, make a note of the number and keep it in your car.

Make sure your driver's license, registration, license plates, and insurance information are all up-to-date. (If you're traveling with a friend, make sure he or she is legally licensed and insured, too.) You don't want to run into troubles on the road. And make a note of your insurance company's telephone number so you have it handy.

Gearing Up

Of course, in addition to getting your car ready for travel, you'll want to bring along other goodies as well. Pack wisely and well and you'll save money on the road, and make your trip more enjoyable. You may want to consider bringing things like:

- *Dramamine™ or motion-sickness medicine*—Better to be safe than sorry.

- *bottled water*— It's cheaper than buying it on the road—and it lasts almost forever.

- *sunglasses and sun block*—You don't want to get a "driver's sunburn" on your left arm, hand, and the side of your face.

- *first-aid kit*—It should contain things like antibacterial gel (to wash your hands without water), antiseptic ointment, adhesive bandages in a variety of sizes, insect repellant, antacid, antidiarrhea medicine, cough medicine, a thermometer, and tweezers.

- *napkins and plastic bags for messy meals-on-the-go.*

- *snacks!*—The more portable, the better. Pretzels, trail mix, travel-friendly fruit like apples, oranges, and raisins, energy bars, and even beef jerky are all good choices.

- *music*—Whether you bring an MP3 player, an iPod™ with an iTrip™ adaptor, or a giant stack of CDs, music makes the drive go faster. If you're traveling with a buddy or two, make sure you agree on your music choices—or trade off what you listen to.

- *beverages*—If you like your stuff cold, bring along a cooler with ice; you can refill it on the road.

- *cell phone*—I know, you wouldn't leave home without it.

- *roadmaps or GPS system to navigate*—Even both in case your technological tool craps out.

- *chewing gum, mints, hard candy*—whatever trips your particular oral fixation.

- *driver's license, car registration, and insurance information*

- *credit cards, traveler's checks, and cash*—You'll need money for the road no matter how cheaply you plan to travel.

- *camera*—to take a photo of that amazing ball of twine.

- *clothing and toiletries, and anything else you'd normally travel with*—You don't want to wear the same ratty T-shirt sixteen days in a row, do you?

THE BIG DAY

Before you head out on your adventure, check the weather along your proposed route. Something may have come up that makes delaying your trip by a day or so—or opting for an alternate route—a good idea.

Check the condition of the roads you'll be taking, especially during the summer. You don't want to lose a day or more due to road construction. Check out the Department of Transportation's Web site at *http://www.dot.gov* (the direct link for National Road Traffic and Road Closure Information is *http://www.fhwa.dot.gov/trafficinfo/index.htm*) or look for the individual states' transportation departments at *http://www.fhwa.dot.gov/webstate.htm*.

Take Off!

The car is packed, your route is mapped out, and you're ready to go. Savor the moment. Then set off for your grand adventure, and enjoy every minute. Whether you spend seven days or seventeen, you'll be making memories you'll remember forever.

Become a Martial Artist

27

Whether you want to feel more self-confident, get in touch with your inner warrior, or simply get in great shape, there's a martial art for you. And you don't even have to have the urge to kick some butt, though that certainly doesn't hurt. The martial arts range from the gentle to the seriously muscle-trembling intense, but knowing what to expect—and what you want to get from your practice—will help you pick the one that's right for you.

PICK YOUR (MARTIAL ARTS) WEAPON

Martial arts are systems of combat techniques; many are thousands of years old while others were developed in more recent years. Some martial arts like kendo use weapons; others rely on the use of your body alone.

But martial arts aren't just about the physical. They also help practitioners develop their spiritual and psychological strength. This mind–body emphasis may explain the growth in interest in the martial arts; more than six million Americans practice some type of martial art. (Just one more reason you don't want to start a fight with someone you don't know!) Consider them exercise for the body and mind.

First things first. Which martial art is right for you? Don't be swayed by Jet Li's mastery of wushu, a Chinese martial art, or Chuck Norris's karate kicks. After all, it's not (only) how cool the martial art looks but what the focus is as well—and whether you're willing and able to take it on.

Aikido

Steven Seagal has helped make this relatively young Japanese art famous. More of a defensive art, it focuses on redirecting an attacker's force with complex, spherical movements that allow you to throw or pin your attacker. If you're good, you use little of your own energy to respond; you simply redirect your attacker's energy against him (or her).

Capoeira

Not all martial arts come from Asian nations. Capoeira was developed in Brazil by African slaves. Unlike most other martial arts, it's more a stylized dance that uses sweeps, kicks, and acrobatics and is performed to rhythmic music. While not as well-known as some other martial arts, it's becoming increasingly popular throughout the world.

Escrima

This martial art, also known as **arnis** or **kali**, is based on the native fighting styles of the Philippines and uses weapons, including sticks and blades. While you do learn to fight without using a weapon, the focus is definitely more weapon-oriented than that of other martial arts.

Hapkido

This Korean art uses kicks, throws, joint locks, and pressure-point attacks. Like aikido, you also learn how to use your attacker's energy and strength against him or her, which makes it a good martial art for self-defense.

Jeet Kune Do

This Chinese martial art was created by the legendary Bruce Lee. With less of a regimented approach than some of the other martial arts, it involves a number of different skills including kicks, punches, traps, blocks, and taking evasive action when appropriate.

Judo

While judo means "gentle way," this Japanese martial art isn't all that gentle. Somewhat similar to wrestling, it involves grappling moves, chokes, and pins—with some throws and strikes thrown in to keep it interesting.

Jujitsu

This is another challenging Japanese martial art, from which sprung others including hapkido and judo. It emphasizes strikes and throws as well as defensive moves.

Karate

This Japanese martial art is one of the best-known martial arts. Karate means "empty hand" (in other words, you don't use weapons), and practitioners use low stances and precise form and balance to perform kicks and blocks; you also get to practice breaking boards with your feet, hands, and head (if you're so inclined). It has a variety of different styles but is recognizable by its focus on fast, hard punches, strikes, kicks, and blocks.

Kendo

This is serious stuff, a Japanese martial art that focuses on sword-fighting maneuvers. If you've always dreamed of being a samurai, this is for you, but it's definitely demanding.

Kung Fu

The term "kung fu" refers to a variety of Chinese martial arts. It means "skill and effort," and the fighting styles are associated with different animals such as the tiger, snake, and monkey. If you practice kung fu, you'll learn how to do everything from punching, kicking, and grappling to using weapons like a knife or spear. Because it involves so many different skills, it usually takes longer to earn a black belt in this art than in any other.

Muay Thai

This is a blend of boxing, kicking, and striking moves, and is sometimes called **Thai boxing**. It's serious stuff—in fact, authentic Thai boxing can be deadly. Muay thai and other forms of kickboxing concentrate on technique and fighting strategies; don't confuse them with the cardio kickboxing taught in aerobics classes, which include kicks and punches (performed to music, no less!) but aren't even close to the same thing.

Tae Kwon Do

This Korean martial art is similar to karate, but includes more kicking and boxing moves; it's the national art of South Korea. It's one of the most popular martial arts in the world and is a great workout for your legs and butt.

Tai Chi

Not just for your granny, this Chinese martial art consists of 108 graceful, slow movements that are performed in a set order. The movements are stylized versions of fighting techniques, but with tai chi the focus isn't on combat but on breathing and relaxation as you perform the moves. In other words, if you're looking for something high-intensity, this isn't it. On the other hand, tai chi can make you more flexible, more coordinated, more centered, and less stressed—all good things.

Wing Chun

This Chinese art was developed several hundred years ago and teaches practitioners to use an attacker's force and strength against him or her. It focuses on close combat and uses both empty-handed moves as well as weapons.

Wushu

Wushu is a general term that encompasses all Chinese martial arts; but today the term usually refers to a type that includes different stances, kicks, punches, balances, and jumps. It's been made popular by actors including Jet Li and Jackie Chan.

FINDING A CLASS

OK, you've selected a martial art that sounds interesting. Now what? Find a class.

If you live in a small community, your options may be limited, but most cities offer a variety of martial-arts options. Keep these factors in mind as you hunt for a class:

- *How experienced is the teacher?* Keep in mind that someone can be a black belt and still be a cruddy teacher. You want someone who can not only demonstrate the techniques but also show you how to do them properly. Ask how long the teacher, or **sensei**, has been teaching the style of martial arts you're interested in.

- *Is the teacher certified?* While most martial arts don't have formal teacher training programs, the National Association of Professional Martial Artists (NAPMA) certifies martial-arts instructors. Not being certified isn't necessarily a drawback, but a sensei who is certified is probably more serious about teaching.

- *What's the focus of the class?* Do you want to learn a sport style, where you can compete in tournaments, or do you simply want to master some self-defense techniques? Some classes focus more on the physical performance of the moves, others play up the mind–body connection more. Consider which feels like a better fit for you.

- *Are there children in the class?* Some classes are open to both adults and kids; others are adults- or kids-only. If it's no big deal for an eight-year-old to flip you onto your back, no problem, but you may feel more comfortable with a grown-ups-only class.

- *What's the schedule like?* Again, some programs are more flexible and meet a couple of times a week; others demand a greater time commitment.

- *How far away is the school, or* dojo, *located?* If it's a forty-minute commute, are you willing to make that drive after a long day? A school closer to home may be a smarter choice.

- *How expensive is the class?* In general, monthly tuition varies, but you should expect to spend between $40 and $90, possibly more. Usually this covers the cost of all classes, but you should double-check to confirm that that's the case. You'll also have to pay for your uniforms as well as for necessary equipment—and testing fees.

- *How often does the school conduct belt tests?* Those tests determine how quickly you move up in belt colors. Some schools offer monthly tests to help you progress more quickly, but the testing fees can be $30 each or more. You may want to avoid "McDojos," which focus more on moving students quickly through belts than really helping them achieve proficiency in the martial arts—unless you're all about the belts, not the art.

- *Are there opportunities to compete?* Some martial arts, including karate, judo, and tae kwon do, conduct competitions worldwide. If you want to experience an adult version of *The Karate Kid* or something close to it, check with the school about competition training.

- **Do you have to sign a contract?** Some schools require you to commit to a year-long contract, but what happens if you get hurt or decide martial arts aren't for you? Read your contract carefully before you sign up.

- **What's the vibe of the class like?** And do you want a serious, stone-faced atmosphere or a more welcoming camaraderie among your fellow students? You may want to visit several schools before you find one that is the perfect fit.

READY, SET, THROW! (OR MAYBE NOT)

Keep in mind that when you start martial-arts training, you're going to start with the basics. That means if you're taking judo, you're going to spend a lot of time just learning how to fall without getting hurt. Stick with it and you will improve.

Many of the martial arts have strong traditions that you should respect. For example, with most martial arts, you bow before coming onto the mat and again before leaving it. Some teachers expect students to practice in silence; others foster a more informal atmosphere. Either way, though, you're expected to wear a uniform to class, so forget about practicing in your ratty sweatpants.

It's normal, too, to be nervous about your first few classes. Or you may be afraid of getting hit. Look for a class where you can progress slowly, at your own pace—and keep in mind that it takes years to progress to black-belt status, if that's one of your goals. On the other hand, if you're interested in competing, you may want a program that will push you a bit harder.

You may have heard of a certain listing of belt colors (from white to orange to green and so on), but the colors can vary among martial arts and different schools. The black belt, though, is almost always the highest belt color you can attain, but some arts then add numbers to the belt color to signify someone who is continually progressing skills-wise.

The idea is that you can always improve upon your skills, which makes martial arts something that you can never completely master. For many people, that's part of the allure—and, of course, the chance to kick some serious tail if you ever need to.

28 Become Politically Active

Have something to say about the way this country is run? Don't just complain about it. Take an active interest in politics and you can make a difference—and no, you don't have to follow in Arnold's footsteps and become the governor of California. Of course, if that's really your dream, don't let me stop you . . .

GET SMART

Regardless of whether an election is coming up, you should know what's going on in the world of politics, both on a national and local scale. The more you know now, the more perspective you'll have when the time to vote comes around. Plus, it's always good to have an informed opinion about the issues that matter to you. While many Americans claim to hate talking about politics, that's probably because they're anxious about being unable to defend their political stances. Maybe you already have an opinion about a major political issue, but right now it's just a gut feeling. Educate yourself more on the topic to get the facts and information you need to defend your views. Who knows? Maybe you'll even change your mind once you know more about it.

Harness the Media

Read newspapers or magazines that focus on current affairs, like *Time* or *Newsweek*, on a regular basis. It's the best—and easiest—way to educate yourself. Now that so many news providers have their own Web sites, there's an infinite trove to choose from.

Whether it's coming from your local newspaper, the *New York Times*, or some obscure news source based in Dubai, make sure the information is objective and unbiased, meaning it's not slanted toward a particular opinion or belief. A truly unbiased news source should offer well-researched stories and information, with all the various sides and facts available to its audience, in order to let readers form their own opinions. Some other politically themed magazines to check out include *U.S. News & World Report*, the *Weekly Standard*, the *New Republic*, and *The Economist*.

Other forms of media like television and radio can also be good sources of news and information. Keep in mind that for news programs to broadcast all the big news stories in a limited time frame, the facts may not be as detailed or thorough as a newspaper or magazine's coverage of the same story. And unless you have access to a twenty-four-hour news channel like CNN, you may only have a limited window to catch a station's news program.

Get Bloggy with It

Although blogs tend to report more opinion than news, many are excellent resources for the most current goings-on in Washington. A few of the top blogs on the net, that span the political spectrum from the left to the right, include:

- http://www.wonkette.com, an unabashedly left-wing blog commenting on all topics related to American politics, often with a humorous and youthful voice.

- http://www.dailykos.com, another liberal blog site, featuring a good deal of community interaction, including discussion threads and links to diaries.

- Daily Dish at http://www.andrewsullivan.com, author and columnist Andrew Sullivan's Web site, featuring articles that take a satirical stab at current issues relating to politics, faith, culture, and more. While Sullivan himself is seen as a conservative, the various articles lean both to the left and the right.

- http://www.talkingpointsmemo.com, featuring discussion forums and links to blogs, in which opinions from all points on the political spectrum are welcome.

- http://www.michellemalkin.com, author and journalist Michelle Malkin's blog, providing political commentary from the far right.

- http://www.redstate.org, a Republican community blog where right-wing thinkers can debate and share information on a wide range of political issues.

MAKE YOUR VOICE HEARD

Now that you've formed opinions about the issues that are important to you, the next step is to find a candidate who can represent your voice. As an election approaches, you'll start seeing more and more news and information devoted to the various candidates and their campaigns, not to mention a barrage of advertisements, flyers, and brochures being circulated by the candidates themselves and by independent groups looking to tip the scales in one candidate's direction.

All this info can be overwhelming. When deciding whether to support a particular candidate, keep these factors in mind:

- *background information*—such as previous professional experience, as well as political experience and positions on any political organizations or committees.

- *where the candidate stands on issues that matter to you*

- *whether the candidate's voting record is consistent with his or her campaign platform*

- *campaign finances and sources of contributions*—i.e., is the candidate receiving a lot of money from businesses to fund his or her campaign? If so, how might that affect his or her interests?

If you want additional information on a specific candidate, many have their own Web sites with data on their agendas. Another helpful site is Project Vote Smart (*http://www.vote-smart.org*), a comprehensive database that provides background information, interest group ratings, voting records, and campaign finance data for thousands of elected officials and candidates on national and local levels.

Register to Vote

Remember, you can't vote in an election until you register. When you register to vote, you're basically providing information about yourself (name, address, etc.) to the government office that manages elections where you live. Your residential information will determine which district you vote in and ensure that you only vote once. Don't let the thought of paperwork (ugh!) stop you from making your opinion count. The process involves four simple "W's" to help you become a legitimate, registered voter.

Who. To register you must be a U.S. citizen, at least eighteen years old by the time the next election occurs, and a resident of the state in which you'd like to vote. Many, but not all, states also have laws that prohibit felons and individuals who are mentally incompetent from voting. To check the rules for your state, call your state's election office; many states also have Web sites with this info.

When. Guidelines for registering vary from state to state. Some states set their registration deadlines as late as ten days before an election; others allow same-day registration (meaning you can register and vote at the same time). Most states, however, require you to register at least thirty days before election day.

Where (and How). There are several places (and ways) to register:

- **At the elections office.** The traditional (and perhaps the quickest) way to register is to go to your local board-of-elections office or county courthouse. Fill out a form on the spot and hand it in; there's no need to mail anything. Bring a photo ID with you, in case it's required.

- **By mail.** Call your local elections office and ask them for a voter registration form. Fill it out and send it back. (Most states also ask for a photocopy of your photo ID.)

- **Online.** You can *start* the registration process online, but you'll still have to print out an application, fill it out, and mail it in. There are a ton of voter organizations with sites that link you to your state's voter registration form. Enter "register to vote" into any online search engine like Google or Yahoo!, and you'll find sites for groups like Declare Yourself (*http://www.declareyourself.com*), a non-profit, nonpartisan campaign initiated to motivate young Americans to vote, and the League of Women Voters (*http://www.lwv.org/voter*), whose site has voter registration forms in English and Spanish, as well as information about important voter registration deadlines (and nope, you needn't be a woman to check it out).

- *In other public places.* When there's an election coming up, you may find volunteers in public places offering to register you. These voter registration drives are an easy way to get registered, and the volunteers can usually answer most of your pre-election-day voting questions.

What Else? Within a few weeks after you send or hand in your registration application, you should receive a notice informing you that you are now officially registered to vote. Hang on to it—it will tell you where you vote and provide other important information as well.

If you can't make it to your designated voting office on election day, you can still vote by submitting an absentee ballot. Call or write your local elections office and request a mail-in ballot. Some elections offices will even allow you to request your mail-in ballot via e-mail. Try to make these arrangements at least a month before the election or at least as early as possible.

JOIN A POLITICAL ORGANIZATION

When you register to vote, you may be asked to choose a party to register under. You have the right to abstain from affiliating with a political party, but in some places you may not be able to vote in a particular party's primary if you're not registered as a voter with that party.

As a registered member of a political party, it is up to you to decide how involved you want to be. This can mean as little as casting a vote, or it could involve a real commitment such as donating money, lending a hand in fund-raising, aiding voter awareness, or performing other administrative tasks. Registering for a party is not mandatory, and you're not bound to a particular party if you have a change of heart.

Although dozens of political parties are currently active in America, the list of parties most likely to show up on ballots includes:

Democratic Party (*http://www.democrats.org*)
Chairman: Howard Dean, Governor of Vermont
Democratic National Committee
430 S. Capitol Street SE
Washington, DC 20003
Main Phone: (202) 863-8000
Contributions: (877) 336-7200

Republican Party (*http://www.rnc.org*)
Chairman: Ken Mehlman
310 First Street, SE
Washington, DC 20003
Phone: (202) 863-8500
Fax: (202) 863-8820

Libertarian Party (*http://www.lp.org*)
Chairman: Michael Dixon
2600 Virginia Avenue, NW, Suite 100
Washington, DC 20037

Phone: (202) 333-0008
Fax: (202) 333-0072

Constitution Party
(http://www.constitutionparty.com)
Founder: Howard Phillips
23 North Lime Street
Lancaster, PA 17602
Toll Free: (800) 283-8647
Main Phone: (717) 390-1993
Fax: (717) 299-5115

Green Party *(http://www.greenparty.org)*
The Greens National Committee (GNC)
G/GPUSA
P. O. Box 3568
Eureka, CA 95502
Main Phone: (866) GREENS2

GET INVOLVED

Work for a Political Campaign

Behind every great candidate is a great campaign staff, and campaigns are always looking for extra help. Most politicos-in-training begin life as lowly interns and unpaid volunteers, performing some of the less glamorous work that goes into getting a candidate elected. Addressing envelopes and canvassing door-to-door might not get you on CNN, but even a campaign maestro like James Carville had to start somewhere. Generally, campaigns from the federal to the local level can use any help they can get during the notoriously fast-and-furious election season, so getting your foot in the door as a volunteer is a piece of cake.

There are a variety of ways to get in touch with campaign offices in your area, but the easiest way is to use the Internet. Check out Politics1, a Web site that will direct you to campaigns in your area and tell you how to get involved (*http://www. politics1.com*). Visit the "State/Federal Candidates" page to receive a comprehensive list of upcoming campaigns. Click on a candidate's name to find out more about him or her and how you can help.

Round 'Em Up

Holding a voter registration drive is an easy way to make a big difference and reach a large number of people. Just be sure to keep the registration drive nonpartisan—the point is to get anyone who is legally able to vote to do so. You and your fellow volunteers may want to coordinate your effort with other organizations to maximize your efforts.

Know the law. Get familiar with federal, state, and local laws that govern voter registration in your community. These guidelines differ from state to state and can even vary among local jurisdictions in the same state.

Work with election officials. Make sure election officials know about your plans. You may be required to contact them in order to obtain voter registration forms, to register voters at special sites, or to train volunteer registrars. In some places, only official registrars may be allowed to register voters.

Select your sites. Use your resources efficiently by setting up registration sites where there are large numbers of unregistered citizens with time to register. Festivals, fairs, sporting events, schools, colleges, public-transit stops, public-assistance offices, and shopping centers are all good places to consider. Visit sites ahead of time, and be sure to get any necessary permission to register people at a privately owned site.

Sell, sell, sell. Advertise your voter registration drive ahead of time, including the sites and times where voter registration will take place. Stage an event—like a band concert, or some kind of promotional giveaway—to attract a crowd. Don't be afraid to approach people.

Keep good records. Keep track of the names, addresses, and telephone numbers of everyone you and your fellow volunteers register by using tally sheets or copying registration cards, where permissible by law. Use this information to follow up with the new registrants.

Follow up and evaluate. Contact the new registrants and remind them to vote, and ask if they need information or assistance. Evaluate your results and determine what worked and what didn't. And don't forget to do something to show your appreciation to your volunteers, especially if you want their help for future registration drives.

YOU CAN MAKE A DIFFERENCE

As you can see, there are a number of ways to make yourself heard in the world of American politics. Some involve a lot of time and effort, but even an easy and painless process like voting is critical to maintaining a healthy and relevant democracy.

The best way to become more politically active is simply to be more aware of the world around you. Think about the political processes you might have taken for granted before, and seek out the answers to the political questions that have been stumping you. Get smart, form your own opinions, and make your voice heard.

29

Travel the World

Feeling cramped? Tired of looking at the same old thing day after day, year after year? Are people around you beginning to bore you? Want to experience life outside the United States? Maybe what you need is a change of scenery, so get out there and see what you've been missing!

BEFORE YOU LEAVE . . .

Before you head out for parts unknown, you'll need to decide on your destination(s) and the length of time you plan to be away. While traveling abroad can be expensive, it can also be surprisingly cheap. In some areas of the world, your daily living expenses are considerably less than what you'd spend in the United States. Keep that in mind when picking your destinations.

Passports

If you plan to leave the United States and its territories, you'll need a passport. Allow at least six weeks to apply for yours if you don't have one. (It's possible to get one in as little as two weeks, but you will pay significantly more.) Visit a passport agency such as a post office, courthouse, or library and fill out an application. The application can also be downloaded from the U.S. State Department's Web site, *http://travel.state.gov/ passport.*

You'll also need two small photos to submit with your application, and, if this is your first passport, you must appear in person. The same is true if your passport has been damaged, lost, stolen, issued more than fifteen years ago, or was issued when you were under sixteen. If none of these applies to you, it may be possible to update your current passport by mail. (Keep in mind that honesty is always the best policy—except when applying for a passport. You will be asked to provide your date of departure, and it's best to write down a date at least a week ahead of your actual departure in case the passport arrives late.)

Regardless, don't let your passport out of your sight. Make a few copies of it before you depart and leave them with friends or family at home, and carry a copy in a safe place separate from your passport in case of theft. It's a whole lot easier to get it replaced if you have copies.

Visas

Depending on where you're going and how long you'll be there, you may have to apply for a visa. A **visa** is a stamp or seal, which is placed into your passport, either before you leave or while you are in the country. It specifies the purpose and duration of your trip. You can usually get a visa before departing the United States at either an embassy or a consulate. Some countries allow you to get a visa abroad, but others require you to obtain the visa before you leave the United States. Check the rules of the countries you plan to visit at *http://travel.state.gov/travel/living/residing*, and be prepared to pay a visa fee.

Immunizations

The requirements vary, depending on where you go. Consult the U.S. Centers for Disease Control, *http://www.cdc.gov*, for its requirements, and then contact a doc for your shots. To be thorough, request the CDC's booklet, "Health Information for International Travelers," for a description of the typical diseases in the regions you will be visiting, as well as how to avoid them.

FINANCING YOUR TRAVELS

Although the amount needed may vary, no matter where you go, you'll always need money! And while it's best to carry local currency, the U.S. dollar is usually very valuable. Consider bringing some hard cash with you if you are going to very economically depressed areas, particularly parts of Africa, South America, or Asia. You can usually get a better deal at markets, hotels, and other places if you flash U.S. cash; just be sure to carry small denominations.

You don't want to carry wads of cash, though, so consider other ways to pay for your trip. You'll get the best exchange rate for your U.S. dollar through an ATM or credit card, but research this as thoroughly as possibly before leaving.

ATM Cards

ATMs are all over the world, and they're an easy way to get local currency. Check your bank's policies about overseas banking before you leave, and be sure to ask how much money you are allowed to withdraw per day.

Credit Cards

Visa™ is truly everywhere you want to be. It's the world's most widely accepted credit card, so get one if you don't have one already. American Express™ is also widely accepted (though not as widely as Visa™!), and has offices in many cities throughout the world that offer services to its cardholders. Its offices can accept and hold mail for you, and can arrange for money to be wired to you in a pinch.

Check with smaller credit card companies to be sure their cards are accepted abroad; certain ones widely accepted in the United States are not accepted overseas.

Traveler's Checks

Traveler's checks are another way to carry money safely. After purchasing them, write down the numbers on a separate sheet of paper; carry that copy in a separate bag from the actual checks and leave one with someone you trust at home. If they're stolen, you can replace them using the check numbers. Regardless, never countersign checks until you're ready to cash them.

GETTING THERE

Unless you're traveling by boat or car, you'll probably be flying, the main mode of transportation for world travelers. Shop carefully for flights; there is a lot of competition. One way to get a good price is to get on the e-mail update list of some of the bargain searchers, such as Travelzoo (*http://www.Travelzoo.com*). Airlines typically offer this free service also. Visit sites like *http://www.cheaptickets.com*, *http://www.expedia.com,* and *http:// www.lowestfare.com* for deals. And watch the travel sections of the newspapers, particularly the Sunday papers, for deals on flights and other packages.

Searching the Internet will generally offer you the most up-to-date info. Web sites like *http://www.gotoday.com* offer last-minute deals on vacation packages if you're willing to travel at the last minute.

If you're young, or still in school, consider joining a travel club to get better deals on flights, packages, and travel advice. One group in particular, the Student Travel Association (STA) (*http://www.sta.com*) offers these services to young travelers under the age of twenty-six. For a $25 joining fee, you get tons of free travel advice and flexibility. STA has offices in over eighty countries where you can get advice on where to stay and what to do—and you can change your flights for either small fees or no fees if you booked them through STA. They can also swing you great deals on one-way tickets, which tend to get very expensive.

GETTING AROUND WHILE YOU'RE THERE

Rail Travel

Many countries outside the United States have a more sophisticated system of public transportation, while some do not. If you're going to Europe or Asia, for example, train travel can be easy, inexpensive, and a great way to meet other travelers. It may be best to purchase a rail pass. This way you can travel on your own schedule and at your own pace without having to buy rail tickets all the time. (Sometimes you'll still need to make a seat reservation for the train, so check before boarding.) Train travel is generally safe and a good way to see the scenery in a new country.

Driving

Depending on the country, you might want to rent a car. Many countries don't recognize a U.S. driver's license alone, however, and require an international driver's permit. Contact the Department of Motor Vehicles in your home state to get information on this. Keep in mind, though, that the price of fuel can be rather high, depending on where you're going—and in some countries they drive on the left side, not the right side, of the street.

Biking

Remember when your bicycle was your only mode of transportation? Many places in the world still rely on bike travel. It's definitely an option to consider, depending on your budget, fitness level, and desire to stay warm and dry.

KEEPING IN TOUCH

You'll want to let the people back home know what you're up to while you're seeing it all, right? Here are some options to keep in touch:

Snail Mail

A letter or postcard can pass the time on long travel stints, but takes time to arrive.

Internet

Get your e-mail on! Internet cafés have become very popular abroad, and are easily accessible.

Telephones/Cell Phones

Telephones are always an option, too. Most pay phones overseas do not accept coins, but instead operate on phone cards, which must be purchased locally. Many U.S cellular carriers now have international roaming agreements, which let you keep your U.S. number while traveling internationally. Check with your carrier to figure out the particulars.

WHAT TO BRING

Obviously what you pack will vary, depending on what activities you plan on, your destinations, and the time of year. Research the weather in the countries you will be going to for the months you will be there at *http://www.weather.com.*

Regardless of when or where you go, always bring at least two types of identification. A combination of a passport, birth certificate, and driver's license will usually suffice. Always split them up into different bags in case one of them is lost or stolen.

You'll always need a sturdy pair of walking shoes and comfortable, preferably lightweight clothing that breathes. In general, when traveling, casual clothes are more useful than dress clothes.

If you're a student at least twelve years old, you may want to apply for an International Student Identity Card. It's a great form of ID and flashing it can also get you significant discounts on sights, transportation, museums, and accommodations. U.S. citizens are also eligible for health insurance benefits; apply by visiting *http://www.myISIC.com.*

You'll also need something to carry your money, ID, and other necessities. A pouch worn around your neck or waist and under your clothes is best to keep these items safe and close to you. And don't pack your bag all the way. You'll need some room for treasures purchased along the way. The general rule is to bring half the clothes and twice the money you think you'll need.

Because electricity voltage varies from country to country, you may want to bring a converter/adaptor to make your hair dryer, razor, and flattening iron work. Remember, too, to bring your eyeglasses and their prescription, maps, guidebooks, a compass, a camera, and extra medication if you take any medications regularly.

You may also want to bring a journal to remember all the fun times and foreign friends you made along the way. A padlock can protect you from theft, and sealable plastic bags are great for wet or dirty clothes or bottles containing liquid. Wet wipes, a small flashlight, and an umbrella are also all good things to pack, as are flip-flops for bathing in questionable showers.

ON THE ROAD

Traveling alone can be a great way to soul-search, and you can definitely do things your way. You must be careful when there's nobody else watching out for you in a strange place, though. Check in at the U.S. Embassy or Consulate (typically in a capital or larger city) upon arrival in a foreign country, which makes your presence known. Leave a copy of your passport, itinerary if you have one, and emergency contact numbers. You can also register online before you arrive at *https://travelregistration. state.gov/ibrs*; visit *http://www.foia.state.gov/MMS/KOH/keyoffcity. asp* for names of key officers and addresses for U.S. Embassies and Consulates overseas.

If You Get Sick

Before you leave, it's wise to check your health insurance and see what medical services it covers overseas. If you're covered outside the United States, remember to carry your health insurance ID card as well as a claim form. If you're not covered, consider purchasing additional insurance.

If a U.S. citizen becomes seriously injured or ill overseas, U.S. consular officers (look for them at the embassy or consulate) are available to help locate medical services, inform emergency contacts back home, and assist in transferring funds from the States. The traveler is responsible for these expenses, such as hospital fees. You can also contact the International Association for Medical Assistance to Travelers, *http://www.iamat.org*, which lists English-speaking doctors worldwide and offers information on sanitation and immunization.

READ UP

Why not invest in a guidebook or two before you leave? There are dozens to choose from; here are some tried-and-true faves. Look for one that covers the country you'll be visiting.

- **Lonely Planet.** Definitely the best; they're written by people who live on the road for at least a year in a given place. Great for background, history, local customs, and the like.

- **Let's Go.** Written by a staff of travelers from Harvard. Excellent for those looking for a bargain, and very good for introductory information.

- **Rough Guides.** Another good guide for local places to stay and eat, and things to see. Not as well-known as the first two, which can be advantageous.

- **Eyewitness Travel Guides.** Your best choice if you're looking for an illustrated guidebook. Shows you all the highlights with spectacular photographs, making it easy to know what you're looking at.

- **Fodor's *Guides*.** A good bet if you're looking for comprehensive coverage. These guides are packed with information on everything from culture and history to off-the-beaten-path treasures.

KEEP IN MIND

Finally, remember, if you travel alone, you're never really alone. Americans can always seek assistance for almost any crisis from the Office of American Citizens Services and Crisis Management (ACS). The ACS can help with matters such as a birth or death overseas, can assist victims of crime, and can help U.S citizens detained in prison. Read more about the office at *http://www. travel.state.gov/travel.*

Traveling the world will broaden your horizons, introduce you to people and places you'd never otherwise see, and give you stories to tell your grandkids. Now get out there and do it!

30

Scuba Dive

So you want to swim with the fishes—and live to tell about it. Become a scuba diver and you'll have access to the water that covers more than 70 percent of our planet and all the fascinating creatures that call it home. Forget those lame snorkelers who have to stick to the surface; scuba diving lets you explore ten, twenty, even a hundred feet down. If you're serious about scuba (**scuba** is actually an acronym that stands for "self-contained underwater breathing apparatus," by the way), there's no substitute for getting certified, or getting your **C-card.**

GET READY TO DIVE DOWN

So you want to join the more than 4 million Americans who are already certified to scuba dive? While just about anyone over the age of twelve can dive, you do have to be reasonably healthy. If you've got certain health problems—like asthma, emphysema, diabetes, or seizure disorders, this isn't the sport for you. Other things, like ear or sinus problems, may also keep you from going down under. If you've got any chronic health conditions, better check with your doc before you plunk down your money to learn to dive. Besides, you've got to have a clean bill of health before you can sign up for a class.

The next step? Finding a class. This is easier than you might think. Most communities offer scuba certification classes through adult education programs, YMCAs and YWCAs, or dive shops. Choose one offered by an organization that is a member of the International Recreational Scuba Training Council, which sets the minimum requirements for diving safety in the United States. Those groups include the following:

- *International Diving Educators Association (IDEA).* http://www.idea-scubadiving.com

- *Professional Association of Diving Instructors (PADI).* http://www.padi.com

- *The Professional Diving Instructors Corporation (PDIC).* http://www.pdic-intl.com

- *Scuba Diving International.* http://www.tdisdi.com

- *Scuba Schools International.* http://www.ssiusa.com

- *YMCA Scuba.* http://ymcascuba.org

While the names of the basic certification classes may vary, depending on the organization that sponsors the class, most classes have two phases: classroom instruction (boring!) and actual practice in a swimming pool (yeah!). You'll probably spend sixteen to twenty hours in class, which may meet one or two nights a week for several hours over the course of several weeks; other programs offer day-long classes that get you in and out in two to three days.

Some questions you may want to ask when choosing a scuba class include:

- *How long is the class?* When does it meet?

- *How much does the course cost?* Be wary of prices that sound too good to be true. Check to find out whether there are any hidden charges, such as for books or equipment rental. An all-inclusive price should cover everything.

- *Where do you do your open-water dive(s)?* Some schools take advantage of whatever body of water is nearby; others will travel to an ocean or other open water to perform the open-water testing.

- *Who is the instructor?* How long has he or she been an instructor? How many students has the instructor certified? The more experience the person has, the better.

- *Is the instructor certified in first aid and CPR?* Most instructors are, but it's a good question to ask.

- *Can I have the names of some recent students as references?* A good instructor will be happy to let you talk to someone who's recently become certified.

- *Do I have to purchase my own equipment or will it be provided?* While most classes supply the tanks and regulators (which provide the mix of gases you'll be breathing underwater), you may be expected to supply your own mask, snorkel, fins, and even a dive knife. Don't skimp on the equipment—you want to make sure it fits properly and comfortably. After all, a mask that leaks or too-tight fins are no fun during class or during dives.

You'll learn the basics of diving in class, and you've got to pay attention because, yes, there will be a test—a written one. A lot of what you'll be tested on involves atmospheric pressure. See, as you descend into the water, the pressure on your body increases. That affects the amount of pressure in the gas you breathe through your regulator, and can affect the amount of nitrogen and oxygen that are pressed into your blood as you descend. The big thing to know about scuba diving is that you can't ascend too quickly, or you'll trap the nitrogen in your blood in your body. This is called **decompression sickness**, or "the bends," and it can make you dizzy and sick—or even kill you. Not good.

After classroom instruction, you get to head to the pool, where you learn how to strap on a scuba tank and regulator, assemble your gear, swim efficiently with fins (basically the less energy you use, the less air you consume), and flush water out of your mask, among other things. You'll also learn safety procedures and different ways to enter the water.

After you master scuba basics in a pool, you'll make your open-water dives. Here you get more practice with your dive equipment in real-water conditions, learn how to solve problems that arise underwater, and what to do in an emergency. You'll also learn how to interact with (or avoid) ocean and fresh-water plant and animal life.

The open-water dives aren't just for fun—you're tested on your skills during them. For example, you have to demonstrate that you can use the equipment properly and show that you can clear your mask if it becomes flooded. This is an opportunity to make sure you know what you're doing, so don't be afraid to ask questions. If you prove that you've mastered all of these skills, you'll receive your certification to dive in open water. Your C-card lets you rent equipment and dive in other locations when you're traveling or vacationing.

There's another option if you're already on vacation and want to scuba dive while you're there, yet lack a C-card. You can take what's called a **noncertification resort course**. Many resorts and large hotels near the ocean offer these for guests who want to learn to dive. Consider them the quick-and-dirty way to get underwater. Typically, you'll spend a half day in the classroom, a little time in the pool, and then go on a dive with an instructor who sticks close by to make sure you can handle everything. This is a great way to discover whether you like it enough to get certified.

Other resorts offer full-certification classes, which cost several hundred dollars. The plus is that you get certified while you're there; the drawback is that you're going to spend a good chunk of your vacation time indoors learning about how to avoid the bends rather than sunning on the beach.

BASIC SCUBA SKILLS

Mastering a few basic dive skills will make you feel more comfortable in the water. You'll learn how to do these in class, but here are a few practice tips to get you started:

Suiting Up

Scuba diving requires a lot of equipment. Donning it in the proper order will save you time and hassles. Start with your wet suit or dry suit, if necessary, then put on your buoyancy control vest (BC), and your tank and regulator. Next, put on your weight belt; then your mask and snorkel. Put your fins on last, when you're about to enter the water, and do a final safety check before you head in. Remember that your air tank should be full of air, be turned on, and have a gauge that works.

Equalize Your Ears

One of the easiest but most important skill is being able to "equalize" in the water, which balances the pressure inside your ears and the water pressing on your body. You probably do the same thing without thinking about it by swallowing or chewing gum as you ascend in an airplane.

As you descend into the water, pinch your nose lightly, and either gently blow against your pinched nose or swallow several times. If you do this as you descend, you shouldn't feel any discomfort in your ears or sinuses; any sort of pain is a sign you've waited too long to equalize. If you have a cold, nasal allergies, or sinus problems, it's more difficult to equalize, so you may want to put off your dive until you're feeling better.

Clearing Your Mask

It's scary when you can't see underwater. When water leaks into or fills your mask, resist the urge to panic. Simply pull your mask away from your face and let water completely fill it. Continue to breathe through your regulator, tilt your head backwards, and press the top of your mask against your forehead. Take a deep breath and exhale through your nose, which will force water out of the mask. When it's clear, replace it so it fits snugly. This is a skill that takes some practice, and you've got to be able to do it to get certified.

Take a Giant Stride

Sure you can climb down the ladder into the water. But you know you're dying to enter the water by doing the giant stride, just because it looks so cool.

Once you've suited up and done your safety check, check the water to make sure it's free of obstructions—like other divers.

Place the balls of your feet on the edge of the entry platform, with your fins about half over the water, and hold your weight buckle and gauges with one hand. Use your other hand to secure your regulator and mask. Looking straight ahead and keeping your front fin pointed up, gently step forward. (Don't look down or your face will slap the water—and it hurts.) Once you enter the water, give the "OK" signal to the crew.

Surfacing

Too bad—it's time to surface. After signaling your buddy, hold your BC inflator hose to release air as necessary as you ascend. Hold one hand over your head, look up, and slowly spiral up toward the surface. Remember to take your **safety stop**, or **decompression stop**, which lets nitrogen be released from your body. (Even for short dives, a safety stop is a good idea because it allows your body to get rid of excess nitrogen.) The length of time you spend at your safety stop depends on how long you've been down and how deep you went; divers use decompression tables to determine how long they can stay at a certain depth and how long they have to decompress before they surface. Finally, continue to the surface, watching for boats and other obstructions.

YOU'VE GOT YOUR C-CARD; NOW WHAT?

Once you've become certified, you're able to dive when and where you like as long as you always have a buddy. Most divers dive with others, often using a local dive shop for equipment and transportation. One of the advantages to this is that the local divers have experience with different sites, dangers, and other potential problems to watch for. They can also turn you on to special sights, wrecks, animals to look for, and the like.

On your first few dives, don't be afraid to ask for help if you have any questions. You can also ask to be paired with a more experienced diver. The **dive master**—the professional diver in charge of the dive—should be able to address any concerns you may have.

You'll find that the more dives you perform, the more comfortable and confident you become in the water. You can also take additional scuba classes such as Advanced Diver, Rescue Diver, and Dive Instructor. Check out the diving education organizations listed earlier in this chapter for more info about advanced training.

Once you start hanging out with the fishes, you may find that you never want to surface. Most people will never witness the amazing world underwater. When you become a scuba diver, though, you become part of it.

31 Break into Acting

Think you have movie star looks, or do you dream of playing Hamlet on stage? Or maybe you'd love to shill for the latest Chia Pet.™ If you want to break into the acting biz, you're not alone. Would-be Hollywood stars are a dime a dozen, but you don't need a perfect face and physique to break into the business. You do need an understanding of how the business works, acting talent, and—let's face it—a dose of good luck.

DO YOU HAVE THE CHOPS?

First things first. Sure, there is plenty of bad acting on television, in the movies, and on stage, but starting out, if you don't have "Hilton" as your last name, you need to be able to act. What does that mean? It means more than playing a role. Acting also means hitting your mark (the place where you're supposed to stand in front of the camera), being able to get into character at a moment's notice, and having some ability to memorize scripts, among other things.

Keep in mind that, while talent may be inborn, acting

skills can be learned. If you're still in school, you can take acting classes or hook up with the drama department. If you're a grown-up (or pretending to be one), you have a variety of options. Community colleges and adult education programs often offer acting classes, as do theaters throughout the country. Established actors and other industry pros who pass on their acting talents to the great unwashed are yet another option. Simply search on Google for "acting class," and you'll find hundreds of choices.

Audition classes can help you work on the skills you'll need to get roles, including improving your skills at **cold-reading** (reading a script and playing a role immediately, with little time to prepare) and enhancing your on-camera technique. **Improv**, or **improvisation**, classes can help you learn how to play different roles, and volunteering at your local community theater will introduce you to the world of show biz. In general, the more you learn at this stage, the better.

YOU, A UNION MEMBER?

While actors are self-employed and can leap from project to project (assuming their contracts allow it), many are members of acting unions. The main union in the United States is the Associated Actors and Artists of America (AAAA); it includes three branches that cover different acting fields:

- *SAG, the Screen Actors Guild, represents actors who work in the movies* (http://www.sag.org). To get your "SAG card," you must have proof that you've either worked on a SAG-recognized production, are wanted for a role in one, or have been a member of another AAAA union like Equity or AFTRA for at least a year—and had at least one principal role during that time. The Web site includes a FAQ section for people new to the business, and other helpful resources.

- **Actors' Equity Association, usually just called Equity, is the organization for stage actors** (http://www.actorsequity.org). You must be a working stage actor to join Equity; the Web site includes the specific requirements to apply and has a helpful FAQ as well as audition notices.

- **American Federation of Television and Radio Artists (AFTRA) covers television and radio actors.** The Web site is *http://www.aftra.org*, but you must contact one of the many local branches, which are listed online, to find out how to apply.

You needn't join a union as an actor, but keep in mind that union jobs will only hire union actors; on the other hand, taking a nonunion gig as a union member may get you booted from the union. If you're serious about making acting your career, you should join the applicable union. If you're doing it for fun, don't worry about it.

SELLING YOUR LOOKS AND TALENT

While some lucky actors are discovered while standing in line for a pretzel in Manhattan, chances are you won't be as lucky. If you want to act for money (and not just in a local theater production of *Streetcar*), you need to invest in a few basic business tools to get your acting career off the ground.

Your Head Shot

A **head shot** is just that—an 8" x 10" black-and-white photograph of your face, with you looking into the camera. It should reflect how you really look, not how you wish you looked (so forget about airbrushing out those acne scars). On the other hand, if you have more than one "look" you want to project (say, sexy and sophisticated versus energetic young mom), consider using more than one head shot.

It's smart to hire a pro for your head shot; look for a photographer who specializes in them. (The Web sites listed at the end of this chapter are a good place to start.) You can also ask around for recommendations. Before you hire a photog, make sure you know what's included in the price of a head shot photography session and how much the head shots themselves will cost. You'll also want to include your name (and contact information) somewhere on the head shot itself, usually in the lower right-hand corner or at the bottom of the photograph.

Your Résumé

Yup, you need a résumé in the world of entertainment, but forget about that stint at Krispy Kreme™. Your acting résumé doesn't address unrelated experience, but instead focuses on your acting experience, training, and skills. Depending on your background and experience, your acting résumé should include the following:

- *Your name.* Make sure you check with the relevant actor's union to make sure your name hasn't been "taken" by another actor. If you were born "Jessica Simpson," you'll need to change your name in order to act, or at least add an initial to prevent people from confusing you with the singer/actress. Same goes if your name is "Brad Pitt," "Russell Crowe," or "Cameron Diaz."

- *Contact information.* If you have an agent, include his or her info; otherwise, list your cell phone or other number where you can always be reached.

- *Membership in any of the relevant acting unions such as SAG.*

- *Relevant physical characteristics, if you want.* You needn't sound like a personal ad ("tall vivacious brunette who loves to laugh . . ."). Include your height, weight, current hair color (we know, it can change!), and eye color. And don't lie. If you're a man who's 5'9", say so. Listing a height of 6 feet may be common in the personals, but it won't help you in the world of acting.

- *Acting experience, listed with the most current roles first.* If you're new, it's fine to list work you did in college (and if necessary, high school) productions. Even a gig as a dancing peanut applies.

- *Acting training.* Have you taken acting classes or worked with an acting coach? Include that information as well.

- *Special skills.* Do you know how to scuba dive? Ride bareback? Can you speak Russian? Include skills you have that might come in handy for a role. Who knows, your long-forgotten moon-walking abilities may snag you a role.

GETTING AN AGENT—OR RATHER, A JOB

An agent can help you get work, but the bottom line is that an inexperienced actor has little chance of snagging one. In the meantime, you'll have to look for work on your own. (All three union Web sites list agents; to contact one, include a head shot, résumé, and a letter of introduction about yourself and why you're interested in that particular agent.)

Your best bet to find work is to look constantly. Read the trade publications like *Backstage*, available online at *http://www.backstage.com*, to locate jobs, and scan the Web sites that list auditions for both union and nonunion actors. Check out the following:

- **http://www.actingdepot.com** This site includes lots of info about the acting biz, resources, and links to acting job boards.

- **http://www.auditionsearch.com** Includes industry news, links to helpful resources, and lets you search for auditions.

- **http://www.hcdonline.com** While you have to subscribe to search the Hollywood Creative Directory, access to the job board is free.

- **http://www.hollywoodauditions.com** This site includes resources and lets you search for auditions near you.

- **http://www.auditionsearch.com** Includes industry news, links to helpful resources, and lets you search for auditions.

THE BIG AUDITION

OK, you've got it. The big audition. Face it—you will be nervous. That's normal, and the casting director expects it. The more you know about the role, the better. What part are you auditioning for? How old is the character and how much do you know about his or her background? How does the character fit into the overall storyline or plot?

And just as important, where is the audition and what time is it? All the preparation in the world won't do anything if you miss the audition itself.

If you're auditioning for television or film, you should realize that a lot of things have to happen before auditions start. First off, a producer finds a project he or she is interested in; the next step is usually to hire a director. The script is polished (or in some cases, written); locations are scouted and secured; a budget is established (which may or may not reflect the eventual costs of the project); a shooting schedule is mapped out; and storyboards (visual sketches of each scene) are created. It's only then that auditions take place, for the big parts to smaller speaking roles including **extras**, or actors who usually play in the background of scenes. (Wanna be one? Check out the "Be a Movie Extra" chapter.)

Looks Matter

But back to the audition. You may be judged more on your looks and less on acting ability, or the other way around. If it's a commercial audition—say, the producer is looking for someone to sing the praises of a new flea dip—a perky, bouncy, energetic appearance may help you. On the other hand, the producer may be looking for a slovenly, out-of-shape actor to play the "before" person whose unkempt pet is riddled with fleas. Just do your best, and try not to take rejection personally—because you will get rejected. We guarantee it.

If you know something about the role you're to play (this may not be the case with a commercial audition, where you may be told your role when you show up), it doesn't hurt to try to look the part. If the role is that of a lawyer, wear a suit and bring a briefcase. You don't have to start spouting off about tort reform in the hallway, but looking (and feeling) the part may set you apart from the other auditioning actors.

Take Your Best Shot

If you're not given a script until the audition, take your time reading it over. Arriving early will give you time to get familiar with the material and practice different ways of delivering it. When you come onstage or in front of the camera for your audition, greet the people there and state your name. (You should always bring head shots and your résumé to an audition.) If it's appropriate, such as with a commercial audition, look into the camera when you deliver your lines—this makes it look like you're speaking directly to the person watching.

If, for some reason, you blow it, ask for the chance to go again. The worst that can happen is that the person will say "no." In other cases, you'll get the role, or be asked for a **callback**, where you'll audition again—and, hopefully, nail it this time.

If you're interested in acting for the theater, you'll need to have an audition piece, or **monologue**, prepared. This is a one-person speech (think "To be or not to be?" from *Hamlet*) that you deliver to show your acting, memorization, and interpretation abilities. There are thousands of plays to choose from, so select one that you feel showcases your unique abilities.

The Rest of the Story

Remember, auditioning for the job is just the first step. Once you get it, you'll be expected to show up on time, know your lines, and be able to take direction. If you act for television or the movies, you'll have to know how to play toward the camera, act scenes out of order, and give a consistent performance. You may have to show up early for makeup and wardrobe and spend days or even weeks rehearsing, including doing **read-throughs** (during which the script is read but not acted) around a table with other actors. The hours can be long and the requirements demanding, but if you believe show business is the right business for you, it's all worth it. And even if you simply try your hand at community theater, you may find that applause is the biggest reward of all.

Save a Life

32

Forget traveling the world or learning to fly. One of the truly extraordinary things anyone can ever do is save the life of someone else. And you don't have to be a fire-fighter, a rescue pilot, or a world-class physician either. There are a variety of things just about anyone can do that can make a difference—and they can be as simple as donating blood or giving first aid to someone who needs it. You just have to know how to do it—and be in the right place at the right time.

JUMP-START A HEART

Learn CPR and you may be able to help someone whose heart has temporarily stopped. **CPR**, which stands for "cardiopulmonary (cardio means "heart," pulmonary means "lungs") resuscitation," is a way to give oxygen and keep someone's heart pumping when his heart has stopped beating and he's no longer breathing. With CPR, you blow air into someone's lungs using mouth-to-mouth resuscitation, and push on the chest to help blood continue to flow throughout the body. CPR saves thousands of lives every year.

The American Heart Association and the American Red Cross both offer CPR classes throughout the country; visit *http://www.americanheart.org* or *http://www.redcross.org* for more information about classes near you. In the meantime, you can learn the basic CPR moves.

Call 911

If someone has collapsed and is not responding to you (talk or touch the person to make sure), the first thing you should do is to call 911. Do this before you start performing CPR, or have someone else do it while you attend to the person who's down.

Position the Person

Before starting CPR, make sure the surroundings are safe—that you're not near a car leaking gas that may catch on fire, for example. Carefully move the person so that she is flat on her back. Kneeling by her side, put one hand on her forehead and one on her chin; gently tilt her head back and lift her chin. Listen for breathing.

Give Two Breaths

If she's not breathing, pinch her nose closed and cover her mouth with yours. Blow two strong breaths of one to two seconds each; watch her chest to see if it rises. (If it doesn't, you're not blowing hard enough.) Then check to see whether she has a pulse and whether she is breathing on her own. If so, stop CPR and stay with her until help arrives. If she's not breathing but has a pulse, continue giving two breaths at a time, which is called **rescue breathing**.

Give Chest Compressions

If the person has no pulse, put your hands, one on top of the other, on her chest between her nipples. Lock your elbows and push down firmly fifteen times in a row, at a rate of 100 pushes per minute (almost two every second). Stop and check to see if the person is breathing and/or has a pulse.

Repeat until Help Arrives

If the person still isn't breathing and doesn't have a pulse, repeat the process, giving two breaths and fifteen chest compressions until help arrives or the person starts breathing on her own.

THEY WANT YOUR BLOOD!

If you're looking for an easy way to make a difference in someone's life—and possibly even save it—consider donating blood. In the United States, someone needs blood every two seconds, and it's a medical supply that cannot be manufactured or harvested. People like you and me create the blood supply in our country, and donating is easier than you might have realized.

While you have to be seventeen to give blood (sixteen in some states), there are few other restrictions—other than good health of course. If you're a type O-negative, your blood is particularly in demand. This type is called the **universal donor** because it can be subsituted for any other blood type. On the other hand, AB-positive is called the **universal recipient** because it can receive the blood of any other type.

The total process of giving blood takes about an hour, which includes registration, a brief medical screening, the actual blood collection, and refreshments (typically cookies, juice, or other high-sugar treats).

How much do you give? Less than you might think. Men have about twelve pints of blood, women about ten, and a typical donation is about one pint—10 percent or less of your total blood supply. You can donate whole blood every couple of months, and it's completely safe to both donate and receive blood. But even if you're a regular donor, you have to go through the same screening process each time. It's part of an FDA requirement designed to help keep the blood supply safe.

BASIC FIRST AID

Knowing some basic first-aid techniques can also help you save someone's life. Obviously you're not a medical professional, nor do you play one on TV, so it's always a good idea to call 911 when someone is seriously hurt. But in many situations, you can help the injured person by taking some first-aid steps.

Abrasions/Scrapes

Rinse the scrape with soap and warm water and bandage it to help prevent infection. If it's a deep scrape or there is material embedded in the skin that you can't get out (picture taking a bad spill from your bike onto a gravel road), let the doctor take a look. Same goes if the wound develops signs of infection, such as swelling, reddened skin, pain, or oozing pus (lovely, huh?), or if you develop a fever, which can be a sign of infection.

Burns

Burns range from first-degree (the least severe) to third-degree, which are the deepest. You can usually treat first-degree burns yourself, but anything more serious should be checked out by a doctor. A first-degree burn feels painful and looks red or discolored; there may also be swelling involved—picture a bad sunburn. Flush the area with cool running water, and apply moist (so they won't stick) bandages loosely. For burns that look more serious, are blistered, or are oozing, don't run water over the burn; instead, loosely bandage the area and have a doctor check it out.

Cuts

For a shallow cut, cleanse the area with warm water and soap, and apply pressure to the cut until it stops bleeding; then put a sterile bandage on it. If the cut is deep or if it won't stop bleeding, seek emergency care right away.

Fainting

If someone feels faint, have her sit down and lean forward, lowering her head to her knees. This will help blood flow to the brain and may prevent fainting. If someone has already lost consciousness, place her in the **recovery position** with her head lower than her legs to help the blood flow to her brain. You can apply a cool, damp cloth to her face and loosen any tight clothing. When she awakens, don't let her get up until she can tell you who she is, what day it is, and that kind of thing. If not, or if she doesn't awaken, call 911.

Frostbite

If someone has frostbite, bring him into a warm place and remove any wet clothing. Immerse the frostbitten parts (often they will be **extremities**, i.e., fingers or toes) in warm water until they regain a pink color, but don't rub the frostbitten areas or try to warm them too quickly. After the frostbitten parts have warmed up, have the person move them to help maintain circulation in the area, and see a doctor immediately to make sure the frostbitten areas heal properly.

Heat Exhaustion/Heatstroke

Heat exhaustion and heatstroke are two different conditions. **Heat exhaustion** is caused by excessive sweating and can cause headaches, muscle weakness, dizziness, nausea, or blurred vision. A person with heat exhaustion may also be sweating profusely. If someone has these symptoms, give her water to help her rehydrate and have her rest in a cool place to lower her body temperature.

Heatstroke can be life-threatening and occurs when the body can no longer cool itself. If someone collapses during physical activity, especially in hot weather, heatstroke may be the culprit. Check to see if the person has an elevated temperature; she may be sweating profusely or have hot, pale, dry skin. If you suspect you or someone else has heatstroke, move the person to a cool place, offer her water, and call a doctor or ambulance right away. To get the person's temperature down, you may want to place her in cool water or sponge her body with cool water or ice packs.

Poison Ivy/Poison Oak/Poison Sumac

If someone is exposed to one of these poisonous plants, he'll know it. Common symptoms include a rash that blisters, burns, itches, and swells. (Sounds fun, huh?) Get rid of any clothing that may also have been exposed to the plants, and rinse the affected areas with soap and cool water to get rid of any lingering plant residue. (Don't use a washcloth, as this can spread the poison over more skin.) Rinse again with rubbing alcohol and apply calamine lotion to ease the itching and burning. If he develops a fever or the symptoms worsen to an excessive degree, have a doctor check him out.

Shock

Shock can occur after any injury, even a minor one. Someone experiencing shock will feel weak and may faint; the person's skin feels cold and clammy to the touch and his pulse may be weak or rapid. If the person doesn't have injuries that prevent you from moving him (such as a suspected neck injury or broken bone), place him on his back with his chest lower than his legs to help blood circulate to the brain, heart, and lungs. Cover him with a blanket to keep him warm, and call 911.

Sprains/Strains

You'll probably know immediately when someone's suffered a sprain or strain. Pain is the first symptom, and it's often intense due to the fact that nerves have been damaged. The affected joint will begin swelling immediately, and may turn black-and-blue. Apply ice to help reduce the swelling during the first twenty-four hours, then alternate hot and cold compresses to help promote healing. It's also a good idea to have a doctor check out the injury to make sure no bones were injured; the doc may also give the injured person a sling or crutches or lightly wrap the strained joint to help immobilize it while it heals—usually at least six to eight weeks.

BECOME AN ORGAN DONOR

You can even save a life after you lose yours. Become an organ donor, and the parts of your body you'll no longer be using can save lives. All you have to do is download, print, sign, and carry an organ donor card from *http://www.organdonor.gov/*; sign the back of your driver's license expressing your intent to be a donor, and register with your state's donor registry if it has one.

Don't forget to talk to your family about your wishes. They'll have the final say, so it's important for them to know what you want and why it's important to you. Even if you never save a life while you're alive, you can be a hero to someone else after you're gone. And that's good karma no matter how you look at it.

Play the Guitar

33

So you want to learn to play the guitar, huh? Good choice. The guitar is versatile, popular, and sexy as well. It's a great crowd-pleaser, light enough to be portable, and can be played alone or with a band. If you're ready to make your fantasies of becoming the next Hendrix, Santana, or Van Halen come true, read on.

BUYING YOUR GUITAR

Well, the first thing you'll need is—drum roll, please—a guitar! Before you buy, it's a good idea to go window-shopping and visit music stores to get an idea of what's out there, and for how much.

For your first guitar, you don't necessarily need an expensive one. But steer clear of a really cheap one as well; it might be of poor quality. A little more cash can buy you a decent guitar to start with; if money is tight, consider a secondhand one. It's a good idea to buy from either a reputable music dealer or have someone who knows guitars with you if you decide to buy from a pawnshop or someone else.

There are other factors to consider in addition to price. Do you want a steel-string acoustic guitar or one with nylon strings? Nylon is easier on your fingers, but steel strings are more common among guitarists who play in bands. They also produce a richer sound with more vibration than nylon strings. If you dream of jammin' out with a band, opt for a steel-string version. Just expect your fingers to be sore for a bit while you learn to play it.

Consider size and weight, also. Usually the lighter the guitar, the better the volume and tone tend to be. Again, your best bet is to ask an experienced guitarist to help you make the right choice.

KNOW YOUR GUITAR

Now that you've chosen your own personal Lucille (B.B. King's name for his guitar), get to know her. Here's a rundown of her parts:

THE HEAD: The smaller end of the guitar, which has six pegs sticking out of it

THE NECK: The long, thin area below the head where the strings are played

THE HEEL: The small area where the neck connects to the main section of the guitar

THE BACK: The back of the guitar, literally; this is the part that faces the musician as he plays

TUNING MACHINES AND PEGS: The six knobs at the top are the tuning machines and pegs. They're numbered one through six. When the guitar is facing you, number one is the lowest one down on the right side; above it is number two, then number three. Directly across from number three is number four; numbers five and six are located below it, in that order. These tuning pegs correspond to the strings, as each is strung into its respectively numbered peg. The first string is the thinnest and highest sounding.

THE NUT: The thin strip located just under the tuning machines and pegs

THE FINGERBOARD: The long, thin area separating the top from the bottom, which has what look like small, segmented boxes in it. Each of these "boxes" is separated by a fret

THE SOUND HOLE: The large open circle underneath the strings on the main section of the guitar

THE FINGER GUARD OR SCRATCH PLATE: The black "blob" area on the face of the guitar, right outside the sound hole

THE BRIDGE BONE: The area underneath the scratch plate that contains the bridge; the strings are screwed into the bridge itself

Before You Strum

What do you play the guitar with? Your fingers, of course, so you should keep them in good string-picking condition.

Right-hand fingernails should be filed, rather than cut, with your nails either level with your fingertips or roughly three millimeters longer than your fingertips for easy playing. Keep your nails smoothly filed; a rough nail will make a scary sound on the strings. With rough nails you also have a greater possibility of breaking both a nail and the guitar string. That makes an emery board part of your guitar-playing tool kit.

The fingernails of your left hand should be kept very short, and should never extend past the tips of your fingers as they'll make it difficult to press strings correctly into the fingerboard. Your fingertips can become a little tender in the beginning, but they will harden with time and practice.

If you wash your hands before playing, wait a few minutes before taking up your guitar—your hands will be soft from the water and it will be harder to play.

Get into Position

The way you hold your guitar and position your hands is an important factor, because it affects how easily you will be able to play. If you're in the wrong position, you'll have less control over your fingers, which makes playing more difficult. It's worth your time to learn how to hold your guitar correctly—that way you'll be both relaxed and comfortable.

Always sit on an upright chair or stool. It's tougher to play in an armchair, easy chair, or sofa because the arms can get in the way. And watch what you wear, too; it may sound silly, but bulky clothes, zippers, or metal buttons may scratch your guitar.

There are two main positions used when holding the guitar. The first is the **casual position**—perfect for you laid-back folks. The guitar may sit on either thigh, with the face of it vertical and the neck angled slightly upward. But the **classical position**, used most often by professionals, is regarded as the proper way to hold the guitar. The left foot should be elevated on a footstool or other object about six inches off the ground; the guitar then rests against the right thigh while sitting on the left leg.

The guitar should always be held close to the body, with your right arm resting on the highest part of the guitar. Your right wrist should be relaxed, with fingers at a right angle to the location of the strings; your left elbow and arm should hang loosely at your side. In fact, the guitar should be supported without the use of your left hand.

At first you'll want to lean forward a little so that you can easily see your fingers, but soon you'll be able to navigate your fingers around more easily on the fingerboard and you won't need to look at them as much.

The Right Hand

The right hand does most of the work when playing the guitar (unless, of course, you're a lefty). The right hand does the strumming and plucking, and your fingers and thumb move to play either one string at a time or several strings together. Start using your thumb only. It's not the best idea to start playing with a pick, properly called a **plectrum**. You want to learn your way around the strings first.

Start with the thumb of your right hand resting lightly on the sixth string. Curve your fingers slightly and let your fingers hang behind the sound hole at a right angle to the strings. Keep your right thumb straight while you're playing, with the rest of your hand away from the strings, and don't move the rest of your hand while you push downward with your thumb. It should stroke the sixth string and come to land on the fifth string, strumming it hard enough to make a distinct noise. After you pluck it, if you touch it again the noise will stop. Keep your hand in the same position, bring your thumb up to the sixth string again, and repeat until your playing gets smoother.

The Left Hand

The fingertips of your left hand will press the strings on the fingerboard behind the frets to change the notes on each string.

A different fret is found at each fret position, and the higher you are on the fingerboard, the higher the notes on each string will be. "High" on the guitar is toward the bridge and "low" is toward the nut.

Put the thumb of your left hand in the middle of the neck, underneath and just past the first fret. Your thumb should be straight, but your wrist should be bent, with your elbow hanging loosely at your side. Arch your fingers over the strings, keeping them separate and relaxed.

Press your fingertip to the first, or thinnest, string, just behind the first fret. Press your thumb gently against the back of the neck while plucking the first string with the thumb of your right hand. Keep the left hand in position, but relax the thumb. If the note doesn't sound clear, you may not be pressing firmly enough, your finger may not be close enough to the fret, or right on the fret, or your fingernails may be too long. Check to see what the problem is and keep trying until you get a clear note after each try. You need to press hard enough to get clear notes every time, but don't use too much pressure, as it will slow down your playing.

LEARNING THE ROPES

There are a variety of ways to learn the guitar. Many people, especially musicians, argue that the best way to learn is from an instructor. There are several advantages to face-to-face instruction—after all, you have someone to watch and learn from as well as ask questions of. Your instructor can also show you exactly how to position your fingers and how much pressure to use. To find an instructor, ask at your local music shop; they'll be able to recommend someone.

Depending on how musically inclined you are, you may be

able to learn how to play from a book, but this may be frustrating for a true beginner. There are also many Web sites that claim to teach through online tutorials; just be leery of those that promise you'll be an expert in something like ten days or sixty minutes. If you want to learn online, shop around for the best deal. Finally, if you're a real music buff, there's a chance you can learn by ear. Play around a bit in the beginning, and see how far you want to go with it before deciding how you want to learn.

Tune It Up

Tuning is an important skill to learn. Any music from folk to rock sounds better when the instrument is in tune. Music stores sell a small inexpensive instrument called a **guitar pitch pipe** or an **"e" tuning fork** that comes with simple instructions.

To tune, you must turn each tuning peg a little at a time; the sound of the string will get higher by turning it one way. Turning the knob the opposite way will give the string some slack, making the sound lower. Make sure you're turning the correct peg for each string.

Be patient with yourself when you are just learning to tune. Like playing, it's a skill that takes time to learn and master. But it's worth it to take the time to do it. Your music will sound much better. Who knows, with a little practice you may be playing riffs like a pro—or at least make the leap from playing air guitar to the real thing.

34

Read Body Language

Want to be able to tell whether you aced that job interview? Whether your date is really interested in you? Or simply communicate better with those around you?

Become a body language expert, and you'll gain insight into how people really feel, and make a better impression regardless of the situation. Paying more attention not to what people say, but to what they do (or don't do) while they say it will give you a leg up in both your personal and professional lives—and even make you a better flirt!

THE LANGUAGE OF THE BODY

In essence, **body language** is the process of sending and receiving wordless messages. It includes everything from facial expressions to gestures and posture—and the way people dress and style their hair. These so-called nonverbal cues provide a window into how people are feeling, whether they're consciously aware of what they're expressing or not.

Researchers say that what we say and the tone and inflection of our voice make up about 45 percent of the message we communicate to others. The remaining 55 percent of the message comes from our body language, including the way we hold ourselves, our facial expressions, and the gestures we make. Other studies show that up to 90 percent of communication is nonverbal.

While most of us don't study body language that closely, it can give you insight into the way people really feel. Body language is essentially a window into our emotions and feelings and moods, and studies reveal it tends to trump the spoken word.

Think about it. If your best friend insists she's not angry about something, but she's standing with her arms tightly crossed against her chest and avoiding your gaze, you're not likely to believe her. While people can (and do) say anything, body language is harder to fake. Part of the reason is that emotions tend to be expressed through more than one specific action. For example, if you're sad about something, your posture may slump, your mouth pull down, and you may hold your head lower—without consciously being aware of it. Sure, you could smile and try to fake it, but your body position would probably give your true feelings away.

We make facial expressions and movements without thinking about it, and some of them appear to be programmed. For example, people throughout the world make the same facial gestures to express disgust and surprise. Other body language gestures can mean very different things: winking your eye or giving a thumbs-up signal has different connotations to people in different cultures. (Even the ubiquitous "middle-finger salute" would mean nothing to an Australian Aborigine; he'd just think you were pointing.)

SPEAK THE LANGUAGE LIKE A NATIVE

The body language you use can also mean the difference between getting that job offer and being passed over; attracting the person you're interested in or being ignored; and having a satisfying relationship versus a not-so-great one. Don't be clueless about the messages you're sending. Here's a primer to help you understand what you're communicating with different parts of your body:

Open Your Eyes

Called "the windows to the soul," your eyes can and do speak volumes. With a glance, you can send a message that says, "I find you attractive," or give a hostile stare that will keep anyone from approaching you. The key is how much eye contact you give. Too much eye contact will often make someone else uncomfortable; think of how you feel when someone keeps looking at you. On the other hand, if you hardly look someone in the eye, you may be thought of as dishonest, impolite, or simply shy. In general, the more you like someone, the more eye contact you'll make.

Someone making eye contact with you invites you to communicate with them. (This is why you avoid the eyes of someone you don't want to interact with.) If someone makes eye contact with you for longer than a second or two, it's likely you'll smile or begin to talk—or you'll turn away, giving a clear message of "not interested" or "don't bother me."

People also make something called the **eyebrow flash of recognition** when they meet someone they're interested in. If you want to signal friendliness, try consciously lifting your eyebrows when you greet someone or smile at him or her. The person may not know what you're doing, but he'll respond favorably. In the same vein, if you see this flash when meeting someone, you know you're halfway there. (Another cue? People's pupils dilate when they see something—or someone—they like, and constrict when they see something they don't like. In fact, dilated pupils are also a sign of sexual attraction!)

Move Your Mouth

The most effective thing you can do with your mouth is to smile. Researchers divide smiles into three types: slight smiles (think Mona Lisa), normal smiles, and broad smiles. Even babies respond favorably to a smile as opposed to a neutral expression, so we may be wired to find smiles attractive. As we grow up, we may use a variety of smiles—even forced ones—depending on the situation.

While smiles are usually used as a greeting or to show pleasure and happiness, your mouth can communicate other emotions as well. Most people recognize a turning down of the corners of the mouth as a sign of sadness. Grimacing or gritting your teeth can express anger or frustration. An open-mouthed expression signals surprise or shock.

If you're in a professional situation—say, a job interview or a meeting—it's good to smile, but you don't want to overdo it. Smiling all the time can make you look, well, like an idiot; a more charitable explanation might be that someone's feeling nervous or unsure and is trying to hide their feelings with a constant grin.

Hold Up Your Hands

Nearly all of us use our hands when speaking. If you're a woman and want to show someone that you're interested in him, try engaging in what's called **preening behavior**, such as using your fingers to stroke your neck or play with your earring. Guys might square their shoulders, run their fingers through their hair, or thrust their chests out. If someone's exhibiting this kind of behavior, chances are they're interested.

On the flip side, if you're not interested in someone, you may want to keep your hands in your lap. The amount you touch someone will also indicate whether you're interested in her. People are more likely to touch when giving information than receiving it, when asking a favor as opposed to granting one, and when listening to someone else's worries rather than expressing their own. In general, the more you touch someone, the more you like him or are trying to convince him of something. (And the less you touch? Do the math.)

Your hands can also give you away if you're fibbing. When lying, people tend to make fewer hand gestures. Interestingly, though, you're also more likely to touch your mouth, nose, or face when you're lying, a stress reaction due to the fact that you're not being honest.

Square Your Shoulders

There may be a reason why men find off-the-shoulder dresses so enticing. Flexing, lifting, or moving the shoulders forward is an expressive move that makes women and men seem friendlier because it's considered submissive. Shoulders are attractive, and they show a lot when they're moved. Also, the muscle that moves the shoulders, the upper trapezius, is operated by special visceral nerves connected to what's called your "emotional brain." The result is that when you experience an emotion, your shoulders may respond without you even thinking about it. Consciously moving your shoulders, however, can show that you're sympathetic, approachable, or friendly.

Open Your Arms—or Keep Them Closed

At one extreme, the way you hold your arms can signal openness and approachability; on the other, it can communicate defensiveness. Crossing your arms tightly will send a message that you're closed off, hostile, or angry—even if you're just trying to stay warm in a chilly office! If you want to show that you're interested in someone or what she has to say, an open-armed posture will help communicate that message. When a woman exposes her chest, she's more vulnerable and, therefore, may be considered more attractive—without a man knowing exactly why. Men, on the other hand, tend to thrust out their chests to display dominance or to attract attention.

Let Your Legs Lie

Crossing or recrossing your legs can be an effective flirting signal because it draws attention to your lower body. Most women will cross their legs without thinking about it, but if you want to look professional, it's better to cross them and keep them that way instead of constantly changing position. Most men, however, will not cross their legs, but instead favor a posture of one foot resting on the other knee, or sitting with both feet firmly on the floor. This is considered more of a powerful position, so if you're engaged in an argument you want to win, you may want to use this technique. In a similar vein, you're more likely to be taken seriously standing firmly on two feet than if you're standing with your legs twisted or bent.

Feet, Don't Fool Me Now

Your feet can give away your true emotions. If you're nervous, bored, or irritated, your feet may tap or move without your realizing it. This is what researchers call **leakage**—when your body reveals your true feelings or emotions. Focus on keeping your feet still during important meetings, even if you're bored out of your mind, and you'll be considered more professional at the office! If you notice someone tapping her foot, there's a good chance she's annoyed or wants to be somewhere else—now.

Your Whole Body

The way you hold your body and move—or don't move—also sends a message. If you shift position very little and don't respond by smiling, tilting your head, or moving your shoulders when someone speaks to you or looks at you, you send a message of "I'm not interested" or "don't bother me." If you really want to be left alone, angle your face or your body away from the person. This is called **cutoff**. Someone positioned this way isn't receptive to what you have to say.

On the other hand, if you align your body with the other person, this shows that you're interested in him or feel he's an ally. Leaning forward a bit shows interest as well, and the appropriate use of hand gestures can also help you make a point. For example, if you hold your hands palms up while speaking, you express rapport with the other person. Using this technique in both social and business situations will make you seem like a good listener, but if you use it too often people may think you're wishy-washy.

Remember, in the world of body language, first impressions count for a lot; most people decide in the first four minutes of meeting a person if they're attracted to or interested in him or her. When you're interacting with people, pay attention to their posture, facial expressions, and gestures, not just the words they're saying. Study people at work, at parties, and on the train to see if you can figure out the hidden messages they're sending. The more you study body language, the better you get at interpreting it. Use your body—and other people's—to your advantage, and people may start wondering just when you got so smart.

Learn Sign Language

35

Want to talk without saying a word? Give your two cents on the guy who's flirting with your friend—without letting him know? Then why not learn the fourth most-commonly-used language in this country—sign language? You can use sign language to speak with the hearing-impaired, communicate with your diving partner under the sea, or even figure out what your baby wants before she can tell you with speech. Chances are your local college offers a course in sign language, and it's a fun skill to learn and master.

THE BASICS OF SIGNING

When you think of sign language, you might think that there's one standard language worldwide. However, just as people in different countries speak different oral languages, sign language varies as well. There is an International Sign Language that was developed by the World Federation of the Deaf, but in the United States, you'll probably learn ASL—American Sign Language.

While it's relatively young language-wise, the origins of

sign language can be traced back to 1620 when a man named Juan Pablo de Bonet published a book about the manual alphabet, a visual way to spell. In the eighteenth century, a Parisian, Abbé L'Epée, founded the first free school for the deaf, and developed a sign system based on hand signs that the deaf were already using; he eventually added a signed version of spoken-language French. In the nineteenth century, major-league baseball player William Hoy, who was deaf, was the reason umpires adopted hand signals for calls like "out," "safe," and "strike." Since then, sign language has been more commonly used and accepted in the United States. In the 1980s, Marlee Matlin, a hard-of-hearing actress who signs, won the Best Actress Oscar for her role in *Children of a Lesser God*, and the popular *Smurfs* became the first cartoon to use sign language on TV.

Enough about the history. Let's get to the technique. Signs are broken into four elements: the shape of the hand, the palm orientation, the relation of hand to body, and hand movement. The message is created by displaying and interpreting these four conditions. By changing just one of these elements, the message itself can be entirely different.

The subtleties of sign language take practice and time to learn. If you're a signing novice, focus on the person's face when someone is signing to you—many signs begin and end there. Don't worry if you don't understand what someone is trying to tell you. As your skills grow, you can broaden your view until you're able to focus on the signer's entire upper body.

To start your learning process, you have several options available. Many colleges and adult education programs offer sign language classes if you want to go the organized education route; check what your community offers. There are also books and videos available, and Web sites offer online classes that can be taken at your leisure. These classes include video of the signs to help you see how they're performed, and they may count as continuing education for educators and people in the health field. Check out *http://www.signingonline.com/* or do a Google search for online classes. The site *http://www.aslpro.com/* is another helpful resource that includes several signing dictionaries with video and quizzes to test your knowledge.

FINGER SPELLING

Books, videos, and classes will introduce you to the world of sign language, but your first step is to memorize the manual alphabet. Once you know that, you can spell out any words you don't know, and so can someone communicating with you.

Keep in mind that finger spelling is not only for beginners. You'll have to spell out people's names and proper nouns because there are no dedicated signs for them. You can find a visual guide to the manual alphabet embedded in the main dictionary at *http://www.aslpro.com/* or at *http://www.masterstech-home.com/ASLDict.html.*

Ready to learn your ABCs in a whole new way? Here's how to make the letters of the alphabet:

A-Make a fist with your thumb held against your index finger.

B-Hold your hand flat by extending your fingers, point them up, and tuck your thumb behind your palm.

C-Curl your fingers and your thumb to form a "C" with your hand.

D-Point your index finger up and curl the rest of your fingers down so that your fingertips touch the tip of your thumb.

E - Curl your fingers down and bring your thumb into your palm, with your fingertips touching the side of your thumb.

F - Curl your index finger down and touch the tip of it to the tip of your thumb, leaving the rest of your fingers up.

G - Point your index finger to the side and curl the rest in a fist, with your thumb nearly parallel to your index finger but sticking out the top.

H - Point your index and middle fingers to the side; curl the other two away and tuck your thumb across them.

I - Make a fist and hold your pinky in the air.

J - Start by making the "I" sign and then swish your pinky in a "J" motion.

K - Point your index finger up, your middle out (90 degrees from your index), and let your thumb rest between them, holding your remaining fingers against your palm.

L - Hold your index finger up, thumb out, with the rest of your fingers curled down to your palm. (Look! It forms an "L"!)

M - Hold your pinky against your palm, with your other fingers held out 90 degrees from your palm, thumb underneath them.

N - Position your fingers like the "M" sign, but tuck both your pinky and ring fingers to your palm.

O - Curl your fingers and your thumb until the tips meet, forming an "O."

P - Curl your pinky and ring fingers to your palm; your index and middle fingers should both point down but be separated, with your thumb next to your index finger.

Q - Point your index finger and thumb down, parallel to each other but not touching; the rest curl to the palm.

R - Cross your middle finger over your index finger and point them up; the ring and pinky fingers should curl down with their tips held by the thumb.

S - Curl your fingers tightly in and wrap your thumb across them.

T - Curl your fingers down and put your thumb between the index and middle fingers, allowing it to stick out and point up.

U - The index and middle fingers point up side by side while the other fingers curl down and are held at the tips by the thumb.

V - Position your fingers like the "U" sign, but split the index and middle fingers in a "V."

W - The index, middle, and ring fingers are pointed up and held apart, while the pinky curls down and is held by the thumb.

X - Point your index finger up and bend it 90 degrees at the knuckle; the rest are curled down and held by the thumb.

Y - Point your pinky and thumb in opposite directions while holding the rest of your fingers to your palm.

Z - Point with your index finger, the other fingers held to your palm with your thumb, and make a "Z" motion through the air.

Once you have these letters down, you'll be well on your way to communicating without sound.

SIGNING WITH YOUR BABY

Sign language was designed for communication in the absence of verbal abilities, so it's a perfect fit for children who are not old enough to talk or whose knowledge of language is still developing. You don't even need to know sign language yourself as long as you know the signs you are going to teach your child. Signing can act as a segue between no communication and talking, just like crawling is a transition to walking.

If you want to sign with your baby, start when he or she is about six months old. Don't worry—if your child is older, he or she will respond to sign language just as well. The first step is to choose the signs you are going to work with. Naturally, you're going to present your child with only a few signs to begin with. Common choices are: "hungry," "thirsty," "change" (for a dirty diaper), "hurt," "tired," "mommy," and "daddy."

To start signing, show your baby the sign immediately before and during the activity. If you're using the sign meaning "food," for example, show the child the sign before and while he or she eats. It is important to remain consistent with your signs; you must make the same motions and make them every time the activity happens. Use the chosen sign until your baby signs back to you. Once she understands the sign, start teaching her another using the same process, while still using the old ones.

Obviously, this learning process takes time. Don't give up if you feel your child isn't learning the signs. As with spoken language, your child understands what you are communicating before she starts to communicate herself. Also, when your child first starts to sign, she may use one sign for everything. This is completely normal and can happen with spoken language as well. Continue using all your signs, and always encourage the child when he or she attempts to sign.

At some point, your baby will realize that by learning and using these signs she can get exactly what she wants. Parents commonly experience a "sign explosion" at that point—your baby may sign frequently and is clearly eager to learn new signs. For example, if you give your baby a new toy, she may look to you for a sign so she'll know how to ask for it later—or, more realistically, so she can tell you to get it.

By using these techniques, you can (hopefully) avoid the frustration that can arise when your child wants something and you can't figure out what it is. Your baby will also have an understanding of the English language at a much younger age than children who don't sign. Some studies even suggest that signing can lead to a higher IQ and a heightened ability to learn new languages throughout life.

Don't worry that signing will delay your child's speech. All the research in this area suggests the contrary. Studies have proven that sign language, rather than delaying a child's speech development, actually enhances it.

If you want to learn how to speak with your baby before she can speak, there are plenty of classes and workshops available to choose from. Check out Web sites like *http://signingsmart.com/*, *http://www.signingbaby.com/*, and *http://www.babysigns.com/* for more info.

Whether you want to learn to communicate with your child, your friends, or the hearing-impaired in a variety of situations, sign language is a valuable skill and one that's actually simple to learn. And the sooner you start, the sooner you'll be bilingual!

36

Play the Market

What's the best kind of money to make? The kind you can make in your sleep. The kind that works for you, producing its own returns while you're off doing other things. If you're not born wealthy, you can get rich—or at least try to get rich—by investing in the stock market.

MASTERING THE MARKET BASICS

First off, the stock market doesn't guarantee anything, but there are a few rules of thumb to keep in mind. The main one is that you want to buy stocks at a lower price than you sell them for. Buy low, sell high—that's how you make money. Another is that the higher the risk, the greater the reward. Of course, the flip side of that is true, too. The smaller the risk, the smaller the reward.

Seems like everybody wants to invest in the market, and nobody wants to lose money, but for every investor who's up, there's someone else who's down. There are no absolute guarantees in the world of investing, despite what your hot tip may say. That's why we suggest you stick to small investments, at least at first. That way, if your super stock winds up tanking, you won't lose your savings along with it.

The Stock Exchanges

There are three major stock exchanges in the United States:

- *NYSE (New York Stock Exchange),* which holds the highest value and largest established stocks. The NYSE is sometimes referred to as the "big board," and it has a value commonly used by the public called the **Dow**. The Dow is a measure of how well thirty **blue-chip stocks** (those with the longest established records of value, such as Dow Chemical, General Motors, and IBM) are performing.

- *NASDAQ (National Association of Securities Dealers Automated Quotation System),* which holds mostly technology and biotechnology stocks as well as many newer stocks, which are primarily growth stocks. This is where you're likely to find stocks of new, up-and-coming companies.

- *American,* which holds many oil stocks and other stocks not traded on the NYSE and the NASDAQ.

While the public tends to view the Dow as "the" measurement of what the stock exchange is doing, a better indicator is Standard & Poor's 500, or the **S&P 500**, which is a measurement of value of the 500 highest-valued stocks on the NYSE and NASDAQ. There's also the **NASDAQ value**, an indicator of how well the stocks on that exchange are performing. Experts recommend looking at all three values each day (Dow, NASDAQ, and S&P 500) to help determine how the market is doing and what it may do next.

Common Terminology

Starting out is a little easier if you know what the experts are talking about. Here's the scoop on some basic Wall Street terms:

BLUE CHIP: A stock that sells for a high price because it belongs to a company that is well-established, highly successful, and reliable.

DELISTED: Used to describe a stock whose price has become so low that it is considered a risk to have on the NYSE; it's therefore no longer listed, making it difficult to follow.

DIVIDENDS: A company's profits that are paid to stockholders, either in cash or in more shares of stock.

GROWTH STOCK: A stock in a fast-growing company that is reinvesting its profits rather than paying high dividends.

HOLDINGS: The stock one has invested in and therefore "holds," or owns.

P/E RATIO: A measure of stock price divided by earnings. The higher the P/E value, the more expensive the stock; lower P/E ratios tend to be lower risks than higher ones, too.

S&P 500 (STANDARD AND POOR'S 500): An index of 500 major U.S.-based companies traded on U.S. exchanges; it's respected as an indicator of the state of the market in general.

SECTOR: An area of the market to invest in, such as pharmaceuticals, technology, financials, and the like.

VALUE STOCK: A stock that has substantial value and that people tend to feel safer holding due to its established earnings. It sells at an undervalued price at the time of purchase, which means it's less expensive than it normally would be.

WHAT KIND OF INVESTOR ARE YOU?

While there's no shortage of theories about how to make money buying and selling stock, there are two major types of investors, creating two main schools of thought: value investors and growth investors.

Value investors want to buy undervalued stocks and hold them until other investors also decide they are undervalued and snatch them up. This raises the value of the stock that the value investor owns. The value investor is generally happy with earnings of 10 percent or less in a year. Many value investors favor utilities and other conservative stocks such as financials, which have a lower P/E ratio; typically they look for a 10 to 12 P/E ratio or lower.

Growth investors focus on buying stocks that will increase in value or have potential in growth. The growth investor looks for returns greater than 10 percent in a year, which will increase the value of the stock, and they tend to be more aggressive than value investors. They're more comfortable with a P/E ratio of greater than 10 to 12, and may take on stocks with a P/E of up to 40 to 50 if they think it's a good risk.

PUT ON YOUR GAME FACE

Not sure where to begin? Almost any well-versed investor will recommend reading and listening to the professionals. Sure, this is a good policy, but in an age where we are bombarded with information, how do you know which pros to take seriously?

Most experts recommend these sources, among others:

- **The Wall Street Journal.** Considered "the" newspaper for business-minded folks; it covers what's happening in the economy and various financial markets (*http://www. wallstreetjournal.com*).

- **Investor's Business Daily.** One of the best sources for keeping abreast of what is going on in stocks and mutual funds. The basis of the economy, banks, and technical funds are also explored, as well as recommendations regarding the hot sectors and the condition of the general economy (*http://www.investors.com*).

- **Fortune** *magazine.* Provides info on very successful companies and business movers and shakers, and advice about the economy (*http://www.fortune.com*).

- **Money** *magazine.* More geared to the general public, *Money* covers financial topics and gives general investment advice (*http://money.cnn.com/magazines/moneymag/*).

- **BusinessWeek.** Check out the editions at the end and beginning of the year, because they recommend the best stocks and mutual funds for the coming year (*http://www. businessweek.com*).

- **USA Today.** A good source of general knowledge, and the "Investment" page provides an overview of the opinions of the country's investment community (http://www.usatoday. com).

- **Mad Money.** There's no shortage of financial pundits on TV, but this popular show on CNBC is hosted by Jim Cramer, who discloses tips on how to value stocks as well as advice on hot sectors and stocks. He's an excellent source of advice for beginning investors. Check local listings for exact times.

- **One up on Wall Street.** There are thousands of investing and financial books out there, but start with this one. Peter Lynch used to run Fidelity Magellan Fund, one of the largest and most successful mutual funds. It's a good introduction to the subject and you can refer back to it as needed.

A FEW MORE TIPS FOR THE SAVVY (OR THOSE WHO WANT TO BE)

Successful investing in the stock market can be summed up in four little words: Buy low, sell high. But how do you actually do that?

Watch the Big Boys

Always keep your eye on **institutional buyers**. They're the groups that actually "move," or impact, the market. Institutional buyers include banks, insurance companies, and holding companies. If you read in a reputable source that these companies are buying several thousand shares of a particular company, chances are that the company's stock will go up in the next day or two.

Smart investors watch what institutional buyers are doing and try to imitate them. Think about it. Banks are out to make money, just like you, so they are very careful which stocks they invest in. Check out *http://www.investors.com* or *http://www.thestreet.com* to see what these big boys are buying—and selling.

Listen Up

Once you've got the basic vocabulary and terms down, read up on the market. Be a sponge. Read and listen to advice, but be willing to make decisions for yourself. (If you're not, no problem—turn to a financial pro. Companies like Edward Jones will help you invest your bucks.) You want to make money, of course, but you also want to balance your portfolio—not have all your investment eggs in one basket—and control risk.

PRACTICE ON PAPER

When you're first starting out, investing can be a little scary. This is real money, remember? That's why it's smart to start by practicing. Begin with a notebook and choose five different stocks from five different sectors such as financials (bank, brokerage houses, mortgage lenders), technology (Intel, Cisco, Microsoft, Google), pharmaceuticals (biotech stocks like Amgen are the fastest-growing sector), defense stocks (Grumman Aircrafts; the group that builds fighter planes), and oil stocks (Apache).

Now you have an imaginary portfolio. Set an imaginary dollar amount (one that you can afford) and decide where you are going to invest specific amounts. Each day, while you are keeping up with your reading and information intake, watch how your stocks are doing and write down your progress as profits and losses. "Play" the market for six months and watch the notes and records you have made. You'll gain confidence and have time to save up your money at the same time. How much to invest is a personal decision that will vary from person to person, but we recommend that you start small—say, $500 to $1000.

THE REAL THING

When you've got your confidence built up and you're ready to ditch the imaginary portfolio for the real thing, try to pick stocks that sell for at least $10 to $15 a share. It's possible to buy stocks for much less ("penny stocks" that really sell for pennies), but stocks that sell for little are at risk of being delisted from the NYSE or the NASDAQ. If the stock is delisted and you can't follow it, it could plummet, taking your hard-earned money with it.

There are a variety of places to buy stocks online; some of the more popular include *http://www.scottrade.com*, *http://www.etrade.com*, and *http://www.ameritrade.com*. Better yet, visit sites like *http://www.thestreet.com*, *http://www.investors.com*, and *http://www.marketbrower.com* for stock quotes and financial news before you buy.

MUTUAL FUNDS

Still sound like too much of a risk? Try a safer way of investing. **Mutual funds** are for the very conservative investor who does not wish to spend a lot of time monitoring his or her investment. Someone else—the **fund manager**—watches and does the homework for you. There is a possibility the yield or return may not be as high as that of investments in the stock market, but the risk is also much less.

You'll find investment advice about mutual funds in the sources listed above, but you may want to check out investment guru Bob Brinker as well. He has over twenty-five years of investment management experience and is the host of *Money Talk*, an AM radio program that can be heard all over the USA and on satellite radio (check local listings). He also recommends books and features authors as guests on his radio show. Brinker can help you pick reliable mutual funds; there are thousands (*http://www.bobbrinker.com*).

Whether you decide to invest a few dollars or a few thousand, you may find that playing the market is an enjoyable hobby—or a way to make some serious cash. Who knows—you might wind up the next Wall Street Wonder!

Design Your Own Clothing

37

Hooked on *Project Runway*, or have a flair for fashion? Lots of would-be clotheshorses dream of designing their own clothing. With a few basic sewing and designing skills, you'll be on your way to creating unique looks for yourself—or maybe even for millions.

YOU NEED MORE THAN GREAT IDEAS

So you want to be the next Donna Karan, Calvin Klein, or Isaac Mizrahi? Good enough. But it takes more than cool ideas to become a designer. You need some basic skills as well. To start with, you've got to have a basic understanding not only of design, but also of fabrics, trims (which include everything from buttons to shoulder pads to zippers to beads), and finishes (what the fabric looks and feels like after it's woven). Do you know what "cut on the bias" means, and why it's so flattering? What's the difference between a dolman and a batwing sleeve? (Ha! Fooled you—they're the same thing.) How do natural and synthetic fabrics differ? Can you recognize the difference between a pattern that is dyed or woven into the material? Did you know that velvet is a finish, not a fabric?

If you don't know your charmeuse from your chiffon, you need to spend more time learning about clothing and design before you try to create your own designs. (To get up to speed, check out the Directory of Fashion Terms, published by Fashiondex Online, at *http://www.fashiondex.com*. At $76, access isn't cheap, but with more than 15,000 fashion terms and their definitions, this directory can help you sound like an established designer even before you hit the big time!)

If you work for someone else, you have a chance to learn these kinds of skills on the job. If you're not working in the fashion field, consider taking sewing classes or spending time at a local fabric store to get acquainted with the different materials you'll be using. That will also help you learn the different properties of the fabrics and how they vary in cost and availability. (Like fashion, fabric trends come and go.) Or check out a fabric or textile trade show, where manufacturers display the new fabrics to designers. Do a Google search; there are fabric trade shows throughout the country at different times of the year.

While you don't have to know how to sew to design, skill with a needle and thread don't hurt. If you're all thumbs, take heart—you can always hire someone to do your stitching.

If you're a relative novice to the design world, consider getting up to speed with some fashion design courses. There are a slew of design schools throughout the country, and some offer online classes as well. You can take classes in a variety of subjects, including but not limited to sewing, computer-based fashion design, pattern drafting, fabric printing, use of textiles, manufacturing, and marketing. If you're serious about making fashion design your career, it may be worth it to pursue a degree in fashion. Even if you don't, you should be able to:

- *come up with new fashion ideas (no fair copying someone else's!)*

- *translate your ideas into sketches*

- *draw and cut patterns*

- *select fabric and trim for garments*

- *work with a flat pattern as well as actually draping it (placing it on a model)*

- *modify and fit the finished garment (and sew the garment, if possible)*

- *know the difference between different fabrics, trims, and other textiles*

- *stay abreast of trends and other happenings in the fashion world*

Check for schools in your area, or visit *http://www.my-career-education.com/fashion-design-schools.htm* or *http://www.design-programs.com/fashion-design.html* for links to programs near you.

CREATING YOUR OWN LOOK

You can't simply copy another designer's look. You have to have your own ideas—your own sensibility. After all, you can't be the next Vera Wang or Giorgio Armani; they've already made their mark on the fashion world. What will yours be?

If you're only designing for yourself, you only have to make yourself happy. But if you're going to design for other people—even a small number—you have to keep your customers in mind as well. First off, who is your customer? Is she a trendy twenty-something? A guy in his thirties who wants to look good without hopping on the metrosexual train? Preteens with weight problems? Or busy suburban moms who want to look good without spending a lot of money?

It takes time to develop your style and your "look." In the beginning, you may try a lot of different things before you stumble onto your signature style. Work on developing your identity and your work will set itself apart from that of your competitors.

While you should be aware of fashion trends, don't allow them to completely dictate what you're doing. Coco Chanel achieved a classic, literally timeless silhouette that has been copied innumerable times but never duplicated. You may want to start with one item and grow your designs from there. Maybe it's a unique purse, a twist on the classic white T-shirt, or a skirt that flatters nearly any body type.

While big-name designers may command most of the media attention, all clothing and apparel are first created by a designer. In fact, the vast majority of clothing designers are names you've never heard of, but chances are you've purchased and worn their stuff.

A fashion designer must have both creative skills (i.e., vision) and technical skills (i.e., ability to execute that vision). Not sure what you should design? The possible lines are practically endless, so narrow your focus to one particular area when you're starting out. Will you design high-profile career suits? Beachwear? Maternity clothes? Baby clothes? Evening dresses?

READY TO LAUNCH YOUR OWN LINE? THINK AGAIN

If you want to design as a career—that is, have a line of your own—it's smart to work for someone else first to gain experience. Designing may look glamorous (all those runway shows and hobnobbing with A-list celebrities!), but launching and running a fashion design business is expensive, time-consuming, and demanding. Quite frankly, most people can't do it. It can take years to develop relationships with people and actually turn a profit. What are you going to live on in the meantime? And if you want to have your own line so you can design full-time, think again. The vast majority of your time will be spent not designing but worrying about production, managing employees, shipping, tracking paperwork, chasing money, and dealing with the inevitable headaches of running your own business. Only a tiny fraction of your time will actually be spent designing.

In fact, nearly all successful designers learned the ropes of the business by working for someone else first. Marc Jacobs designed for Perry Ellis, and Donna Karan worked for Anne Klein. You can learn on the job, and save money to help launch your own line eventually. You can also build connections and develop a reputation that will be invaluable when you launch your own line.

STILL WANT TO DO IT?

If you're convinced you want to run your own design shop, there are a few things to know. Launching a design business takes a significant amount of money. If you're not independently wealthy, you'll need to borrow from friends and family, take bank loans, or look for backers for your business. Once you've secured financing, you need to get to work on your designs.

Have you considered how much work is involved in the actual production process? After you develop your initial designs, you have to choose fabric and create your patterns. Then you sew your **samples**, the garments that are used to place orders.

After you collect orders, you need to purchase enough fabric and materials to produce your collection, finalize your patterns, and adapt for different sizes, if applicable. Then you can actually cut and sew your line. Expect this process to take at least six months, and, since the fashion world basically works around the spring and fall lines, you want to plan on selling your fall line early that year and actually producing the line in spring and summer. If you're designing for spring, you'll start selling your line in the fall of the year before, and produce the clothes that winter.

Hiring Help—and Getting the Look Book

If you know how to make patterns, that's great. You can also hire a professional patternmaker who can alert you to possible flaws and problems. The best design on paper may not work with the particular pattern or fabric you've chosen. Contact a fashion school for a recommendation, or ask more established designers for referrals. If you can't sew, you may also need to hire freelance sewers to design your line.

You'll also need a **look book**, which includes photos of all of the items in your collection. Look for a photographer who has experience in this area. Your look book should be professional yet eye-catching; it's your strongest tool for actually selling your designs.

You'll also need publicity—as much of it as you can get. If you don't hire a publicist (which costs more money), you'll have to do this kind of work on your own, which means you'll spend more time getting your name and your designs out there. All this work may mean that you decide to start off small, designing just for friends, or that you work in the industry while getting ready to launch your own business. Either way, you'll have the satisfaction both of creating and seeing your designs come to life.

Fortunately, there are plenty of Web sites to provide information and help you navigate your way in the fashion world:

- **American Apparel and Footwear Association,** a national trade organization that represents manufacturers of apparel, footwear, and many other sewn products, *http://www.apparelandfootwear.org/*

- **Apparel Job Board,** which lists job openings in the fashion industry, *http://www.appareljobboard.com*

- **Council of Fashion Designers of America,** a nonprofit association of fashion and accessory designers, *http://www.cfda.com*

- **DNR,** the leading magazine covering the men's fashion industry, *http://www.dnr.com*

- **Fashion Career Center,** another place to search for jobs in the fashion biz, *http://www.fashioncareercenter.com*

- **Fashion Group International,** an international nonprofit organization of more than 6,000 people who work in the fashion, accessories, beauty, and home industries, *http://www.fgi.org*

- **Gen Art,** an arts and entertainment organization that showcases new fashion designers and other creative pros, *http://www.genart.org*

- **Women's Wear Daily, or WWD,** the leading trade magazine covering women's fashion, *http://www.wwd.com*

THE FINAL CUT

So, what's your pleasure? Depending on your interests and abilities, you can work in other positions in the field while honing your design skills. Job possibilities range from technical designer to cutter to patternmaker to trend researcher, and your employment options are also wide open. You might work for a retailer, an apparel manufacturer, or for another designer before you decide to go full-time—or you may decide to keep your fashion designing a hobby that brings you pleasure and satisfaction. Even if you don't become the next Tommy Hilfiger or even close, you'll find that you can make a statement with your designs and the way you wear them.

Become a Blogger

38

Your best friend has one. So does your little brother, not to mention pundits, celebrities, and people obsessed with celebrities. These days, there are blogs that cover every topic imaginable, from politics to raw foods to pregnancy to celebrity gossip to Target (Really! Check out Slave to Target's blog at *http://slavetotarget.blogspot.com/*).

If you want to voice your political agenda, highlight overlooked news in your community, talk about your hobby, weigh in on what's happening in the world, or simply have a personal diary for only a select few to read, become a blogger. With a blog you can make your opinions known to as many or as few people as you want.

WHAT THE HECK IS A BLOG?

Blog is simply a cooler way to say "Web log." Simply put, a blog is a customizable journal where the most recent entry appears at the top of the Web page. Often you'll find the ten most recent entries on the page; older ones are accessible by links to archives.

Blog entries can contain any combination of text, pictures, and links to Web sites. And blogs are interactive—

readers can make comments about the entries as well as comment about other readers' comments.

Some blogs are titled; some are not. Many are anonymous, but others include a profile of the author with a photograph or picture. Most include links to other blogs or Web sites. When you build a blog, what you include, and what you omit, is up to you.

THE BIGGEST BLOGS

In 2005, there were at least 4 million blogs on the Internet and the number is skyrocketing. Yet the most popular blogs get thousands—even hundreds of thousands—of hits every month. The vast majority of bloggers are under the age of thirty; in fact, many are teenagers. But both men and women and boys and girls enjoy blogging.

Before you begin, you may want to read some of the most popular blogs out there to get ideas for your own. Check out the following Web sites for lists of popular blogs by number of "hits," or visits:

- http://www.blogarama.com/index.php?show=most_popular Blogarama's list of popular blogs, by number of readers. (Just be warned: The top one hundred all feature naked teenage girls and gay porn.)

- http://www.bloglines.com/topblogs Bloglines' list of most popular blogs.

- http://www.blogstreet.com/top100.html The BlogStreet ranking of top blogs.

- http://www.bloogz.com/rank/ Bloogz Rank constantly analyzes and ranks the most popular blogs.

YOUR BLOGGY'S MOMMA

Ready to join the "blogosphere" of the collective hive of blogs? There are countless Web sites that host blogs. A **host** is simply the site that provides a home for your blog. Many hosts provide the service for free, but often that "free" service means putting up with Internet advertisements. If you decide to go with a fee-based host, make sure you don't have to put up with advertising—or at least not as much of it. Other hosts offer a free service as well as an upgraded fee-based service that offers more options. Before making the upgrade, consider whether you'll use the expanded options.

Here are several host options:

- *Blogger.com* (*http:www.blogger.com*). This is the mack daddy of hosts. Blogger is a member of the Google family. It is entirely free, offers a tremendous amount of options, and has no advertising, unless you choose to have advertising on your site, and is a great place to start your first blog.

- *Livejournal.com* (*http://www.livejournal.com*). This is another popular host that offers free basic access; to receive all possible options, you must pay a fee. At LiveJournal, you can create an extensive profile of yourself with as much or as little personal information as you like. You can then use this information to search for people with similar interests and people can search for you, so it's a great online community if you're looking for online buddies.

- *Deadjournal.com* (*http://www.deadjournal.com*). Yup, a cynical spinoff of LiveJournal, it has many of the same features. The catch is that to join you either need to pay for a membership or obtain an account code, which can only be obtained from existing DeadJournal members.

- *Angelfire.lycos.com* (*http://www.angelfire.lycos.com*). Here, you can build a blog or Web site for free, but you'll have advertisements on your site. For a monthly fee, you can ditch the ads and gain some extra features.

- *Spaces.msn.com* (*http://www.spaces.msn.com*). This is Microsoft's host, which features many of the same options as Blogger and is free. Your blog will have ads at the top and bottom pages, and the service isn't as user-friendly as Blogger.

- *Yahoo360.com* (*http://360.yahoo.com*). This site lets you build a blog, write local reviews, or even have Yahoo 360 automatically post information from one of your other blogs through a feed. The service is free and easy to use.

BIRTHING YOUR BLOG: HOW TO DO IT

So, you've chosen a host. Now what? Let's assume you choose Blogger. Now we'll walk you through the process.

The first step is to create an account. Click on the link called, "Create Your Blog Now." You'll be prompted to choose a user name, password, and display name, give your e-mail address, and check a box to accept the site's terms of service. Your **user name** is essentially the name of your account. This is what you will type in, along with your password, when you log into Blogger to update your blog. People who read your blog will not see this name. Your password ensures that you're the only one in total control of your blog.

For safety's sake, choose a case-sensitive password that contains random letters and numbers. Using your dog's name (or something equally obvious) as your password is a good way to let people into your blog to write silly things that make you look like an idiot.

The **display name** is the name readers will see as the author of the blog. It can be your first and last name or something totally wild—say, "Crazy First Time Blogger Dude." Don't sweat picking the perfect name—you can always change it later. You have to agree to Blogger's terms of service to create a blog; check the box and move on, or be one of the rare few who actually reads the terms of service!

After completing the page, you'll continue on to name your blog. This title will appear at the top, unless you prefer the untitled rebellious look. Then you're asked for your blog address, which will be *http://*[what you enter].*blogspot.com*. You can use whatever address you like, provided it's not already taken. To make it easy, many people prefer to make their address something related to their title.

The next task is to choose a **template**, a preconstructed layout for your blog. After choosing the one you find most appealing, continue—you'll see a screen stating your blog has just been created. Score!

If you'd rather start a blog with another host, you'll see that the setup process is similar. Some hosts promote a community feel where you can meet online pals; others are focused on the privacy of what you write. Hosts like Blogger simply provide a way to get your words out there; anyone can see your posts, and there's no focus on community-building. Hosts have links on their home pages about what they offer; with a little time, you can find a host that fits what you're looking for.

POST IT! YOU'RE ABOUT TO BE PUBLISHED

When you log into your account at Blogger, the first screen you see presents several options. You can search for blogs, learn how to make money through advertising on your blog, read about blogger news, edit your profile, include your picture, and even change your password.

Click on the title of your blog to begin posting. The next screen will list your most recent posts by their titles; each post has an "Edit" button adjacent to it. Click it to make changes to your posts. You can also delete your post entirely.

At the top of the page is the "Create new post" button, which is your ticket to getting published. In the "new post" screen, you'll find a text window where you'll type the content of your post. This screen looks like the screens used in word-processing software; along the top of the text box are options to change the font, font size, text (i.e., bold or italics), and font color, and many other handy formatting tools. At the bottom of the box, you can change the time of your post and decide whether readers will be allowed to post comments about it. Some hosts even allow you to limit who will be able to see the new post; you can make it totally private, viewable to friends you have identified, or viewable to the public.

When you have completed your post, there are two courses of action: save your post as a draft, or publish your post to your blog. If you choose to save it as a draft, Blogger will move your post into the "edit posts" list; however, the post will not be posted on your blog or be viewable to readers. You can access your draft later, edit it, and post to your blog whenever you feel like it. If you publish your post, it will be added to your blog. Sure, you will be able to go back and edit your post if you decide you look like a goof, but no matter how many spelling errors are in it, it will be viewable in the meantime.

Make sure you take advantage of the other settings available. For example, you can make changes to the title of your blog, write a description of it, decide how many posts will be shown, change its appearance, and give other people the ability to post on your blog, among other things.

LET'S BLOG TOGETHER!

At Blogger, you can use **group blogs**, which are great for families or teams of any kind. These provide an online space to share ideas, news, and photos. You can even send Blogger text and picture messages from your mobile phone. Simply send a message to go@blogger.com and the text and picture you send will be stored for you to retrieve later. Blogger will send a text back with a claim code; when you're ready, log on to Blogger and enter your claim code.

Finally, if you want to be heard, or rather read, you need people to actually find your blog. Register it at sites like:

- *Blogarama* (*http://blogarama.com/*)

- *Globe of Blogs* (*http://globeofblogs.com/*)

- *The Open Directory* (*http://dmoz.org/Computers/Internet/On_the_Web/Weblogs/*)

To search for other blogs, try Google's blog search at *blogsearch.google.com*. (Note: If you use any of the major blog hosts, you'll already be listed in Google's blog search.)

That's all there is to it! Now that you've created a blog, you just have to figure out what you want to say. But I assume you'll be able to handle that one on your own.

39

Design Your Own Web Site

So what if there are already more than 64 million Web sites out there? What the World Wide Web is missing is yours—and designing one is easier than you might think. Launch your own Web site and you've got a place to spout off, showcase your talents, meet like-minded friends, display photos of you and your family, or educate the world about your favorite hobby or interest.

BUT I'M NOT A GEEK!

First things first. Why do you want a Web site? Is it going to be a place to showcase recent holiday photos, or do you want the site to share information about one of your interests? Some people have Web sites only devoted to their families; other people "think big" and want to attract as many visitors as possible. The decision is yours. (If you're designing a Web site for your business, you've got other issues to consider. I've got some tips for you later in the chapter. And if you're more interested in having a **blog**, or Web log, I've got a whole chapter dedicated to that, too.)

If your heart is set on a Web site, there are a few basic Web design principles to keep in mind.

Let the Program Be Your Friend

So you're not a techie? No problem. While you can spend hours learning **HTML (hypertext markup language, or coding language)** to create your site, there's a much easier way to do it. There are Web design programs that do the heavy lifting for you. They provide **templates**, or starter documents, to help you design your site. Basically, they walk you through the process page by page; after you enter the required info, graphics, and other data, you'll have a Web site with as many pages as you like that's ready to launch when you are.

The great thing about a Web design program template is that a lot of decisions have already been made for you; you don't have to decide how far down the screen to place navigation buttons, for example. Templates also give your site consistency and address important elements like headlines, headers, and footers that a newbie might forget about.

Keep in mind that a template is just a starting point. Don't be afraid to choose a color scheme and cool elements that will make your site unique and prevent it from looking like every other site out there.

There is such a thing as too much originality, though. For example, a vibrantly colored or busy background may make it hard to read the text on your site. Blinking or flashing text or buttons may look cool, but to most viewers they're simply an annoyance. If you have any questions about your site, ask a couple of your geek friends to check it out before you launch it and go live.

Check out Web design programs like Microsoft's FrontPage (*http://www.microsoft.com*), Sausage Inc.'s HotDog (*http://www.sausage.com*), NetObjects' Fusion (*http://www.netobjects.com*), or

Macromedia's Dreamweaver (*http://www.macromedia.com*) to get started.

What Do You Want to Say?

Here's the thing. Forget how your Web site looks for a minute. Bottom line is that it's what is actually on the site that matters—and makes your site "sticky," meaning it attracts repeat visitors. And when it comes to content, that's totally up to you. That's why you should think about the subject matter you want to cover before or during the design process.

Feeling stuck? Well, if you're designing a Web site about a hobby or interest, think about what someone would want to know about it. Let's say you're into ultramarathons (races of more than 26.2 miles) and you want to build a Web site about the topic. Your site might include:

- *a list of ultramarathons throughout the country or world, with links to each one*

- *a suggested training program, or a description of how you train*

- *photographs from ultramarathons (just don't use gigantic graphics—more about that in a bit)*

- *a rundown on equipment ultramarathoners use*

- *your diary of your personal ultramarathoning experience*

- *links to other relevant sites—say, of other ultramarathoners or running organizations*

See? It's easier than you might think. Check out other Web sites for possible format ideas, and to see what you like and what you don't. You can always take an idea and put your own spin on it.

Streamline Your Site

Just because you have a cable or DSL connection doesn't mean everyone who visits your site does. Some people still have (gasp!) dial-up connections, so don't go crazy with bandwidth, which is eaten up by those super-detailed, eye-popping graphics, and other add-ons like sound and streaming video. In general, the more amazing-looking the graphic, the more bandwidth is required, which means that the page that pops up in just a second on your cable modem connection takes minutes on a dial-up connection. What happens? Would-be visitors get frustrated and move on, and who can blame them?

When designing your Web site, check that each page contains less than 200 kilobytes of graphics. (Web design programs usually have **page stats** on the bottom of each page showing the file size and load times.) That will ensure that your page will load quickly regardless of how a visitor is accessing it.

If you do have a large or detailed image or graphic that you want visitors to see, convert it to a .jpeg or .gif file. You'll lose some detail, but the files will be compressed, which means they're smaller in size and take less time to download. And if you have sound on your Web site, make sure that visitors can easily opt to shut it off.

Finally, make sure the text is large enough to read! It should be at least ten points in size, depending on what type of font you use. Skip the most exotic-looking fonts in favor of something simple and legible.

Help Visitors Find Their Way

Always keep easy navigation in mind as you design your site, meaning that a visitor should know where he or she is on your site and be able to jump to other pages with no problems. The most common navigation setup includes a navigation toolbar at the left-hand side of the page, and another at the top and/or bottom of the page. That lets the viewer quickly move to a different page on your site; speed and ease of getting around are important.

And here's another issue to think about. Just as people access the Net with different types of connections, computers, screen resolutions, and browsers vary as well. What does that mean for you, the fledgling Web designer? That you should make sure your Web site looks decent not only on a twenty-one-inch monitor and a high-speed cable modem connection, but on a fifteen-inch monitor with a dial-up connection as well. If your site has graphics (as opposed to being all text) like clickable images (where the viewer simply clicks on the image to jump to another site), make sure that you have text-based links on the same page. That way, if someone's browser can't "read" the link, the viewer will still have the text-based option.

When you've got your Web site ready to launch, or "go live," consider asking friends who use different browsers or have different screen resolutions to take a look at it to make sure it looks consistent on different setups.

HOW TO GET MORE VISITORS

Designing a Web site takes time and effort, and of course you want people to visit yours, right? After all, if you're only doing it for yourself, you wouldn't have to make it available on the Web. So how can you bring back plenty of repeat visitors?

- **Add new content.** People come back to blogs because they're updated frequently. Consider adding a blog to your site. If you don't, at least update your site regularly—say every week or so, or more often—to get people to return. Readers want new info, so be willing to give it to them.

- **Keep your dates to yourself.** You know those "last up-dated" tags many Web sites include? Unless you're updating your site frequently, they can be a turnoff. A visitor may think a Web site that hasn't been updated in months can't possibly offer relevant info, and surf on his or her merry way.

- **KISS your visitors.** In other words, "Keep it simple, stupid." Web surfers come back to sites that are easy to navigate, read, and enjoy.

- **Think style and substance.** Each Web page should be short, no longer than a couple of typed pages. If you have longer text, break it up into pages, with buttons to navigate forward and back, or use frames to make it easier for visitors to read.

- **Tell them why they want to go there.** You need more than a table of contents to entice viewers to check out your site. Give a little information about each page of your Web site to encourage them to visit it.

- **Skip the Web counters.** You can monitor how many people are visiting your site without making it public knowledge to everyone who visits. If a visitor is only the thirteenth viewer ever, she may never return. (On the other hand, if you have a wildly popular site, a counter advertises that fact!)

- **KISS 'em again.** It bears repeating, not just with navigation but with the various bells and whistles you have to choose from. Streaming audio, animated files, and movies may be more of a nuisance to viewers than you think. Give them an opportunity to choose whether they want to take advantage of all your exciting Web site features—or whether to skip them.

- **Add links, but be choosy.** Adding relevant links to your site makes it more useful for visitors, but when they leave your site they may never return! Choose links carefully, and check them occasionally to make sure they still work and aren't "broken."

CHOOSING YOUR HOST

Don't forget you'll need an **ISP**, or **Internet Service Provider**, and hosting company for your Web site as well. Your ISP may already provide low-cost hosting options, or you can look for others online. Check out *http://www.dslreports.com* for unbiased reports about DSL providers from current and previous subscribers, along with a DSL provider locator feature with pricing and ranking to make it easier for you to make a smart choice. Or do a Google search for "hosting companies," and you'll find sites that offer side-by-side comparisons of the top companies and their offerings of Web, e-mail, and even e-commerce sites.

If you want to register your own domain name for your site (such as *http://www.ultrasrock.com* for the ultramarathoning example we talked about earlier) instead of simply using the site name that your ISP provides, registering your unique domain name on the Internet is easy. Your ISP can probably do this for you; if not, there are Web sites that will do it. Visit *http://www.*

netsol.com to see if your desired site name is available. If not, come up with alternative names (would *http://www.ultrasrule.com* or *http://www.iloveultras.com* work instead?) and see if they're taken. Once you find a unique name, plan to spend about $35 per year for the privilege.

WORK YOUR WEB SITES

If you're hoping to use your Web site to help attract business, keep a few additional tips in mind:

- *List your contact information in prominent places on the Web site.* Include a telephone number and a fax number (if you have one) in addition to your e-mail address; it's smart to include an e-mail link on every page.

- *Don't mix business with pleasure.* If you're a photographer hoping to score more weddings shoots, omit your personal "girls-gone-wild" stuff.

- *Let potential clients know who you are.* Your bio is a great place to highlight your relevant experience and background. Or consider having a "former/current clients" or "testimonials" page, which features the words of happy customers singing your praises. (Ask customers for permission to put their comments online.)

- *Consider an FAQ, or "Frequently Asked Questions," page.* This will tell people about your business, rates, and other relevant info.

- *Market your Web site.* Use your Web address on your business cards and letterhead. And make sure you use

META tags (which describe your site's content) and keywords that will help potential customers find you, and that you submit your site address to different search engines.

Once your Web site is designed and online, expect to hear from visitors. You may even want to consider including a guestbook where viewers can post comments. Either way, you'll have established your own presence on the Web; what you do with it is up to you.

Become a Sailor

40

Want to whip along the high seas under nothing but the harnessed power of the wind—or land a backflip on your windsurfer? Learn to sail and you'll have the power of the wind and sea at your disposal, and look cool doing it, too.

YOUR FIRST STEPS

If you're a sailing novice, you may learn the basics on vacation. Some resorts will give you a crash course and send you out on a floating device with a stick in the air. But let's get real. You want to be a sailor, and that means manning an actual boat.

As graceful as a sailboat looks splitting through the open waters of your nearby ocean or lake, getting it where you want to go isn't as simple as holding a large piece of fabric in the air. Fortunately, there are sailing classes that start with the basics—boating rules and safety tips—and work their way up to teaching you how to sail around the globe.

EDUCATIONAL OPTIONS

There are numerous sail schools scattered across the United States and the rest of the planet. Even if you live in a landlocked state, you may be surprised at the sailing options available. While there are hundreds to choose from, the top two training associations in the United States are the United States Sailing Association (US Sailing) and the American Sailing Association (ASA). Each claims to provide the top training and be the most authoritative sailing voice in the country. Choose either and you're assured quality training with licensed instructors.

Each association has a building-block program that starts with learning to sail a small boat in familiar waters; you can then move up to larger boats in unfamiliar water, fog, or the great blue yonder. Upon completion of one of their courses you'll receive a certificate, and it does more than just look pretty on your wall. The certificate means you've proved yourself competent (to sail, anyway) and can rent sailboats without the pesky owners requiring a "check ride" to prove yourself and your skills.

US Sailing (*http://www.ussailing.org*). US Sailing has its roots in racing, and I'm not talking about the ponies. I'm talking about yacht racing. Originally formed more than a century ago, the organization has gone through name changes, but it became the United States Sailing Association in 1991 to better describe the broader activity of the organization. In other words, while US Sailing remains the governing body of racing in the United States, it is also involved in many other aspects of the sport, including teaching newbies how to master sailing skills.

ASA (*http://www.asa.com*). The American Sailing Association began training sailors in the early eighties, and has taught over 200,000 students since 1983. ASA formed a partnership with the Coast Guard Auxiliary, a volunteer civilian wing of the U.S.

Coast Guard dedicated to nonmilitary duties such as boater education. In fact, the Auxiliary beginner sailing class uses ASA materials.

Finding Your School

Ready to take a class? Both the US Sailing and ASA Web sites include search features that enable you to find sailing schools near you. The best option is to use both to make sure you find all your available options. Once you have a list, make some calls. Narrow your search by asking questions like the following:

- *Does the school teach a US Sailing or ASA program with certified instructors?*

- *When is the class offered?*

- *How many classes must you take to get certified?* (In other words, what's your time commitment?)

- *What type of training boats do they have?*

- *Have their boats been safety-inspected by the U.S. Coast Guard Auxiliary or the United States Power Squadron?* (This is a free service.)

- *Are their courses held in a sheltered bay?* (If you're learning to sail for the first time, you don't want to be out on choppy open water.)

- *Do students have to contend with boat traffic?* Same as above. You want a safe, comfortable learning environment.

- *What about windy or bad weather days?* How are those classes made up?

- *Do they have a dependable rescue boat?*

- *How much time is spent in the classroom versus on the water?* Learning safety rules and sailing terminology is great, but you're there to get actual hands-on skills.

- *Can you provide me with references?* Other students can be a great resource to help you decide on the right school for you.

- *How long has the instructor been teaching classes?* What kind of sailing experience does he or she have?

- *How much is the class?*

Consider the answers to these questions—and others you have—and you'll find the class that's right for you.

ALL ABOUT THE BOAT

You'll learn about boats in class, but here's a brief intro. There are four basic categories of sailboats: small boats, keelboats, windsurfers, and multihulls.

Small Boats

Small boats are the best way to learn the basics of sailing. Obviously, they are far less expensive than the yacht monsters that can tour the world, but that's not what makes them the best for beginners. At under twenty-five feet in length, small boats are less forgiving when sailors make a mistake, and most instructors agree this instant feedback provides the best learning curve.

Here's why: When you correct a mistake or are sailing properly, small boats yield positive results right away. A large boat's momentum and sail size can hide mistakes and changes in the conditions, such as wind direction. Without proper training (and remember, you don't have it yet), these problems could easily go unnoticed until it's too late to correct.

Most small boats are **dinghies**, which are totally open (or "open cockpit"), also called **day sailors**. They may have foredecks and enclosures for gear, but they have no cabin. Most of these small boats can be piloted alone or with one other person; their range of stability can provide anything from a relaxing sail to a wet-and-wild rocker.

If you find yourself in a dinghy, your job is bigger than just piloting the boat. Without a **centerboard** or **keel**, a vertical fin at the bottom of the boat that helps with stability, the people or person in the boat become the stability of the boat. Their weight and where they position themselves make the difference between cruising along the water and taking a dip. (Don't worry. Most sailing schools have dumping-practice day, during which you learn to right your boat after it has tipped over.)

Keelboats

Keelboats start at around twenty feet in length and range all the way to the size of massive yachts. They are called "keelboats" because of the weighted keel, the vertical fin at the bottom of the boat. The weight and size of the keel is enough to counterbalance the effects of the wind in the sails.

The first class of keelboats is the **basic keelboat**, which is twenty to thirty feet in length. These boats have one mast and a self-bailing cockpit, and most also have a small outboard motor for docking purposes. Most basic keel boats have an enclosed cabin below deck. This may be a storage area or can include bunks, a toilet (or "head"), water tanks, and a small kitchen.

The next class is the **cruising keelboat**. Ranging from thirty to sixty feet, these boats all have auxiliary engines, most of which are inboard diesels. Cruising keelboats can spend multiple days at sea and have the same facilities you can find in your own home. Before you become a modern-day Magellan though, you should know what you're doing. The good news? Both US Sailing and the ASA offer a seven-step keelboat training process, starting with the basic keelboat.

Windsurfers

Windsurfers are the extreme-sports addition to a craft hundreds of years old. You don't have to do backflips on your surfer—it can actually provide a calm ride. Essentially, a **windsurfer** is a fiberglass board, much like a surfboard, with a rotating sail attached. The rider stands on the board and holds onto a handle built off the sail.

The size of the board varies by width and length. For beginners, the longer and wider the board the better, because a longer and wider board is more stable. You'll find that many resorts rent windsurfers with little instruction, but whether you're renting or buying (windsurfers are the cheapest sailboats), it can't hurt to get some reliable instruction. Fortunately, US Sailing offers a class just for you budding windsurfers, or even those who want to brush up on tricks and skills.

Multihulls

As the name implies, **multihulls** are simply vessels with more than one hull. There are two basic varieties: **catamarans**, which have two hulls, and **trimarans**, which have three. These boats can literally be any size from nine to one-hundred feet. Most catamarans run between thirteen and twenty-one feet. Often called "beach cats," these boats are light and fast.

Once over twenty-one feet, there are countless varieties of cats and tris. The extra hulls eliminate the need for keels, so many are built to be lightweight racers. Others are built heavy and make use of the larger deck space; these ships are designed more for a relaxing cruise. And wouldn't you know it? Lessons are available for sailing these multihull beauties as well.

TALK LIKE A SAILOR

Now that you've got the basics of the boats down, let's drop some sailing lingo into the mix. Everyday language is peppered with boating terminology (for example, **aboveboard** literally means "above the deck," or "in plain sight"), but here are some terms you'll probably need to know:

AFT: in the direction of the stern of the boat

AHOY: nautical for "Hey!"

BACKSTAY: a cable that secures the mast to the rear of the boat

BOOM: a pole (or "spar") attached to the mast and the bottom of the mainsail

BOW: the front of the boat

CAPSTAN: a wheel that rotates to reel in heavy objects

CAREEN: to tilt the boat on its side; this can be intentional (to clean the hull, for example)

FATHOM: nautical term of measurement denoting six feet

FOOT: the bottom of a triangular sail

HEAD: the top of a triangular sail

JIB: a triangular sail set ahead of the mainsail

LANYARD: a short rope used to fasten something

LEAGUE: another nautical term of measurement denoting three nautical miles

LEE SIDE: the side of the boat opposite from the wind

LIST: the amount the boat is leaning to one side

MAINSAIL: the biggest or most important sail on a boat

PORT: in the direction of the left side of the boat

RIGGING: the masts, sails, and other equipment used to sail the ship

SCUPPERS: holes in the side rail that let water run off the deck

STARBOARD: toward the right side of the boat

STERN: the rear of the boat

WINDWARD: the direction the wind is coming from

ADDITIONAL RESOURCES

Other than the Web sites of US Sailing, *http://www.ussailing.org*, and the ASA, *http://www.asa.com*, here are a few more online resources to learn about the art and sport of sailing:

- **http://www.sailnet.com.** Buy all kinds of neat gadgets and gear for your boat and sailing experiences here. Check out the site's features, where seasoned sailors write about everything from learning to sail, to buying a boat, to racing. The site also provides cool services like a boat manager, message boards, and classifieds.

- **http://nws.cgaux.org/index.html.** This is the U.S. Coast Guard Auxiliary's home page. Look into its boating education classes and find out how to get a free vessel safety check. You can even learn how to join the volunteer group.

- **http://www.sailing.org.** This is the home page of the International Sailing Federation. Stay up-to-date on the current racing action, from windsurfers and dinghies to keelboats to multihulls—now that you know what they all are.

- **http://www.usps.org.** The United States Power Squadron is a nonprofit organization whose goal is to make boating safer and more pleasurable through education. Look into this site for classes and how to help make your boating as safe as possible.

BON VOYAGE!

Once you've learned to sail, you'll probably want to get on the water every chance you get. You'll find that sailing is an art and a skill, and you may enjoy it so much you wind up becoming a boat owner yourself. Can't afford it? Just rent one when you can—or hang out at the dock or harbor until you become best friends with a multihull or keelboat owner.

Master Poker

Ever fantasized about living in a mansion in Vegas and driving your Porsche to the casinos for a few short hours to make a living? While it takes years of practice to become a poker master, you can become a decent player fairly quickly. And the sooner you start, the sooner you'll be big time.

THE RULES OF THE GAME

As Kenny Rogers once said, "You got to know when to hold 'em, know when to fold 'em." Understanding the rules of the game is the first step to becoming a player.

What Tops What?

There are several types of poker games, the most popular of which are Texas Hold 'em, Omaha, Stud, Razz, and Draw. The first three are the ones most commonly played in casinos. Regardless of what style you're playing, the way a hand wins is the same—that is, regardless of the number of cards available to you, the best five-card combination wins.

Surprisingly, the best hand doesn't always have to be the strongest. In **high/low poker**, for example, the strongest five-card combo wins half the pot; the weakest five-card combo wins the other half. Hence the name, "high/low."

So what beats what? Possible winning combinations are described below, from weakest to strongest:

High card. If you don't have any of the other hands, you have to beat the other players with your highest card. The ace is the highest card in the deck, followed by the king, queen, jack, and the numbers ten to two in reverse order. If two players have the same high card, the person who has the second-highest card wins.

Pair. Any pair of cards beats any high card. Obviously, a pair of jacks beats a pair of eights. If two people have the same pair, the person with the highest third card wins; this card is often known as the "kicker."

Two pair. Two is better than one. If more than one player has two pairs, the pot goes to the player with the highest pair. In other words, aces and twos beat kings and queens. Ties are once again decided by the kicker.

Three of a kind. Three of a kind of the same card is better than just a pair or two pair.

Straight. A straight is five cards in consecutive order. If two players have straights, the pot goes to the person who has the highest straight; for example, queen/jack/ten/nine/eight beats ten/nine/eight/seven/six. If two players have the same straight, the pot is split between them.

Flush. A flush is five cards of the same suit. In the event of two flushes, the highest card in the flush takes the pot.

Full house. A full house is three of a kind combined with a pair—for example, king/king/eight/eight/eight. If two people have full houses, the pot goes to whoever's set of three is higher. So, ace/ace/ace/two/two beats king/king/king/queen/queen. If the players have the same three-card combination, the one with the higher two cards wins.

Four of a kind. Like it sounds, this is four of the same card.

Straight flush. This is five cards in consecutive order, like a straight, and of the same suit, like a flush.

Royal flush. This is the highest possible hand, ace/king/queen/jack/ten, all of the same suit. If you get one, take a picture—it will likely be years before you see another.

PLAY LIKE A TEXAN

While there are a variety of poker styles, Texas Hold 'Em is the most popular game in casinos and television—and it's time you learned it. Texas Hold 'Em can be played with two to ten players. With the exception of tournament play, there is no **ante**, or amount you have to put in the pot to start play, in Texas Hold 'Em. Instead there are two forced bets called **blinds**.

The blinds are posted by the two players to the left of the dealer. In a casino the dealer doesn't move, so a large disk called the **dealer button** sits in front of the person who has the dealer's position. This essentially means the person gets dealt last and plays last during the betting rounds. After each hand, the button rotates to the next player in a clockwise fashion and, thus, the blinds rotate as well. The person to the left of the dealer's button is the **small blind** and the next player is the **big**

blind. The amount of the small blind is usually half that of the big blind.

In Texas Hold 'Em you get two down cards, known as **hole cards**. These are the cards that are exclusively yours, and no other players can see them. After the blinds are out (i.e., the opening bets are on the table) and the hands are dealt, the first round of betting occurs. The person to the left of the big blind is first to act. This position is said to be **under the gun**.

After the first round of betting is complete, the dealer places one card face down. This is known as a **burn** card. You'll never see or be able to use a burn card. Then the dealer deals three cards faceup in the middle of the table, known as the **flop**: These are community cards that can be used by anyone. After the flop, there is another betting round, starting with the player to the left of the dealer's button.

The dealer then burns another card and deals one card, called the **turn** or **fourth street**, faceup. After another round of betting, a burn and a final community card are dealt; the latter is called the **river**, or **fifth street**. After the river, there is a final round of betting; if there are players still remaining, their cards are revealed in a showdown.

Betting the Farm (or Not)

Let's talk about the betting itself. During a round of betting, players have four options: fold, bet, call (or check), and raise. By **folding**, you toss your hand away and are out of the game until the next hand. If the first person to act in a betting round wants to bet, he or she puts money into the pot. The other players, in order, can now choose to fold, call, or raise. If they **call**, they put in the same amount of money as the bet. If they want to put more money in the pot, they **raise**.

After a raise, the player who initially bet then has to decide if he or she wants to fold, call the raise, or reraise. During the first round of betting in hold 'em, players have to at least call the big blind if they want to see the flop. After the flop, if the first player to act does not want to bet, he or she can check. A **check** is basically like a pass; because no one bet before them, they are not obligated to put in money to stay in the hand. If everyone in the hand checks, the next card is dealt; if everyone checks on the river then there's a showdown.

What Are Your Limits?

With Texas Hold 'Em, there are three types of betting limits: limit, pot limit, and no limit. In a **limit** game, there is an exact amount that players can bet and raise. In the first two rounds of betting, before and after the flop, the amount is equal to the big blind. In the last two rounds of betting, the limit is double the big blind. For example, if the blinds are $5 and $10, the player under the gun can fold, call $10, or raise $10, making his or her bet $20. The next player to act can then fold, call $20 (if the first player raised to $20), or raise another $10 to $30, and so on. After the turn has been dealt, the first player to act can check (there is no need to fold if there hasn't been a bet), bet $20, or raise $20, making the total bet $40. Most limit games allow a maximum of four raises.

In pot-limit hold'em, players are allowed to raise the total amount of the pot. So if the blinds are $5 and $10, the initial pot before betting is $15. The player under the gun can fold, call $10, or raise up to $15, making the bet $25. Players are not obligated to bet the pot, but the minimum bet is the size of the big blind.

Here's an example. Let's say the player under the gun raises by $15. The pot is then $40, because the blinds are equal to $15 and the player raised the pot for a total of $25, making it $40. The next player can fold, call $25, or raise up to $40. If this player wants to raise, he or she has to raise a minimum of what the previous raise was—in this case, $15.

No-limit is pretty simple: Players can bet any amount at any time. The player under the gun can fold, call the big blind, or bet any portion of his or her chips. If a player bets everything they have, they move **all in**. Again, the minimum bet is the big blind; if someone wants to reraise, they have to raise at least the same amount as the previous raise.

LEARN FROM THE EXPERTS

Of course, there's a lot more to playing poker than simply knowing the rules. You've got to develop a feel for reading people's body language, looking for **tells** (gestures that give away someone's hand), and developing a betting strategy. You can become a better player by spending some time with these resources:

- *Doyle Brunson,* Doyle Brunson's Super System: A Course in Power Poker *(Cardoza, 1979),* the first great poker strategy book.

- Harrington on Hold 'em: Expert Strategy for No Limit Tournaments: Strategic Play, Volumes 1 and 2 *(Two Plus Two, 2004),* considered by many pros the best book ever on the subject, but geared more toward experienced players.

- *Mike Caro,* Caro's Book of Poker Tells *(Cardoza, 2003),* covers strategy and figuring out what competitors are holding.

- *David Sklansky,* The Theory of Poker *(Two Plus Two, 1994),* addresses the psychological, mathematical, and chance aspects of playing poker.

- *Barry Greenstein,* Ace on the River: An Advanced Poker Guide *(Last Knight, 2005),* covers how to play the game and describes life as a professional poker player.

In addition, there are countless books on the subject of poker, many written by other top professionals who play on TV in the World Series of Poker on ESPN or the World Poker Tour. Pay a visit to *http://twpplustwo.com,* a free Web site run by the publishers of Sklansky's books. It's a new resource for poker players and provides several message boards for poker players to communicate online.

PRACTICE YOUR PLAY

Sure, you can play with friends, but there are also online servers that provide poker gaming. Nearly all have free-play options. In most cases, after you sign up, the server allots you play money that you can use in tournaments or ring (nontournament) games. If you run out, the play money can be refilled.

The disadvantage is that, because no real money is on the line, many players play recklessly. These games don't accurately reflect the type of play you'll see at casinos or even in most home games. If you decide to deposit money at one of these sites, you'll find the play becomes more serious, with the exception of some of the small-limit games, and small buy-in tournaments. Either way, spending some time online will help your game. The more hands you see and play, the better you will become.

Of course, I have to note that online gambling is illegal in most areas of the United States. (Obviously, if you're using play money, there's no problem.) However, most players consider online play with real money as driving 56 mph in a 55 mph zone. The government has never acted against online players, and many live solely on their online income in areas where it's illegal. While the risk is currently low, it should be considered, so check your local laws before depositing money.

Here are a few of the more popular sites:

- **http://www.pokerstar.com** This is where both 2004 and 2005 World Series Main Event Champions Chris Money-maker and Greg Raymer won their entries into the tournament.

- **http://www.fulltiltpoker.com** Many top professionals who have earned fame by playing in televised tournaments play on this site regularly.

- **http://www.paradisepoker.com** A popular site with a tropical theme.

- **http://www.partypoker.net** One of the largest poker sites; you don't have to look far to find some action.

Finally, for a well-rounded game, you need a well-rounded poker background. This means studying the game, learning strategy, and playing lots of hands. And, of course, calling on Lady Luck doesn't hurt either.

Get on a Reality Show

42

You don't need a pretty face anymore to be noticed in Hollywood. As a matter of fact, put on a few hundred extra pounds or develop an affinity for creepy animals or outlandish stunts, and you might wind up on *The Biggest Loser* or *Fear Factor*.

WHY GET REAL?

What's your reason for wanting to get on a reality show? Maybe you have a secret desire to exist in bitter animosity with total strangers on a desert island—or to live in a really cool house and get drunk, naked, horny, and angry—all on camera—again with total strangers.

There are also people who look at reality TV as their way to break into showbiz. It's not completely unrealistic. After all, people will recognize your face around town after seeing it week after week on TV, and that could lead to other careers. Take Jacinda Barrett from *Real World: London*. She's made an acting career for herself starring opposite John Travolta and Joaquin Phoenix in the movie *Ladder 49*, and she's nabbed other acting contracts after that big break. A reality show can be one way to break into Hollywood, even if you just wind up doing commercials for NutriSystem™ like Zora from *Joe Millionaire* did.

Finally, there are those who see a reality show as a chance to get something they either need or want and wouldn't be able to get otherwise—like a new house, a new face, or a chance to travel around the world. If that sounds like you, there may be a reality show that fits the bill.

ARE YOU REAL ENOUGH FOR REALITY TV?

There are two main ways to get on one of these shows. Either they notice you and ask you (rare), or you apply to them (much more likely). Most reality show stars wind up there by applying, but you may not have to be anyone extra-special to get on. For example, Tyson Mao, a Caltech astrophysics student and Rubik's Cube champion, was recruited to appear on *Beauty and the Geek*, a show in which eight beautiful and social women are teamed up with eight supposedly socially handicapped geeks to try to win a $250,000 grand prize.

Mao had heard of the casting calls on a Rubik's Cube Internet forum, but had decided against trying out because of the two-week filming period. Geek to the core, he didn't want it to interfere with his studies. That was before a producer at the show e-mailed him after finding him through Caltech Chess Club correspondence and encouraged him to try out. He did, and made it on the show.

Usually, however, producers don't come to you. You have to go to them and apply. This process can be relatively simple, or more complicated, depending on the show. You can attend an open casting call where you simply show up and try to wow the producers. Otherwise, you generally need to send in an application (you can usually find them online) along with a short video of yourself.

The sophistication required of your video varies. For example, if you want to work for Trump, *The Apprentice* asks you to make a video to "wow" and "dazzle" the producers while guiding them through a memorable tour of your life. (How many of us have lives that are really all that memorable on a day-to-day basis?) On the other hand, *Fear Factor* asks for a five-minute video explaining why you and your partner would be good candidates for the show. (The more outrageous—within reason—and memorable you are, the better. They're looking for drama, remember?)

To find out what each show wants, visit its official Web site; every show has one now. Do a Google search or check out:

- **http://www.realityblurred.com** for info on a ton of reality shows, including recent updates.

- **http://www.realityshows.com** gives a rundown of both current and past reality shows and includes a page for shows that are currently casting, at *http://www.realityshows.com/castingcalls.htm*.

- **http://www.RTVstar.com** strives to simplify the tedious reality show application process. Brian Ostrovsky, who actually won a coveted spot on *The Apprentice* but missed the deadline due to work and school (oops!), launched the site. Hopefuls can post profiles and videos into a database that is available to more than eighty reality TV casting professionals.

But don't just wait to be discovered; make sure you pursue the shows you're really interested in. Follow the directions, and make sure that your application and video make a strong case for why you're the perfect candidate for the show.

WHICH ONE'S RIGHT FOR YOU?

Think of a subject, and chances are there's a reality show about it. Whether it's treasure hunting, decorating your house, looking for a date, or applying for a job that you're interested in, you can find it all on reality TV. While there are dozens of shows to choose, here's a short sample of a few in the giant vat of reality show soup.

The Amazing Race

Got a thin wallet but a yen to travel the world? *The Amazing Race* (h*ttp://www.cbs.com/primetime/amazing_race6/*) recruits teams to travel the globe on a quest to solve a puzzle for a $1 million prize, circumnavigating roadblocks, detours, and other obstacles along the way. A typical mission might involve starting in New York City, flying to South Africa, and then having to make your way through extreme conditions to reach other destinations in Africa. Teams can consist of married couples, families, best friends, or other combinations.

The Apprentice

"You're fired!" If the idea of having one of America's biggest business tycoons say this to you in front of millions of television viewers doesn't bother you, look no further! Twelve contestants from various career and educational backgrounds are selected to compete as Donald Trump's apprentices for one year, for a salary of over $200,000. They're divided into two teams that compete against each other on various business projects that range from creating an ad campaign for a private jet company to being judged by an airline's executives to working with celebrities on charity auctions to raise money. Each week a contestant (or two or three) is "fired" until one lucky sap gets to become The Donald's new henchman or henchwoman (*http://www.nbc.com/nbc/The_Apprentice_3/*).

The Biggest Loser

This show's name is kind of a misnomer, because if you can win, you've not only won $250,000, but possibly your health and your life back. This show targets severely overweight people and has them compete against one another to lose weight. Contestants are offered ten weeks with two motivational personal trainers, all meals, and a weekly stipend. Whoever loses the most weight at the end (the biggest loser—get it?) wins. This show also offers special editions such as a family competition (*http://www.nbc.com/The_Biggest_Loser/*).

Fear Factor

Teams of two compete against each other by doing all sorts of weird and unnerving activities—from being buried alive to having rats crawl all over them while they're blindfolded—to win cash prizes. These teams can be different sets of people; depending on the show, they may be twins, couples, or siblings. If you've got a strong stomach or nerves of steel (or both), this may be the show for you (*http://www.nbc.com/Fear_Factor/*).

Project Runway

Skilled with a needle and thread and have great fashion sense? Supermodel Heidi Klum developed *Project Runway*, a unique reality show. For ten weeks, up-and-coming fashion designers compete in weekly challenges. The three finalists are given all the resources a top fashion designer would have to prepare for a competitive runway fashion show for the next New York Fashion Week. The prize is $100,000, a fashion spread in *Elle* magazine, and a mentorship from Banana Republic (*http://www. bravotv.com/Project_Runway/*).

Queer Eye for the Straight Guy

Not a metrosexual? You can become one with a little help. A team of gay guys (the "Fab Five") will come to your house to make you over, get rid of your unibrow and back hair, and teach you how to dress, cook, decorate, and entertain. Occasionally, the Fab Five even stray to helping women and other gay guys get with the program (*http://www.bravotv.com/Queer_Eye_for_the_ Straight_Guy/*).

The Real World

This is one of the original reality shows. As MTV puts it, it's the "true story of seven strangers picked to live in a house and have their lives taped." The chosen seven live in a totally hip house in a cool city, usually in the United States, but some seasons have been filmed in Europe as well. The roommates are supposed to work on some kind of project that somehow benefits the community they live in, but really the show usually ends up being a lot of arguing, gossip, fighting, flirting, and sometimes even fornicating, all on camera (*http://www.mtv.com/onair/realworld/*).

Road Rules

In this series, six twenty-somethings (three guys and three gals) travel across the country on various missions in a quest for cash and prizes. They are given a definite route and MTV funds the trip; they don't have to front the money themselves (*http://www.mtv.com/onair/rwrr_challenge/inferno/*).

Supernanny

Are your kids—or someone else's—little terrors? Maybe it's time to call in *Supernanny* (*http://abc.go.com/primetime/supernanny/*). Jo Frost, an English nanny, will come to your house for a week and work with you and your kids to get them to behave. While teaching the kids manners, she also shows the adults how to be better parents. You'll learn how to remain in control once she's gone without a whip and a chair. The prize? Less screaming, fewer meltdowns, and a home you can actually invite people to—now that they won't want to run screaming into the streets within five minutes!

Survivor

This one is not for the faint-of-heart. Eighteen Americans are deposited into some of the most unforgiving places on the globe, such as an island off the coast of Thailand, with virtually no creature comforts. They are divided into teams, or "tribes," and participate in tough challenges (e.g., standing still in the baking sun with one hand on a post all day, without moving). Every three days, the losing tribe must vote members of its team "off the island." Alliances end up forming among people who are left, and this is when the drama begins. Eventually, when enough people are gone, the tribes merge into one, making it every player for him- or herself. A jury is formed, and it ends up coming down to two people, one of whom is voted out by the other participants. The prize for the survivor is a whopping $1 million (*http://www.cbs.com/primetime/survivor2/*).

Trading Spaces

Is your house in desperate need of a makeover? Maybe some friends or neighbors feel the same way about their house. If so, why not call in the professionals! To qualify for this show, you must have friends or neighbors who live within a ten- to fifteen-minute drive and want parts of their house redone as well, because two different residences are worked on during each episode. You must have three rooms per residence available to renovate, and each team works on the other party's home (literally trading spaces) with professionals there to guide them. The prize? A new look for part of your home—hopefully one you like (*http://tlc.discovery.com/fansites/tradingspaces/tradingspaces.html*).

Getting on a reality show takes some time and effort, but with dozens to choose from, you may just find that you're the flavor of the month. Even if you get voted off immediately, you'll have a great story to tell your grandkids someday.

Become a Vegetarian

43

Chances are you know someone who's a vegetarian. Maybe your best friend recently announced she's given up all animal products or one of your coworkers is avoiding meat for health reasons. Perhaps you've flirted with the idea of a vegetarian diet, but the idea of soy balls or tofu treats for dinner doesn't thrill you. Or you're not sure what you'd replace your regular chicken sandwich with every day.

But vegetarian diets are becoming increasingly popular—in the United States, about 5 percent, or 15 million, Americans say they don't eat meat, poultry, or seafood. Millions more have reduced the amount of meat they eat. The good news is that today's vegetarians have many more choices than before. The days of subsisting on tofu and bean sprouts are over. Besides, a veggie diet may be cheaper, more environmentally sound, and better for your health as well.

GOING VEGETARIAN:
PROS AND CONS

Health is the number-one reason cited for going vegetarian. A plant-based diet can add years to your life, and vegetarians have a lower risk than meat-eaters of many diseases including heart disease, high blood pressure, diabetes, digestive disorders, and asthma. Even the American Dietetic Association has stated that vegetarian diets provide health benefits to prevent and treat certain diseases.

It makes sense when you think about it. Fruits, vegetables, and whole grains are loaded with vitamins, minerals, fiber, and phytochemicals (natural plant substances), yet are low in fat. In their natural state, these foods don't contain cholesterol (which comes from animal products), preservatives, or chemicals. Base your diet on them or around them and, because they're naturally low in calories, you'll also find it easier to lose or maintain your weight.

Some people become vegetarian for humanitarian or religious reasons. For example, both Buddhism and Islam promote vegetarianism. Other people do it to help save the planet. They cite ecological concerns, pointing out that a plant-based diet uses up fewer natural resources than a meat-based one. For example, it takes about sixteen pounds of grain to produce just one pound of beef. It's also cheaper to grow vegetables than to raise cattle; as a result, it's less expensive to eat a plant-based diet than one centered around animal products.

Whatever your reasons for becoming a vegetarian, you can expect to encounter some resistance from others in your life, especially if you've grown up eating meat. In our culture, meat-eating is the norm. You may face pressure from friends, family members, or even coworkers, and may have to learn how to diplomatically refuse turkey at Thanksgiving, much to your mom's chagrin, or how to respond to friends who tease you about being "off hamburgers" or who insist that animals were put on Earth for us to eat.

The best approach is not to make a big deal out of your diet, and to have a few standard responses for work, family, and social situations. "I'm trying to eat healthier" is a good answer to nearly every obnoxious question; if people are truly interested, you can always go into more detail about your diet.

LACTO-OVO WHAT? TALKING VEGETARIAN

Even the label "vegetarian" can be confusing. Some people call themselves vegetarians because they don't eat beef; others eliminate all meat but continue to eat eggs and dairy products. Here's a short list of common terms:

FRUITARIAN: a person who only eats plant foods that can be harvested without killing the plant (such as apples, oranges, and green beans)

LACTO VEGETARIAN: a person who doesn't eat meat, poultry, eggs, or fish but does eat dairy products like milk, yogurt, and butter

LACTO-OVO VEGETARIAN (OR OVO-LACTO VEGETARIAN): a person who doesn't eat meat, poultry, or fish but does eat eggs and dairy products (Lacto-ovo vegetarians are probably the most common "type" in the United States.)

MACROBIOTIC: refers to a diet that eliminates nearly all processed foods and focuses on unrefined, unprocessed foods like beans, whole grains, seaweed, some vegetables, and fermented foods like soy sauce and miso (While macrobiotics and vegetarianism are sometimes thought of as the same practice, a veggie may not practice macrobiotics, and a macrobiotic-diet follower may eat fish occasionally.)

MISO: a thick fermented paste made from soybeans; also called "bean paste" (It's used in sauces and soups.)

PESCETARIAN: a person who doesn't eat meat or poultry but does eat fish

SEITAN: also called "wheat gluten" or "wheat meat," a product created by soaking, kneading, and boiling high-gluten wheat flour (Seitan and tofu are common meat substitutes.)

SEMI-VEGETARIAN: a person who has cut back on meat or poultry consumption, or may not eat red meat (Not considered a true vegetarian.)

TOFU: a high-protein food created from soybean curd; often used as a meat substitute

TEMPEH: a high-protein food created from partially cooked, fermented soybeans (It has a stronger taste and firmer texture than its cousin, tofu.)

VEGAN: a person who eats no animal products, including honey, and usually avoids wearing animal products (e.g., leather) as well (When used to describe a food, it means that it contains no animal products of any kind.)

VEGETARIAN: a person who doesn't eat foods containing meat, poultry, or fish, and may not eat dairy products or eggs as well

(When used to describe a food, it usually means that the food contains no meat, poultry, or fish.)

VEG OR VEGGIE: short for "vegetarian."

BEYOND ICEBERG LETTUCE: EATING OUT

In the past, it was more difficult to find vegetarian options when dining out. Happily, that's less of an issue today. Restaurant owners are realizing that many people are seeking veggie dishes, and now even small-town restaurants may feature hummus, soy burgers, or even tabbouleh, a Middle Eastern salad made from cracked wheat.

Start with the menu, but don't stop there. Most restaurants are happy to cater to your dietary desires. Ask questions about the ingredients and the way dishes are prepared. For example, many vegetable soups may have a chicken or beef base or contain small pieces of bacon and ham. If you can't find anything on the menu that sounds appealing, ask if the cook can prepare a dish just for you.

Eating breakfast out? Opt for oatmeal, muffins, toast with jam, cereal with soy or rice milk, pancakes, veggie sausage or bacon, and fruit; lacto-ovo veggies can enjoy scrambled eggs or a vegetable omelet.

For a quick lunch, look for a veggie burger (many restaurants now offer a veggie version of the standard hamburger) or soy dog. Look for dishes based on beans or vegetables, which are often vegetarian. Bean burritos or enchiladas, vegetarian chili or vegetarian soups, grilled vegetable sandwiches, stir-fried vegetables, hummus in a pita, and portabella mushroom sandwiches are all delicious choices. Start with a salad of spinach or mixed greens and add as many vegetables, beans, and other toppings (sunflower seeds, anyone?) as you like. Add a hearty pumpernickel roll and you'll never miss the meat.

At dinner, look for pastas that feature vegetables (such as veggie or spinach lasagna or pasta primavera) or stir-fried dishes; often you can ask your server to simply skip the chicken or beef in favor of extra veggies. Even steakhouses offer a variety of side dishes ranging from baked potatoes to macaroni and cheese to steamed broccoli. Don't be afraid to ask for what you want—you'll probably get it.

STOCKING UP: THE VEGETARIAN KITCHEN

At the grocery store, you're likely to find dozens of veggie versions of everything from hot dogs to chicken nuggets—and they're surprisingly yummy! Most stores have an entire section with meat substitutes including ham, turkey, bologna, and four or five different types of grilled and flavored tofu. In the dairy case, there are now refrigerated soy milks, soy yogurt, and soy cheese. Other vegetarian or vegan foods may contain TVP, (texturized vegetable protein) and other plant-based proteins.

If you choose not to eat meat, there are plenty of easy ways to do so. Order cheese pizza instead of sausage, or try spinach lasagna rather than the meat version. If you take a lunch to work, it's simple to use soy bologna or turkey instead of the "real thing." Manufacturers like Morningstar Farms, Boca Burgers, and Amy's all offer delicious vegetarian selections of foods like "chicken" pot pies, bacon, and ground beef as well.

NUTRIENT KNOW-HOW:
GETTING ENOUGH

However, simply giving up meat doesn't guarantee that you'll eat healthier than someone who includes hamburgers and chicken as part of their regular diet. After all, Coke and french fries are vegetarian, but that doesn't mean you can live well on them! It's important to eat a variety of fruits, vegetables, and whole grains, and to make sure you're getting enough protein from nonanimal sources.

Basic principles of nutrition still apply, so that means limiting junk food like chips, soda, candy, and high-fat fast food, and focusing on including a variety of fruits and vegetables, whole grains, and nonanimal protein sources. A well-balanced diet will provide most of the nutrients you need, but vegetarians, especially vegans, may need to pay special attention to getting enough of the following nutrients:

- *Calcium.* This nutrient helps build and maintain bone. Aim for the recommended dietary allowance of 1,000 to 1,300 milligrams per day of calcium. (A cup of nonfat milk has 300 mg of calcium; a one-ounce slice of cheddar cheese, 204 mg.) This usually isn't difficult for lacto-ovo vegetarians, but vegans may need to focus on getting large servings of calcium-rich foods like collard greens and kale, or include fortified soy milk or calcium-fortified orange juice to make sure they're getting enough.

- *Vitamin B_{12}.* Vegans in particular may not get enough vitamin B_{12}, which helps form red blood cells, because it's found in animal products. If you're a vegan, you'll need to rely on a supplement or B_{12}-fortified foods like cereals or Red Star Nutritional Formula yeast to consume enough.

- *Iron.* Iron helps deliver oxygen to all the cells in the body and is particularly important for women who menstruate every month. However, it's easy to get enough iron in a vegetarian diet; foods like blackstrap molasses, broccoli, raisins, spinach, chickpeas, and pinto beans all supply this nutrient. Eating foods high in vitamin C at the same time helps your body absorb iron.

- **Protein.** While nonvegetarians wonder how veggies get their protein, it's actually easy to consume sufficient protein. Assuming you choose a reasonable variety of foods in your diet and get enough calories to meet your energy needs, it's pretty easy to get enough protein. Good sources of protein include cheese, yogurt, milk, eggs, beans, nuts, tofu, chickpeas, peanut butter, and soy products like soy bologna, turkey, and "chicken" nuggets. Your body can't distinguish between animal and nonanimal protein, but active women need more than sedentary women for muscle growth and repair—about 1.2 to 1.4 grams of protein per kilogram of body weight, more if you're trying to gain muscle.

MAKING THE TRANSITION

Want to try a vegetarian diet? Some people go cold turkey and simply give up meat entirely. You may find it easier instead to ease into it by gradually reducing the amount of meat you're currently consuming. A serving of meat is about the size of a pack of playing cards, but most people eat far more than this at a sitting. Start serving yourself smaller amounts, and when dining out, try eating only a portion of your meal.

As you do so, experiment with meatless meals. Select dishes that usually don't include meat, or make one with some of the meat substitutes available. There are "hamburger" and "turkey" versions you can use for meatloaf, meatballs, and chili recipes. Some simple ways to do this include:

- *Replace meats with protein sources like beans, tofu, nuts, or dairy products.*

- *Make pasta with marinara instead of meat-based sauce, and use refried beans in place of beef in burritos or tacos.*

- *Next time you grill out, try some veggie burgers and hot dogs.* There are a number of different brands and versions, so sample several to find your favorite.

- *Choose veggie alternatives of your favorite dishes.* Top your pizza with olives, spinach, garlic, and peppers instead of pepperoni, or cook vegetarian chili.

- *Have to eat bacon with your eggs?* You're in luck! There are soy versions of breakfast meats available, including links and sausages.

- *Invest in a wok for stir-fry dinners made with loads of vegetables and tofu; you may not even miss the meat.*

Remember, you don't have to give up meat all at once to reap some of the heath benefits of a more vegetarian-like diet. If you're jonesing for a cheeseburger and give in, don't beat yourself up. Give yourself time to experiment and realize that these kinds of dietary changes are more likely to succeed if they're gradual. Even if you decide to eat meat occasionally, focusing more on a vegetarian diet can only make you healthier in the long run.

44

Climb a Mountain

Why climb a mountain? Because it's there, of course. Besides, mountain climbing is the latest thing. If Sarah, Duchess of York, can celebrate her thirty-fourth birthday by climbing Mt. Everest, can't you tackle at least a small mountain? Maybe you're approaching a big milestone—say, your thirtieth birthday?—or you're looking for a way to add some spice and adventure to your careful, seat-belted, antibacterial-obsessive life. After all, life is made meaningful by the quest for constant improvement. The next step for you may be a step up—literally.

NO MORE HANDRAILS

Mountain climbing, more commonly called "mountaineering," is an ages-old outdoor activity that entails climbing up the steep sides of a mountainside in hopes of reaching the top, or **summit**. Basic mountain climbing usually includes climbing steep snow slopes with the help of **crampons**, which are frameworks of metal spikes that attach to your boots, an ice ax, and other equipment (more about that in a bit).

Just because you can scale the StairMaster™ for an hour doesn't mean you're ready to tackle a mountain. Sure, introductory mountain climbing is often composed primarily of hiking, but there are still some difficulties to consider such as the distance you plan to cover, how much elevation you'll gain (in other words, how high you'll be climbing), and how to handle environmental hazards like bad weather. You may encounter extreme conditions, from subzero temperatures to extreme altitude, so you must make smart decisions before leaving for the day, such as whether to venture out at all, and what gear you'll need to be comfortable and safe. These kinds of decisions—call them "mountain smarts"—can mean the difference between a challenging climb and a life-threatening one.

Shape Up Before You Go

Before you even consider climbing a mountain, particularly one involving a high peak and steep terrain, you've got to be in good physical shape. It's smart to consult your physician before beginning the training regimen to be sure you are physically up to it. Depending on the altitudes you plan to tackle, your physical condition is a major factor in whether you'll be able to complete the climb.

For your own sake, and to ensure a smooth and enjoyable climb, follow a training regimen well before you set out. You need to develop both strength and endurance to maximize your climbing potential. Underestimate the importance of your physical condition and your trip may become drudgery rather than pleasure. You're also likely to slow down your fitter climbing buddies, which isn't a good way to endear yourself. Besides, you don't want to miss your chance to try for the summit after you've spent time and money traveling to an out-of-the-way place to fulfill your dream.

The altitude you plan to tackle, the steepness of the mountain, and the number of days you plan to climb will affect how you prepare. Obviously, physical preparations for a one-day trip on a beginners' climb in California versus an expert eight-day trek up Mt. McKinley (aka "Denali") will be quite different. For either, though, you'll want to use both cardio and weight-training exercises to maximize your fitness.

To start, you'll need good cardiovascular (CV) training. This gets your heart and lungs in shape for the rigors of climbing. As you ascend, the air becomes thinner, so the more efficiently and effectively your CV system functions, the better. Aim to spend forty-five to sixty minutes four to five times a week participating in a demanding cardio activity such as running, biking, swimming, or aerobics. A simple stroll around the block isn't going to cut it.

Using a variety of these exercises (commonly called **cross-training**) is the best way to build up endurance while reducing your risk of injury. For example, do twenty-five minutes on the bike followed by twenty-five minutes of running up and down stairs. The following day, try thirty minutes of swimming laps followed by a half hour of aerobics, and so on. The key is consistency; better to exercise four times a week regularly than to miss a week or two and then try to work out seven days in a row. After all, if you get hurt, you'll have a hard time keeping up with your training plan, let alone tackling the mountain.

In addition to cardio work, it's a good idea to do sport-specific exercise. In this case, that means actually climbing. That will strengthen the muscles you'll use both ascending and descending. Hike steep outdoor trails to simulate the real environment; carry extra weight by stashing full water bottles in your pack. When you reach the top of the trail, you can pour out the water to make the descent easier on your knees.

Start out this hill climbing gradually; work in five- or ten-minute increments, and slowly increase the steepness of your climbs. As you get stronger, you can add items to your pack to increase the weight so you become accustomed to carrying it by the time of your official climb.

Scaling Strategies

As you get in good shape, you can also learn climbing techniques. Scrambling over rocks is one thing; using an ice ax and learning to belay, or secure, yourself and other climbers is another. Don't try to learn these skills on the mountain—take a class with an experienced mountaineer or guide first. Check out your local gym, YMCA, or sports outfitter; many offer climbing classes. Or check out the following Web sites for more information about climbing classes and techniques:

- *http://www.amga.com/guides/index.html.* Looking for a mountaineering guide? Check out the American Mountain Guides Association for trained, certified professionals.

- *http://www.uiaa.ch/weblinks.aspx.* The International Mountaineering and Climbing Federation Web page includes a "links" page; put in "United States" in the "states" field and you'll pull up all of the U.S.-based organizations and resources.

- *http://www.aai.cc/.* The American Alpine Institute is a well-respected climbing school that offers classes throughout the United States and in other countries.

- *http://www.alaskamountainguides.com/.* Alaska Mountain Guides and Climbing School offers training courses throughout the world for climbers of all abilities.

GOING FOR THE SUMMIT

So, what kind of climb are you aiming for? Do you want to tackle a several-day highly technical climb, or simply have a leisurely one-day climb with no goal of reaching a summit? Consider what your local area offers in terms of mountains (or molehills), or look into a trip centered around your climb.

Either way, start at the beginning: Try several easy climbs before buying your plane ticket to Kilimanjaro. Before you head out, even for a short hike, check with the local ranger station for current weather and climbing conditions. (Visit *http://www. nps.com* for the U.S. National Park Service.) Make sure you consider avalanche conditions before climbing anywhere with snow. Both *http://www.wrh.noaa.gov* and *http://www.csac.org* report on snow and avalanche conditions.

As with scuba diving, it's best to hike with at least one buddy. You're safer in the event of an injury or emergency. Carry plenty of water, because proper hydration is crucial for climbing; if you bring too much, you can always dump some at your highest point to make your pack lighter for the descent. High-calorie, easily portable foods like energy bars, the ever-popular **gorp** (for "granola, raisins, and peanuts," or any similar combination), fig bars, and even energy gel (you don't even have to chew; just squeeze it into your mouth, lazybones) are all good choices.

If you're climbing in an area that requires a trail pass or climbing permit, purchase it ahead of time. Ranger Rick issues some pretty hefty fines if you don't have the necessary proof in some parks.

Gearing Up

You'll need a variety of equipment to ensure a safe, comfortable climb. Don't try to summit a mountain without the proper pieces of equipment. You're bound to fail, or possibly even fall. Not a good thing.

Don't wait until the day before you're leaving to buy your equipment, either. Training with it will help you get accustomed to it and break in your gear as well as acclimate you to the load you'll be carrying. When it comes to clothes, dress in layers; they help keep you warm and can be removed when you start to get sweaty or when the weather heats up. Look for fabrics that wick sweat away from your skin; even in cold weather, you'll sweat when climbing. Avoid fabrics like denim and cotton, which absorb moisture, become heavy, and can even bring down your core temperature, eventually leading to hypothermia.

So, what will you need? Your gear list will vary, depending on the weather, length of route, type of terrain, and your climbing ability. For example, you probably won't need a headlight or flashlight if you're taking a daylight trek through California's Sierra Mountains. If you're not sure about what you'll need, ask your outfitter, guide, or an experienced climber. To save money, you may want to opt for basic equipment now; you can always choose stuff with all the bells and whistles another time.

You'll definitely need the following, though:

- *Backpack, or pack.* Don't skimp here. A quality backpack is worth the money. Have a guide or experienced climber help you choose it to make sure it fits you properly.

- *Climbing clothing and footwear.* Assume the worst-case scenario—like you'll need a waterproof jacket even if it doesn't rain. Dress in layers, and wear comfortable hiking boots that have been broken in. Carry an extra pair of socks in case your feet get wet, and remember gloves and a hat in case the weather gets cold.

- *Cell phone.*

- *Compass.* OK, you swear by GPS, but a compass always works—and is tons cheaper, too.

- *Emergency blanket.* It doesn't take up much space in your pack, but can literally save your life.

- *First-aid kit.*

- *Flashlight or headlamp.*

- *Matches.* Even if you don't smoke.

- *Sunglasses and sunscreen.* You can get a terrible burn if you're not careful; the air is thinner, so protect your skin well.

- *Trail map.* Your local ranger station or outfitter will have one.

- *Water and food.* Bring more than you think you'll need in case the climb takes longer than expected.

In addition, you may need the following equipment. Again, ask a guide or experienced mountaineer for advice when gearing up:

- *Camp stove and cookware for climbs longer than a day.*

- *Crampons.*

- *Helmet.* It could save your life if a big rock drops on your head.

- *Ice ax.* You should practice using this before the day of your big climb, too.

- *Internal frame pack, for longer climbs.*

- *Mountaineering boots, if necessary.* They're designed to keep your feet warm in extreme conditions, and provide good traction.

- *Sleeping bag—and sleeping pad for comfort.*

- *Tent, for longer climbs.*

Talk like the Real Thing

You don't have to scale Denali to sound like an experienced climber once you know some of the lingo:

APPROACH: the route to the beginning of a technical climb

BAIL: to ditch, or give up, on a climb (a smart move when you know you're in over your head)

BELAY: the practice of keeping a climber from falling using an anchor, rope, and friction device (It's necessary to master this skill before you attempt extremely technical climbs.)

BOULDERING: like climbing, but done close to the ground (It's a good way to safely practice your climbing skills.)

CLIMBING WALL: a facility to climb on made from artificial rock (usually indoors)

CRAMPONS: the spikes that attach to your boots for better traction

GUMBY: a novice climber—for now, you

RAPPEL: to descend using a rope and friction device

SCREE: loose rocks—they may fall on your head.

SUMMIT: the high point of the mountain! (This word can also be used as a verb, as in, "I summited!")

YOUR FIRST CLIMB—AND THE NEXT, AND THE NEXT . . .

You're setting out for your first climb. Just don't make it your last. Climb with a more experienced mountaineer or guide, follow the safety rules you learned in climbing class, and, when in doubt, err on the side of caution.

Once you reach the first summit, you'll probably look forward to the next, and the next, and the next. After all, those mountains are meant to be climbed, aren't they?

Become a Surfer

You may not be able to walk on water, but if you learn to surf, you can get darn close. Learn how to catch a wave and you'll probably wind up a surfer for life. Whether you shuck it all to be a full-time beach bum or simply want to enjoy the water, this addictive sport reeks of cool. If you're ready to get gnarly, you can hook up with a surfing instructor at just about any surf shop or decent-sized oceanfront hotel or resort. Check out *http://www.surfing-waves.com/* or *http://www.surfingschoolsdirectory.com* for a list of surfing instructors near you; or, if you're ready to go it alone, read on.

GET YOUR BODY READY

The pros make it look effortless, but surfing demands you be in kick-butt shape. Think about it. Over 90 percent of your time in the water is spent paddling on top of your board or swimming back to it after a wipeout. If you want to be a serious surfer you need to be, or at least become, a strong swimmer.

If you're still dog-paddling, it's a good idea to prepare for surfing by swimming a combination of long-distance swims and short sprints three times a week. Use a pool or train in the ocean (always with a buddy!) to get stronger and boost your endurance. Remember, for all its beauty, the ocean can be a dangerous place. The more familiar and confident you are in it, the safer you'll be when you hit your local **break**—the breaking, surfable waves.

The shape and speed of the waves depend on the ocean floor beneath them, but all waves rolling in on a break vary between two extremes—plunging and mushy. **Plunging waves** occur if there is virtually no slope to the bottom, such as with a reef or sandbar. Plunging waves are ideal for experienced surfers, but they're too fast and difficult to ride for beginners. You want to start with the **mushy waves**, which are the result of a gradual bottom slope. They may sound boring, but they have a softer feel and will allow you to develop your wave-riding skills as fast as possible.

GEARING UP

Now you know more about the water you'll be surfing in. Now let's talk about what you'll be surfing on. When you're first learning, it's all about stability. The **long board**, or Malibu, is one popular style of large board. While these boards are stable, they're made of fiberglass (like most surfboards) and can easily become a sharp surface-riding torpedo. For your safety, the best beginner board is a **soft board**, often called a "Morey Doyle" or "BZ Board."

Your feet will need some help staying put on your new board, and the most common solution is surf wax. Apply the bar of wax to the top of your board, or **deck**, by making semi-circular motions forming small beads. Before hitting the water, rub the deck with a wax comb to develop some texture. The other option is **surf traction**, a textured pad mounted on your board.

You'll also want to have a **leash**, the line connecting your ankle to your board. Your leash should be a foot longer than your board, and a quick-release model is a good idea in case it gets caught in rocks or a reef.

A few more gear details: If you choose a Malibu or any pointed style of board, look into a noseguard to turn that piercing sharp point into a blunt one. And while you may want to look cool in your bikini or bare chest, you'd better wear a shirt or rash guard or splurge on a wet suit, because the big rash on your chest from your board is anything but cool. Finally, consider a protective helmet as well. Even if you're riding on water, you may crash into your board—or have it crash into you.

READY TO SURF? THE BASICS

Prepare to Pop-up

The **pop-up** is the transition between paddling away on your stomach and actually standing on your board. To increase the chance you'll actually stand your first time in the water, practice the pop-up on land. If your board has detachable fins, take them off and lie on your board. Otherwise, make a line in the sand to represent the center of your imaginary board. Center your body on the line and put your hands in a push-up position. But, instead of having your arms sticking out to the sides, you want your hands behind your shoulders and on the edges of your board, called the **rails**. Your hands should be flat on the deck of the board, not wrapped around it.

Now for the pop-up. Push your torso up so your back arches like a seal's. Just before your arms are fully extended and you feel your hips begin to lift off the board, suck your legs in under your body. Your initial stance will be very low and nearly sideways. One foot should land in front of you with your arch across the center of your board and almost perpendicular to the center line. Your rear foot should be centered as well, and virtually parallel to the other foot. Your stance should be slightly wider than your shoulders.

Which foot you put forward is entirely up to you and what feels most comfortable. If you put your left foot forward, you're a **regular foot**; if your right foot is forward you're a **goofy foot**, or goofy. Pick what feels natural and stick with it. If you're struggling with the pop-up, prop your hands on a couple of books or mounds of sand. The extra height will help get your front foot in position and help you understand how to move.

Paddling Basics

When paddling on your board, the idea is for your board to be flat on the water. If you're too far forward, water will wash over the tip (**pearling**) and if you're too far back the nose will be airborne (**corking**). Your head will likely be three-fourths of the way up your board, and you should be centered on your board with your feet resting over the tail.

To paddle, make freestyle strokes with your arms. Cup your hands and let your arms go about elbow-deep; be sure to follow through with your stroke. Try to keep your body still. Any unnecessary movement will waste your needed energy and create extra drag for your arms to have to pull. Always keep your head up to look out for waves, obstacles, and other surfers.

From Land to Sea

Ready to try the real thing? When you arrive at the beach, take a few minutes to survey the ocean. Look where the surf is breaking and reference the point with landmarks such as palm trees or lifeguard stands. Wait for a lull in the waves before heading out, and don't forget to pick up the slack on your leash. Hold your board to your side and don't let it get in-between you and an incoming wave.

Before you can position yourself to catch a wave, you must get past the breaking ones. Try to paddle toward the broken parts of waves, or **white water**; they'll be less likely to toss you back toward shore. To get through the waves, try these moves:

- *Push-up.* This is a good option for small waves. Start by getting as much speed as possible by paddling as the wave approaches. Head directly into the wave, push your entire body up, and allow the wave to roll over your board and under your chest.

- *Turtle or Eskimo roll.* If your board is too buoyant to push underwater, try the turtle roll. As the wave approaches, grab the rails of your board above your shoulders. Roll over with your board so it is upside-down with you underneath. Do a frog kick to help fight the momentum of the wave. When it's passed, roll yourself back over.

- *Duck dive.* As you gain experience, try the duck dive. Gain as much speed as possible; then, a few feet before your impact with the wave, grab the edges of your board, your hands in-between the nose and the midpoint. Use your weight to force the nose of your board underwater and bow your head to let your body follow. Once your body is just below the surface, use your dominant knee or your foot to push the tail of your board down. Once the wave passes, let your board carry you to the surface.

Surfing White Water

Hopefully, you'll be smart enough to start at a beach that slowly slopes away into the sea. That way you can further enhance your learning curve by trying to ride the white water before paddling out to the break.

Sit on your board with your feet dangling, barely touching the sand. You'll have to sit farther back on your board to balance the weight. As a wave approaches, push off from the bottom and ride the white water in.

After getting comfortable riding this way, try a few pop-ups. When you fall off or wipe out, as you will more often than not, try to fall toward the back of your board and get as much distance from it as you can. Then try again!

Riding the Curl

Now that you can handle the white water, move up to the **curl**, the stage between the incoming swells and the white water. Paddle out to where the waves are breaking; the idea is to be on top of the wave right as it's about to break.

Timing is one the most difficult things for beginners to master, but your judgment about when to start to paddle for a wave will come with experience. The angle of your board to the wave will vary, based on the shape of the wave. If the wave has a lot of slope and is slow-rolling, your board will basically be perpendicular to the wave. The steeper the wave you're trying to catch, the more angle is necessary to prevent yourself from pearling.

When you feel the momentum of the wave, start your pop-up. The timing of this is critical. Remember to arch your back to take some of the weight away from the nose of the board.

Once you're up, you must turn your board across the wave, more parallel to the beach, to stay on the curl. Be sure your stance is low. Your head, shoulders, and hips will lead your board, so start by turning your head and leading arm in the direction you wish to turn. Put as much weight as you can on your back foot and push the tail of your board opposite the direction you want to turn, thus rotating the nose in the correct direction.

A long fast wave will require a more extreme angle than the slow mushy waves you should be starting on. Every wave has a speed and angle that will keep you on it for as long as possible; this is called **trimming**. Once you've turned into the wave, keep your weight forward and toward the inside edge. If you're facing the wave, guide your board with your front toe; if your back is to the wave, guide your board with your heel. Once you've established your trim, you can begin trying to climb up and down the surface of the wave using your turning techniques.

Alas, all good things must end, and there will come a time when you need to stop. To end your ride, try a kick-out by turning your surfboard out toward the ocean. This should get you off the wave and into smooth water. Or put your rear foot on the very tail of your board and lean back; you'll slow down and the wave will move on without you.

KNOW THE UNWRITTEN RULES

Surfing may be a rebellious free-spirit sport but it does have guidelines. For example, often you'll find several surfers at the same break. To avoid total mayhem, a **lineup** will form—surfers waiting in line for their chance to catch a wave.

With a lineup, the surfer closest to the curl has the rights to the wave. If someone who isn't the closest to the curl catches the wave, that's called a **drop-in**. It can be dangerous and it's definitely not a good way to make surfer friends. Wait your turn in the lineup.

One of the most important unwritten rules is that a surfer up on a wave has the right-of-way. So, if you're trying to get past the white water and the breaking waves and see a surfer riding toward you, it's your duty to paddle around him or her.

Remember that your surfboard is not only your equipment—it's also your responsibility. It is up to you to hold onto it at all times and keep it from becoming a water-riding rocket. The only time you should not be in contact with it is if you wipe out. Letting go of it, especially around other surfers, is a cardinal surf sin.

Finally, always help out another surfer in trouble. Assist someone who is injured to shore. If someone is drowning, get them something that floats; don't try to save them alone. If you find yourself in trouble, turn toward the shore and remember the universal signal for help is waving one arm in the air.

Now you're ready to speak, act, and (hopefully) surf like the real thing. Go get gnarly, dude.

Get Your Name in Print

You're reading a magazine and think, "I could have written this article!" Or you've been scribbling short stories for years and now you're ready to publish them. Or maybe you simply want the satisfaction of seeing your name in print. It's easier than you might think. Obviously, you need to be able to write, but knowing how to market your work is essential. Locate the markets where your voice and work are a perfect fit, and you'll be bragging about your byline in no time. (I'm assuming you want to publish articles, essays, or short stories. If you've got a book inside you, check out the "Publish a Book" chapter.)

LOCATE MARKETS

New writers assume that writing comes first. But if you want to get published, it's important to consider the markets to help you figure out where your particular piece belongs. In fact, if you write articles, you'll want to pitch an idea before you write it. (Sounds crazy, but I'll explain in a bit.) If you write essays or short stories, though, go ahead and write the piece before looking at markets.

The book *Writer's Market* is a fat, annually updated volume that lists thousands of markets for short stories, articles, essays, and poetry. While reviewing guidelines is helpful, it's no substitute for actually looking at books, magazines, newspapers, or Web sites themselves to get a better feel for the kind of material they publish.

The type of market you're pitching to will determine your approach. Here's a quick rundown on potential markets:

Magazines

Thousands of magazines purchase freelance work. Consumer magazines are those you can find on the newsstands; trade publications are aimed at people in a particular industry or profession and are often available by subscription only. With magazine articles, you usually send a query letter first, and then write the piece after you receive an assignment. (Or an editor may offer to look at the piece **on spec**, or on speculation, meaning that he's willing to read it with no guarantees of purchasing it.) Essays, short stories, humor, and poetry are the exceptions to the rule; with them, you send in the completed work with a brief cover letter introducing it.

Newspapers

Newspapers are a great place for new writers to gather writing experience and gain clips. Most local publications pay modestly (usually ranging from $5 to $10, but up to $125 for features), but they're often looking for freelancers, or **stringers**, and it's a good way to hone your reporting and writing skills. Call your local newspaper with a list of story ideas and express your interest in freelancing for the publication. (Ask the editor if she's on deadline before you start your spiel.) She may want you to write about an idea you've pitched or send you out to cover another story.

Web Sites

With Web sites, you'll make your approach via e-mail. Depending on the site, you may send a query or the completed manuscript. Many Web sites don't pay for submissions and many more pay very little, so you may want to make online publishing your last resort.

ANALYZING MARKETS

When looking for potential markets, consider their guidelines. Many publishers now have writers' guidelines available online; if not, you can also obtain a copy of guidelines by sending an SASE (self-addressed stamped envelope) to the magazine or book publisher and requesting them. (For online publications or those with Web sites, send an e-mail requesting the same info.)

Guidelines in hand, you should also consider these factors when analyzing potential markets:

- *What type of material do they accept?*

- *How many words do they want?*

- *Who's their audience?* (This is particularly important with magazines, which tend to have a specific readership.)

- *How do they want you to submit material?* For example, a nonfiction book publisher may want a book proposal as opposed to a full-length manuscript; a magazine may specifically request query letters, not completed articles.

- *What do they pay for material?*

- *What's their response time?*

Keep all your market information in one place. Then you'll have it to refer to when you're preparing your work for submission.

MAKE YOUR PITCH

Magazine Query

So, you've got a great idea for a magazine article. While some magazines accept completed manuscripts, most prefer query letters. A **query** introduces your idea, demonstrates why readers of the publication will be interested in the story, outlines how you'll approach the story, and convinces the editor that you're uniquely qualified to write the piece. Note: many magazines accept queries by e-mail, but if you e-mail a query, include it in the body of the message, not as an attachment.

Cover Letter

If you're submitting a completed piece—say, an essay, a humorous piece, a poem, or an article that's previously been published—a simple cover letter will suffice. You can use a brief lead and include information about where the piece has been published before.

Another issue to consider is whether you'll submit your query by e-mail or by regular mail. It depends on the publication. Some specify that they prefer one or the other. E-mail is quicker, but not all editors like e-mail queries. Double-check the guidelines of the publication before you submit work.

The Format of Your Work

If you're submitting a completed piece, such as an essay or short story, keep these formatting guidelines in mind:

- *Your name, address, and contact information should be in the upper-left section of the first page of your manuscript; include the word count of the piece in the upper-right section.*

- *The title of your work should be centered a few lines below your contact information, followed by the word "by" and your name, centered on a separate line.*

- *The manuscript should be double-spaced to make it easier for an editor to read.*

- *Use 11- or 12-size Times New Roman or Courier font; both are commonly used in the publishing business.* Avoid fancy, difficult-to-read fonts.

- *Include page numbers at the bottom or top of the page.*

- *At the end of the piece, use "30" or "###" (which means "end of the manuscript").*

WHAT'S NEXT?

Submitting work to a publication can be a nerve-wracking business, so once your query or piece is on its way, either by snail mail or e-mail, do something to celebrate! You may get rejected (all writers do), but continuing to write, submit work and ideas, and find new potential markets will boost your chances of getting published. If you're serious about seeing your name in print or want to write as a part-time (or even full-time!) job, keep these strategies in mind:

Set Your Own Deadlines

As a new writer, you may not be working on anyone's schedule but your own. However, the time will come when an editor gives you a deadline you'll have to meet. Get used to writing on deadline by setting your own targets for the writing that you're working on. If you're working on a big project, like a book, break it into smaller chunks—say, chapter by chapter—and set deadlines for each one, plus a deadline for completing the whole thing.

Overcome Rejection

Trust me, you will get rejected. All writers do. The first step to coping with rejection is expecting it. That doesn't mean that you shouldn't have faith in your work. It does mean that you realize your odds of having work turned down are high, especially if you're a new writer. By remembering that it's normal, you ease its sting.

And don't take it personally. Any rejection you receive is only of that particular piece by that particular editor at that particular publisher. It's not a reflection on you or your abilities as a writer. The timing may be wrong, the editor may not care for the idea, or she may already have something similar in the works. A rejection can even be a positive sign if the editor took time to write a personal note like "sorry, not quite right for us" or "nice essay, but we're overstocked." Instead of stewing over why your work was turned down, find another market for it. Taking action is the best way to overcome rejection.

Calm Writer's Anxiety

Call it writer's block, performance anxiety, or plain old-fashioned self doubt: Every writer suffers from it at one time or another. Anxiety is common, normal, and part of the writing process for all of us. When you're beginning work on a piece, some nervousness is normal and to be expected. If you're afraid you don't know enough to write what you intend to write, then you'll naturally be anxious. Maybe you don't have a handle on your subject yet. But if your research is almost complete and you're still too anxious to write, your fear may be due to a number of factors.

Are you afraid to offend someone? Do you continually worry that what you write isn't good enough? That means your internal censor is at work, the nasty little critic that's always telling you you're not good enough.

Perfectionism is another major source of writing-related anxiety. If you expect your first draft to be perfect, you're setting yourself up for disappointment. Good writing is rewriting—and sometimes rewriting again (and again). Give these techniques a try next time you're feeling anxious, stuck, or blocked:

- *Schedule your writing.* Having a regular writing habit works for nearly everyone. You'll start training your brain to turn on and get creative—say, every morning at 6 A.M. or each night at 9:00 P.M. Instead of worrying about when you'll write, you simply stick to the schedule.

- *Just do it.* Sometimes you just need to write. You can't write and feel angst at the same time.

- *Switch gears.* Do something different: vacuum, walk, read, do a crossword puzzle. Or write something else for a while.

- *Break it up.* When an assignment appears overwhelming, you're likely to feel anxious. Break the work up into smaller steps—conducting research, doing interviews, transcribing notes, writing a draft, and so on—and focus on one step at a time.

- *Move your body.* Nothing conquers writer's anxiety like physical exercise. Take brief movement breaks away from the computer, even if it's only five minutes to get up, stretch, and take some deep breaths. You'll feel calmer and more able to focus on your work.

- *Be gentle.* Writers are often their own harshest critics. Be nice to yourself. If you picture an audience for your work, think of someone who gets it—your best friend, spouse, or someone who thinks like you do.

Stay Motivated

Writing well is a demanding job, and sending out work and getting published, even tougher. The writers who succeed are resilient, dedicated, and more than a little bit stubborn. Those qualities will help you survive the ups and downs of freelancing.

One of the most effective ways to stay motivated is to set two types of goals for your writing. Set an outcome goal and then design production goals to get you there. An outcome goal is often what you're striving for in terms of publishing your work. It might be "I'll publish my work in a national magazine" or "I'll write and sell my novel." A production goal, on the other hand, is a small, measurable, specific goal that will help you reach your overall or outcome goal—like "I will send out three queries each month" or "I will write for thirty minutes every day."

When you're writing for publication, you need both. The production goals, although seemingly minor, will help keep you on target to reach your overall, or outcome, goals. They also give you a way to track your progress. After six months of working on your novel, for example, you may not have achieved your goal of publishing it (yet), but you will have met your production goal of writing every day. That kind of success helps keep you on track while making you a better writer and improving your chance of getting published in the process.

TAKE THE NEXT STEP

You may feel nervous, maybe even terrified, the first time you mail off an essay or hit "send" to e-mail an article query. That's normal. Remember, though, to become a published writer you have to take the first step and actually submit work to a publication. Chances are slim that you'll run into an editor at the grocery store who, after staring at you intently, will approach you with the words, "You appear to be a writer of some talent. Would you like to write for me?" You might laugh at the idea, but many writers secretly hope that they won't have to make the effort to publish their work. They'll know someone, or meet someone who knows someone (who knows someone), and magically be "discovered."

Hey, you can be discovered, but it won't be in the grocery store, dry cleaner, or even the bookstore. You'll be discovered by making yourself visible—by honing your writing skills, researching the best markets for your work, and getting your work in front of editors. There's no mystery to how unpublished writers become published writers; it simply takes time, work, and a refusal to give up. But the reward of seeing your first byline (and your tenth, and your fiftieth) makes it well worth it.

47

Do Stand-Up Comedy

So you think you're funny. Your friends say you're funny. Your family says you're funny. Even people who hardly know you say you're funny. But are you funny enough to do stand-up? Because any successful comedian knows that there's funny—and then there's funny. If you're sure you're the latter, and you're willing to work late nights, deal with hecklers, and spend endless hours crafting jokes, you may be able to get paid for making people laugh.

MAKING THE CUT

Stand-up comedy is one of those careers that most people think they could succeed at—if only they tried. Time to get real. Just because your girlfriend or your buddies or your family members think you're a riot doesn't mean you're ready for prime time—or even amateur night at the local comedy barn. To succeed as a comedian, you need to be funny to people who don't know you, have never heard of you, and may have nothing at all in common with you. If you can make those people laugh, then you may have the ability to succeed as a stand-up.

Still, there's more to comedy than simply "being funny." First off, you've got to have material. Stand-up comedians like Jerry Seinfeld may appear to toss out hilarious observations effortlessly, but every comic spends the majority of his time writing, honing, practicing, and revising his jokes, or **material**. Only a few minutes of a typical day are devoted to actually presenting the material to an audience.

In other words, you can't just get up there and figure you'll think on your feet. You need to have some kind of act. That doesn't mean you have to juggle or tap dance or do impressions. It does mean that you have to have a cohesive routine that you can perform. The more comfortable you are with it, the more natural you'll sound.

DEVELOPING YOUR PERSONA

The first step is writing your material, and part of that is developing your comedy persona, or **image**. What kind of image do you want to project? What will you be known for? Roseanne Barr started out as the angry housewife, doing jokes about raising kids, arguing with her husband, and struggling with bills. Jeff Foxworthy has made an entire career based on his "You Might Be a Redneck . . ." jokes. Jerry Seinfeld turned his status as an "observational comedian" into one of the most successful sitcoms of all time—and it was actually "a show about nothing."

As you develop your comedic alter ego, think about what your life experience has been. Are you single, still on the quest for Mr. or Ms. Right? Are you making the transition from wild-and-crazy girl to a mommy of little monsters? Do you want to tell jokes, or do you want to be more a storyteller a la Bill Cosby or Richard Pryor? Or do you want to do biting social commentary like George Carlin, or make esoteric, intellectual jokes like Dennis Miller?

The great thing about comedy is that you can be whoever you want to be. But deciding on some kind of persona will help you hone your material and give you an identity. Don't try to be another Seinfeld or another Richard Pryor. You won't win audiences over by doing the same old thing. A persona that grows out of your unique sense of humor is more likely to be successful.

Think about the comedians you find funny and what attracts you to them. Dane Cook is hugely popular with the college and twenty-something crowd, and his bits range from his high-school stint working at Burger King (where his older brother, the manager, "really was the Burger King") to lines like "Why do people with bad breath always want to tell you secrets?" Steven Lynch's routine consists of comical folk songs accompanied by a guitar; it sounds like it wouldn't work, but it does.

Plan to spend lots of time honing and developing this persona. Among other things, consider how "blue," or raunchy, you want to be. Bill Cosby is known for a clean act. Comedians like Dane Cook and Chris Rock are definitely R-rated. There's nothing wrong with either approach. The key is to do what feels right for you. You want to be unique and, hopefully, memorable. Think of the comedians whose names you know. Even if you don't like their material, you remember them because of it.

WRITING YOUR MATERIAL

As you're developing your persona, you should also be writing material. And that means writing. A joke in your head is likely to be forgotten. The more you watch other comedians, the more you learn what works and what doesn't. Jerry Seinfeld said that he learned how to craft a joke by watching other comics perform: seeing the importance of every word, as well as timing and delivery.

So, what are you going to actually write about? The door is wide open. Several golden opportunities include:

- *Your love life—or lack of such.* Whether you're single and looking, single and given up, happily coupled (except for those annoying quirks of your partner), or coupled and bemoaning it, relationships are a great place to start.

- *Your job.* Does it suck? That's actually a good thing. Think of what makes you laugh at work—and what has universal appeal. Bad boss? Unreasonable expectations? Those dreaded TPS reports? Insane coworker who keeps stealing your stapler? Anyone who's ever worked—and that's about all of us—will relate to these kinds of jokes.

- *Your family.* Hey, now you can get back at your older brother for all those noogies or for your parents being so unreasonably strict. Once again, family jokes work because, well, we all have families. And most of our families are a little demented.

- *Your needy pet.* Your attempts to get back in shape. Your lack of coolness. Your obsession with Cheetos. It doesn't matter what exactly it is—as long as you think it's funny, and other people do, too. Remember, too, that part of what makes a comedian funny is the universality of humor. We laugh because we realize what she says is true, or because we can picture it. Look for material that not just a close friend will laugh at, but that anyone (with a sense of humor) will appreciate.

Remember to write down your stuff! Carry a notebook or a tape recorder to capture your great ideas and write them up when you get home.

Don't steal material from other comics, and don't overuse certain setups for jokes. (Jokes about the farmer's daughter, or the priest, the rabbi, and the Polish person are outdated, overexposed, and overdone.)

As you're writing your material, consider how you'll perform it. Are you a natural storyteller? Do you thrive on back-and-forth with the audience? Do you do great impressions? There's more to comedy than just writing and telling jokes. Sure, you can take comedy classes, but the thing that will set you apart can't be taught. In a word, your act is you.

Improv, or improvisation classes, though, can help you learn to think fast on your feet and make your mind more creative. Check out your local community college's offerings; local comedy clubs sometimes offer them as well.

FINDING YOUR FIRST GIG

So, you've got some material down—say, five minutes of good stuff. It's funny. You're funny. You've polished it and practiced it and you're ready for the stage. What's next? Finding someplace to perform. Depending on where you live, there may be clubs that offer "open-mic" nights that are primarily for amateurs. Don't be a snob. This is a great way to get up there and practice your material. If you impress the club owner or booker, they may ask to you come back—this time for pay.

Otherwise, as a new comic, you may be asked to take a "try-out" or "open" spot, which may be five or ten minutes long. You won't be paid for these either; it's just a way to determine whether they might want to hire you.

To look for comedy clubs in your area, check the yellow pages, or do a Google search for "comedy club" and nearby cities or locales. Local clubs, restaurants, and bars may have open-mic nights. Look for a local club that can be your "home club." Show up on time, be willing to take any open slots, and basically make the owner or manager's job easier. Do all that and make people laugh and they'll come to rely on you, which is what you want.

GETTING ONSTAGE—
WITHOUT PASSING OUT

Hands shaking? Stomach in knots? Mouth dry? All are normal before you take the stage, especially for the first time. Even if you lose your lunch, keep in mind that the more gigs you do, and the more times you get in front of an audience, the more likely you are to improve.

Think about it. It's either get better—or get out of the business.

Basically, your act itself should have a beginning, middle, and end. Start off strong, and project confidence as you walk on the stage, unless you've got a depressed or downtrodden stage persona. You should have your opener down cold. Throughout the middle, you may do **callbacks**, which refer to earlier jokes or bits. Close with something that will get a big laugh, usually a callback to an earlier joke. Then get off the stage.

If someone heckles you, ignore it or give the individual a snappy comeback. Have a few choice ones ready, and if the heckler continues, call on the club management for a hand. If you're flopping or just can't seem to make anything work, get off the stage. There will be other nights, other shows, other audiences. Don't give up because of one bad experience; you wouldn't give up on the opposite sex after one bad date, would you? On the other hand, if you flop ten, fifteen, twenty times, maybe it's time to try something else.

A FULL-TIME GIG?

Doing stand-up as a hobby is one thing. If you want to make it your career, though, prepare to pay your dues. Expect to spend late nights in no-name towns waiting for your chance to do a few minutes of material, and playing at clubs where audiences will hassle, heckle, and harass you.

How many comics are working today? Estimates vary, but it's probably about 5,000 who are actually working—and getting paid for it—and countless more who are trying to break in. If you're serious about making a living as a comedian, you may have to take on a day job to pay the bills in the meantime, or do temp work between gigs.

You'll also need some business basics to help promote you and your act. At the least you need a business card, a résumé, and a booking sheet, which shows your availability. As you gain experience (or want to gain it), you'll need a photo (usually an 8" x 11" black–and-white head shot) and a video, and a Website doesn't hurt, either. Your video should be professionally shot, and should showcase audience reaction; in other words, the more the crowd laughs, the better.

As you gain bookings and exposure, you may want to consider taking on a manager or agent, but neither will be interested in someone who's just starting out. Getting gigs will be up to you. Contact clubs, colleges, and other venues by calling or sending a cover letter with your head shot and video, and ask talent bookers or club managers who've seen you perform to write letters of recommendation. Two excellent resources that cover the basics of the business are the books *The Comedy Bible: From Stand-up to Sitcom—The Comedy Writer's Ultimate "How-To" Guide* by Judy Carter (Fireside, 2001) and *Comic Insights: The Art of Stand-up Comedy* by Franklin Ajaye (Silman-James, 2002). Both are available on Amazon.com.

One of the most appealing aspects of stand-up comedy is that you're the master of your domain. You control everything, from your material to the way it's performed to the way you change it over time. The creative aspect of the business, along with the undeniable satisfaction of making people laugh, may draw you to stand-up even if you're just doing it for fun, not for money.

48

Make Kids Love You

Sure, we share the world with them, but unless you have kids of your own—have grown up in a family with lots of younger siblings or cousins—you may be mystified by drooling rug rats. A few short years later and they're popping three-foot ollies on skateboards or rolling their nine-year-old eyes at your lack of knowledge of Britney Spears's latest album. Kids are cute—usually. But some people just naturally seem to have the gift with children. If you'd like to enhance your Pied Piper skills, I've got ways to make almost every kid love you—and, more importantly, think you're the coolest.

UNDERSTAND THE ENEMY

Let's face it. Kids can be tricky people. They may look like little adults, but their brains work differently. They haven't had the life experience you have, and their perspective is probably completely different from yours. So how does one gain access to the kiddie brain?

Think back to when you were their age. Was it a crisis when you weren't invited to the most popular kid's party? Did you dream of playing first base for the Red Sox? Did you preen while crooning "Lucky Star" in your bedroom, plotting to be the next Madonna? You may not have been concerned about things like your career and finding Mr. or Ms. Right, but you had worries that were just as critical and pressing. Try to put yourself in a kid's Rocket Dogs or Skechers (those are both types of shoes, in case you didn't know).

Don't talk down to them. Remember how you thought you knew everything when you were eleven? Kids today think they know it all, too. Don't insult their intelligence or act as if the weighty matters of your all-so-important life are beyond their comprehension. They won't like it—and they won't like you.

But do use discretion. Believe me, your sister will get upset if you brag to your eight-year-old nephew about the strip bar you and your buddies visited last weekend. Adults do plenty of things—experiment with drugs, have casual sex, cheat on their taxes—that you really don't have to share with kids. They'll figure it out soon enough.

Find out what they're into. Some careful questioning will reveal whether tickets to Tony Hawk or *Sesame Street on Ice* will be joyfully received. Is the kid into Harry Potter? (If he or she is between the ages of eight and fifteen, that's a safe bet. And if you've read the series and can talk potions, hexes, and Quidditch with the best of them, most kids will be duly impressed.)

Kid not talking? Check out her room, or the way he's dressed. If he's still wearing a Jordan 23 jersey, he's either a basketball or a Bulls fan. And if she's carrying a Powerpuff Girls backpack, ask which one's her favorite. "Who's your favorite singer?" "Who's your favorite sports team?" "What's your favorite video game—and what level have you attained?" You don't have to grill the kid, but try to find out what kids really care about. It makes getting to know them much easier.

Share your own secrets. It's great to put yourself in a kid's shoes, but go a step further. Tell him or her what you enjoyed doing when you were his or her age. Just because you played records (be prepared to explain what those are) doesn't mean you don't share an interest in music. Kids, especially older kids, are more into music today, especially classic rock, and you may find that the music you dug growing up is now the music they dig growing up. Which is either really cool, or really scary, or both.

Be prepared. Know a few games—especially portable ones— and you'll be everyone's favorite relative. If you have paper and pencil, you can always play a quick game of tic-tac-toe or hangman, depending on the kid's age. Or bring along a deck of cards. A six-year-old is a bit young for a rousing game of Texas Hold 'Em, but don't forget these old favorites:

- *War.* Divide the deck into two halves and flip cards over simultaneously. Aces are high, deuces low; the high card wins both. If the same card comes up, then you place three more cards face down, then the fourth cards faceup; same rules apply. (Warning—kids four to ten can play this game for hours. You'll give up, bleary-eyed, while the kid is still chanting for "one more game!")

- *Old Maid.* Take all but one queen out of the deck. Deal the remaining cards out to three to five players. Each player puts down any pairs (two threes, two tens, and so on). The players then take turns drawing from other player's hands, going either clockwise or counterclockwise, trying to pair up every card in their hands without winding up with the queen, or "Old Maid." It's fun for kids ages six and up, and they love it when an adult winds up with the Old Maid.

- *Crazy Eights.* Each player (two to four) is dealt eight cards. Then one card is flipped over to start the game; each player must play a card on top of the starting card. If the card is the two of hearts, you can play a two or a heart; if you don't have either in your hand, you must draw until you get one to play. Each of the four eights is "crazy," and with it you can change the suit of the play card. The object of the game is to get rid of all the cards in your hand before the other players do. Ages six and up.

- **Gin Rummy.** Seems like everyone had a grandma who taught them this classic game. You're dealt either seven or ten cards, depending on style; the object of the game is to turn your hand into a group of either three of a kind or more (by collecting the seven of spades, hearts, and clubs, for example), or a straight of three cards or more of one suit (e.g., the three, four, and five of spades). To start play, a card is turned faceup; you either select the card (if it helps you create a group of three or a straight) or choose from the deck. The object is to complete your hand, upon which you say "gin" and put down your hand. For older kids, keep track of points—the number of cards left unmatched (that aren't in a series or set of three of more cards) in the losers' hands are added up. Points are bad; make the game more exciting for an older kid by playing for a "penny a point" or more, if your wallet is fat. For ages eight and up.

MORE WAYS TO DELIGHT (AND EXHAUST) ENERGETIC YOUNGSTERS

Part of being a supercool adult is having a stash of fun (and time-wasting) ideas at the ready. Consider these:

- **Kids too young for cards?** Wow and amaze them with simple magic tricks, like making a coin "disappear" by rubbing it into their arm. (Palm the coin or slip it between your fingers or into a shirtsleeve; then pull it out of their ear, nose, or other orifice with a flourish.

- **Whip out your stopwatch.** Kids love to be "timed" doing things, whether it's riding their bikes down to the corner and back or racing upstairs to put on their pajamas.

- **Run around like crazy people.** A game of freeze tag or "duck, duck, goose" for younger kids (ages three to six) will keep them entertained for hours. (Don't know how to play? Ask them! They'll tell you!)

- **Play "I spy" when you're outside.** "I spy, with my little eye . . . a basketball." Wait for the kid to find the object; then it's your turn. This is a fun way to distract kids during a long car or train ride, too.

- **Whip out the board games.** There's a reason *Monopoly*™ has sold millions and millions of games. People love to play. Check out games like *Othello*™, which teaches strategy; *Rummikub*™, a twist on gin rummy with tiles; checkers; backgammon; and the favorite of many boys, *Battleship*™. Ask what games the kids like to play and be willing to lose graciously.

- **Turn on the tube.** Ask any parent of a four-year-old, and he or she will tell you there have been times when *Finding Nemo* has saved the day. Depending on the age of the kid, *A Shark's Tale*, *Toy Story*, *The Little Mermaid*, *Aladdin*, *Shrek*, or *The Incredibles* may be a fit. In a pinch, just about any Disney or Pixar feature will entertain a kid for nearly ninety minutes.

- **Make a day of it.** Consider an appropriate venue and offer to take the kid someplace fun. (Remember, it's supposed to be fun for him or her first and foremost.) Whether you go to a baseball game or a science museum, talk to the adult in charge (you know, the parent) and make sure you're equipped for the day. An adult may be able to go anywhere with a cell phone and a bottle of water, but depending on their ages kids may travel with bottles and diapers, snacks and toys, or MP3 players and BlackBerries™.

BE A FUN GROWN-UP—WHO'S STILL A GROWN-UP

A few words of warning. Most kids love it when adults relate to them on their level. But hanging out doesn't mean letting it all hang loose. For the clueless, here are a couple of guidelines for dealing with kids on your own. Don't:

- *get drunk or do drugs* (Smoking isn't great, either. Come on! You're a role model!)

- *swear like a sailor* (Sure, you know seventeen variations of the f-word. Your adorable little niece doesn't need to hear any of them.)

- *spill your secrets* (Kids are like little voice-activated recorders. Say something in front of one of them and it will be repeated. Watch what you say—and what you do.)

- *let the kid out of your sight* (Sure, you can let your sixteen-year-old cousin check out the T-shirts a few aisles away at the Gap. But keep younger kids close by. Sorry, but there are freaks and weirdos out there, and your job as kid-sitter is to make sure the little munchkins don't encounter them on your watch.)

- **pass out** (This is a follow-up to not letting the kid out of your sight. You agreed to babysit, and the little tyke's out cold. You settle down for a nice snooze, only to wake and find the two-year-old has crawled out of her crib to de-stroy—but oh so quietly!—the entire apartment. Or worse yet, gone for a stroll down the hallway—or down the block. Trust me, you do not want to be in the position of not knowing the whereabouts of the kid you were sup-posed to be watching.)

OK, enough about the don'ts. Don't let the safety and respon-sibility aspects of hanging with the shorties dissuade you from hooking up with kids now and then. A little time with a two- or ten-year-old and you'll probably come away amazed at how smart, fascinating, hilarious, and even fun kids can be. Who knows? You might even be convinced to have a few of your own someday.

Be a Dog Whisperer

49

Animal experts may make it look easy, but they don't have some special Dr. Dolittle-like ability to talk to birds and beasts. Sure, they communicate with animals, but they do so by reading and understanding their body language and using that knowledge to make the animals respond the way they want them to. (Animals have body language just like humans. That shouldn't be surprising. We all descended from the same primordial ooze, right?)

If you want to be the next dog whisperer—or just understand your pet better—read on.

DECODE YOUR DOGGY

Each animal may have a slightly different temperament, depending on its breed, the way it's been raised and disciplined, and its own personality quirks, but here are some doggy emotions and what they're likely to look like in any canine.

Aggression

Look closely and an aggressive or angry dog will let you know to stay away. His body will be tense, tail stiff, and he'll hold himself to look as big as possible; his hackles may be raised and he'll snarl, growl, or bark—loud. His ears will be laid back and his eyes may be narrowed or he may stare directly at you. (Avoid eye contact, which is taken as a challenge to an aggressive dog.) His teeth will be exposed, too, to show off his most fearsome weapon.

Excitement

An excited or eager dog is ready for action, and wants to investigate further. (Picture a drug dog at work—all business.) Her ears will be perked up, eyes wide open to gather as much information as possible, and while her mouth is open her teeth will be covered. She'll hold her body in a normal position—not stiff or relaxed—and her tail will be up. Some dogs will whine or bark in excitement.

Fear

A fearful dog will give you a lot of clues about her emotional state. Her ears are likely to be laid back close to her head, and her tail will be low, between her legs. She may avoid eye contact, and may crouch in a submissive position. She may tremble, whine, or yelp, and may show her teeth.

Friendliness

A friendly dog will have his ears up, and his tail will be up and most likely wagging. He'll make eye contact, and his mouth will be relaxed, his body relaxed-looking—unless he's wagging so hard his back end is wiggling, too. He may whimper or yap excitedly, depending on the dog.

Happiness

A happy dog looks like a friendly dog—with more energy. Her eyes will be open, mouth relaxed, and she may be panting. Her body will be relaxed, or she may drop her shoulders and front end in invitation to play. She'll be wagging her tail and may bark excitedly.

THE WAY YOUR DOG SEES THE WORLD

It's important to remember that communicating with your pet is more than just understanding what your dog is thinking. Communication is a two-way street; in fact, what you say to your animal through your actions and body language is more important than understanding what your pet is saying to you.

Sure, we love our pets. We talk to them as if they understand English, we care for them as if they were children, and sometimes we love them as soul mates. Basically, we fall into the trap of humanizing our pets, and dogs do the same thing—they "doggy-ize" us. Just as we think of them as human, they think of us as dogs, and members of their pack. Dogs are pack animals and members of the pack fit into two categories—dominant and submissive.

Believe it or not, many family dogs consider themselves the pack leaders. Does your dog get tense or protective when new people come near you, is he overly protective of your home, or does he freak out when you leave? These are all symptoms of a dog who thinks he's the boss. Think about it. It's the leader of the pack who protects the members, who defends the cave, and who worries if his pack disappears.

The problem is that many dog owners usually don't realize their behavior is interpreted as submissive by their dogs. For example, do you feed your dog before you eat? (If so, you're telling him he's the boss—in a pack, the leader always eat first.) Does your dog run out the front door first or drag you behind him on his leash? Once again, you're letting him think he's in charge. Does your dog stuff his cold, wet nose under your arm when he wants some affection? It may be cute, but the fact that he demands attention means he feels he's in an authoritative position to do so.

The good news is that you can take back control. Dogs are not power-hungry like so many of us Homo sapiens. Few care if they are top dog or at the bottom of the power pyramid. To climb back on top, always eat before you feed your dog. And take charge of petting and play time. If you want to pet your dog, have it follow a few simple commands, like "sit," "roll over," or "lie down." Then reward your dog by petting him. This way the animal understands that you are petting him because he was obedient.

When you walk your dog, you must lead him, not the other way around. That means your pet must walk beside or behind you so that you decide where you're going to go—and how fast you walk. You may have to keep your dog on a short leash until your dog adjusts. If your dog starts to pull, don't pull back—this lets him resist you. Instead, pull the leash to one side or the other. This forces the dog to step sideways, breaking his forward movement, and reminds him that you're in charge.

THE PACK LEADER

As the pack leader, it is your responsibility to keep your animals healthy. Every day you need to assert your pack leader status, and give your dog plenty of exercise. Your dog can be submissive to you and yet be unhappy and/or unhealthy. Domesticated dogs spend most of the hours of the day lying around, when the reality is that dogs love to work and play.

Have you seen the way a herding dog looks when she's taken out to the field, or how excited a hunting dog gets when he sees a gun? Dogs love having purpose, even if their "job" is retrieving a tennis ball over . . . and over . . . and over. Exercise your dog for as close to an hour as you can, and take her new places when you can to let her explore her migratory instincts. Don't forget to always reward your dog—being dominant doesn't mean that you can't show affection.

When you discipline your dog, remain calm yet stern. Your pet will not respond well to anger or yelling. If you give a command and the dog ignores you, don't raise your voice. Simply move closer to the dog, and assert your command again.

If need be, you may touch the animal to get her to respond, but never do so in a harmful way. A pack leader would never try to harm one of its submissive members. The same is true for training. Positive reinforcement, such as a treat when the dog obeys a command, has proven a much better training tool for dogs than threatening or hurting them when they do not obey.

To learn more about dogs and why they do the things they do, check out *http://www.digitaldog.com/* or *http://www.hsus.org/pets/*. (The latter site is that of the Humane Society of the United States, which offers a slew of "Dog Behavior Tip Sheets" on the Web site under "Pet Care/Dog Care.")

UNDERSTANDING YOUR CAT— AS MUCH AS YOU CAN

It's said that dog owners train their dogs, and cat owners are trained by their cats. Getting a cat to do what you want is a lot trickier than working with a dog. Face it: some cats just don't care, even with the promise of tuna or catnip. At least you can have some idea of what's going on in your favorite feline's mind with these three common emotions:

Anger

Cats don't just get disgusted. They get mad, too. He'll flatten his ears against his head, and will puff out his tail and arch his back in an attempt to look larger and more menacing. He'll breathe faster and his body will look tense; he may flick his tail or yowl. If you (or the dog, or whatever is threatening him) don't give him a clear path, he may pounce.

Anxiety

An anxious cat may flick her tail or meow. Watch her body language; her ears will flatten against her head and the muscles of her body may ripple. An anxious cat is more likely to bite or scratch, so take care with her.

Happiness

It's actually easy to tell when a cat is happy. He'll purr. (But purring doesn't guarantee a happy cat; your cat will purr when he's scared or anxious, too.) A contented feline will have relaxed body language and his ears will be perked forward, his breathing slow. He may bump or nuzzle you with his head as well.

GETTING KITTY LOVE

It turns out that cats aren't always standoffish; they can voluntarily show affection and some even do! But it takes time to build a relationship with a cat. Patience is a virtue whether you are holding the door for her to slip outside or seeking his praise. How do you know you're getting through? Look for these kinds of actions that show that maybe, just maybe, they like you.

The Leg Rub

The leg rub is probably the most common action a cat will take when she meets someone—that is, if she does anything at all. The feline will rub the entire side of her body across your leg, saying, "I acknowledge your existence." If she chooses to purr, you're off to a fine start.

Stroke My Chin!

While petting your cat, you find that she stays still so you can rub under her chin. She may even position herself on her back for easy access. This is a clear sign of trust and friendship.

Watch Me Chow

If your cat permits you to watch her eat, you've definitely made progress. This means you've got some kitty-cat status.

Lap Naps

If your cat chooses to curl in your lap to nap, you're almost there. This means there is trust, affection, and even warmth between the two of you—even if not equality.

Let's Rap

This is the Everest of cat affection. Your cat will put her face in yours and talk—not like in *Alice in Wonderland*, but a simple meow. You've now achieved the highest bond with your cat—whenever she finds it convenient at least. For more on cat behavior, check out *http://www.catsinternational.org/articles/index.html* or *http://www.hsus.org/pets/pet_care/cat_care/* for their "Cat Behavior Tip Sheets." You may be surprised at what you learn!

The bottom line is that, if you make the effort, you'll find that you can build a relationship with your dog—even your cat. Whether your dog is your best friend may depend on who leads the pack. Your feline friend may take a bit longer, but with some patience (and possibly tuna), you'll find that eventually she'll deem you . . . well, acceptable.

Give a Great Massage

50

Want to turn someone into putty in your hands? Learn how to give a great massage, and you've got a seduction tool at the ready. But massage isn't just for the single guy (or gal) who's looking to get lucky. Massage can reduce stress, soothe aching muscles, and speed recovery from a hard workout—plus, it feels awesome. Learn the basics of massage and you'll boost your popularity—and maybe discover a skill you want to practice full-time.

GET THE RUB ON RUBBING

Massage is more than simply touching someone; it's controlled, thoughtful touch that defines massage. Even Hippocrates, the father of medicine, prescribed massage, and Chinese practitioners using forms based on **pressure points** and **body meridians** (the pathways on your body that **chi**, or body energy, travels along) have been around for thousands of years. While there are a variety of massage types (more about that in a bit), most people in the United States tend to think of Swedish massage when they think of massage.

Here's the skinny on popular types of massage:

DEEP TISSUE: This is a serious massage, using heavy finger pressure and slow strokes to release tension. Deep-tissue massage usually concentrates on one specific muscle group or area.

REFLEXOLOGY: This type of massage only involves the hands and feet. Reflexologists apply pressure to specific points along the hands and feet that correspond with the ends of the meridians that run throughout the body; these points are believed to correspond to specific body organs. Reflexology is used to treat specific health problems or to simply reduce stress and improve energy.

ROLFING: This isn't for the fainthearted. Named after the scientist who invented this technique, Rolfing is a type of extremely deep massage that stretches connective tissue to release lactic acid. You'll be sore afterward, but this technique is thought to improve body alignment and boost energy.

SHIATSU: This type of massage involves finger pressure that is applied along certain points of the body along meridians, or pathways. Pressing on specific points along these meridians is believed to restore energy, or chi, which helps with healing. Shiatsu practitioners use their elbows and feet along with their hands to apply pressure to the various pressure points.

SPORTS: Sports massage is massage in which the focus is on particular areas of the body; the strokes are similar to those used in Swedish massage but may be more intense than those of typical massage.

SWEDISH: As mentioned above, Swedish massage is the best-known type of massage in the United States. Swedish massage includes several types of strokes, but the most commonly used are called **effleurage**—long strokes on the muscles that are applied in the direction of the heart, along with several other techniques (see below).

TRAGER: Named for Milton Trager, MD, this technique uses gentle shaking and rocking motions that are designed to release tension held in the body, particularly in the back, neck, and shoulder areas.

TRIGGER POINT: Somewhat similar to acupressure, in trigger-point massage pressure is applied to specific painful areas. By stimulating the trigger points, you can relax other areas of the body.

Massage does more than just make you feel good. Research has found that massage can reduce swelling, increase blood flow and improve circulation, and prevent scar tissue from forming. It also stimulates lymph circulation, especially with techniques that are specifically designed to do this (called **lymphatic drainage**), and may improve your body's immune system as well. Just as importantly, it can help strengthen muscle tissue and reduce muscle spasms, which can both prevent injury and promote healing.

Because massage is so pleasurable, people feel better afterward, too. Premature, or preemie, babies who are massaged grow faster, are more active, and are less irritable than preemies who are not massaged. Other studies have found that massage can relax both children and teens. In fact, massage reduces anxiety; lessens the perception of pain; and reduces heart rate, breathing rate, and blood pressure. And it takes little more than a pair of hands and a caring attitude.

DIFFERENT STROKES FOR
DIFFERENT FOLKS

Before you start rubbing on someone, though, it's a good idea to have an idea of what the massage techniques actually are. Shiatsu and other massage styles can take years to learn, but most people can give a basic Swedish massage fairly easily. This type of therapeutic, relaxing massage can be performed on the entire body, or just one spot—say, the back, or even the hands.

You'll use up to five basic strokes, with the idea of relaxing the person, not trying to work out any major muscular problems. (Leave that to the pros.) You shouldn't massage someone who has health problems like diabetes or heart disease without a doctor's OK. And, obviously, don't massage any part of the body that's bruised or swollen, or any open sores (um, which you wouldn't want to touch anyway, right?).

While it may sound romantic to give a massage on a bearskin rug in front of a roaring fire, you don't have to wait for the perfect atmosphere. Do take a few steps, though, to ensure that your "massagee" will feel relaxed and get more from the experience.

First off, consider where the person will lie. A massage table is the best choice, but a firm mattress or even the floor (put a thick blanket underneath for comfort) can be used. Place an old sheet under the person to protect your linens, and make sure that you can move around the person's body easily.

Use oil or lotion to reduce the friction between your hands and the person's skin. Place another sheet (and blanket, if necessary) over the person to keep him warm, and provide some modesty. That way you can keep him covered; only the part of his body you're working on should be exposed. Apply lotion or oil to your hands first, where you can warm it, before touching his skin. (The big no-no? Squirting cold oil directly onto his back. Not relaxing at all!)

Check the temperature and light in the room, too. Ideally, the lights should be low, with no bright lights shining in the recipient's face. Candles are a nice touch, and scented ones can add to the relaxing atmosphere. The room should be warm enough so that the person can relax. Finally, consider playing light instrumental music or a "nature sounds" CD (you know, ocean waves, babbling brooks, and bird calls) to cover any background noise.

To give an effective massage, relax and try to listen to the person's body. Massage can be relaxing for both the giver and receiver, and the technique isn't as important as the intent—and the results of the massage. You should start and end your massage with effleurage strokes; the rest of the massage is up to you—and the person receiving it.

- *Effleurage is commonly used in Swedish massage, and involves sliding your hands along the person's muscles in broad, sweeping motions.* It is a soothing, relaxing stroke. To do it, place your hands, elbows slightly bent, on the person's body, and slowly slide over the area you're working on, increasing and decreasing the pressure you apply by leaning into or pulling away from the person. Push through the area, applying more pressure, and then return to the starting point using very light pressure. You'll find it easiest to do this stroke if you keep your elbows stable; when stroking someone's arms or legs, always move toward the heart.

- *Friction helps release muscle knots and can penetrate below the superficial muscle layers; it can also help improve joint mobility.* It's important to only perform friction techniques after the area has been warmed up, say after some effleurage and petrissage strokes. To perform a friction stroke, press your thumb and index finger together, or use your index finger with your middle finger over it. Exert pressure, making sure that it isn't too much, and never press directly on a joint or bone.

- *Petrissage is a firm, friction-creating stroke.* It involves **kneading**, or lifting and squeezing, someone's flesh, and can be performed across muscle fibers, not just along them the way effleurage is. Petrissage is the most complicated stroke and is usually only used on the largest muscle groups, such as those in the thighs, butt, or upper back. While petrissage can reduce muscle fatigue, it shouldn't be used on overworked muscles. Start with effleurage to warm the muscles before trying petrissage. To do it, grasp the muscle in one hand and squeeze it, then quickly switch hands and repeat the move. Keep a rhythmic pattern going, and make sure that the pressure isn't uncomfortable. Follow with a few effleurage strokes before moving on to the next area of the body.

- *Tapotement (or percussion) involves quick, brisk strikes to the body, which can mean anything from slapping to tapping.* For a relaxing massage, you'll use the latter—say, light fingers drumming over a person's back—for a relaxing sensation.

- *Vibration is a technique that involves shaking a large muscle area; the key is to do it gently and rhythmically.* Place your hands on the person's body with your wrists, fingers, and arms stiff, elbows bent. Start a small circular rotation with your fingertips, gradually increasing your speed so that you're vibrating the area. Keep the pressure light, and control your movement; you shouldn't be flinging the person's body around. You can also apply vibration by holding a person's hand or foot and gently shaking it.

However you perform the massage, you should finish with effleurage strokes. Give the person a few minutes afterward to relax and bask in the post-massage glow. If you're lucky, he'll offer to switch with you—or at least owe you one.

GETTING PAID TO TOUCH PEOPLE

If you feel you have a natural gift for massage, or simply want a career that enables you to make people feel good, you may want to consider becoming a massage therapist.

What does it take? More than the desire to give pleasure. You've got to be in decent shape, first of all. Giving a massage may look easy, but doing it all day is physically demanding work. It takes strength and endurance, and you can develop overuse injuries in your hands and wrists. You can reduce the risk of injuries by making sure that you work at a comfortable height and that you keep your hands and wrists positioned properly. Because it is so demanding, you probably don't want to work eight hours a day; many therapists work four to six hours a day, and schedule breaks throughout the day.

Becoming a massage therapist isn't as simple as deciding you want to do it. You'll have to attend massage therapy school, where you'll master subjects ranging from kinesiology, the study of body mechanics, to anatomy and physiology. You'll also learn different massage techniques and perform plenty of hands-on massages for practice. Expect to spend nine months to a couple of years mastering massage techniques. For more info about schools near you, visit *http://massagetherapy.com/careers/training. php* or *http://www.amtamassage.org/schools.html.*

The majority of states require that massage therapists be licensed. Many require you to have at least 500 hours of classroom instruction; some require 1,000 hours or more. You also have to keep your license current, which may involve continuing-education courses; regardless, most massage therapists take additional classes to learn new techniques.

The good news, though, is that with the aging population and an ever-increasing interest in alternative healing techniques, there is an ongoing demand for massage therapists who work anywhere from hospitals to gyms. Massage therapy also gives you an opportunity to be self-employed, working as much or as little as you want; some therapists work from their homes while others carry their table and call on people at home or work. For more information, check out the American Massage Therapy Association's Web site at *http://www.amtamassage.org/*.

Whether you decide to go pro or simply learn some techniques to please your partner, giving an awesome massage is a skill you can use the rest of your life—and a way to connect with people. And the ability lies in your own two hands.